TRAINING FOR ORGANIZATIONAL TRANSFORMATION

TRAINING FOR ORGANIZATIONAL TRANSFORMATION

Part 1: For Policy-makers and Change Managers

ROLF P. LYNTON
UDAI PAREEK

Sage Publications
New Delhi/Thousand Oaks/London

First published in 2000 by

Sage Publications India Pvt Ltd
B-42, Panchsheel Enclave
New Delhi 110 017
www.indiasage.com

Sage Publications Inc
2455 Teller Road
Thousand Oaks, California 91320

Sage Publications Ltd
1 Oliver's Yard, 55 City Road
London EC1Y 1SP

Published by Tejeshwar Singh for Sage Publications India Pvt Ltd, typeset by Line Arts, Pondicherry, and printed at Chaman Enterprises, Delhi.

Sixth Printing 2006

Library of Congress Cataloging-in-Publication Data

Lynton, Rolf P.
    Training for organizational transformation/Rolf P. Lynton and Udai Pareek.
    p. cm. (cl.) (pbk.)
    Rev. and updated ed. of Training for development, 1990.
    Complete in 2 vols.
    Contents: v. 1. For policy-makers and change managers
    Includes bibliographical references and index.
    1. Employees, Training of. 2. Organizational change. I. Pareek, Udai: Narain, 1925- II. Lynton, Rolf P. Training for development. III. Title.

HF5549.5.T7 L9   2000   658.3'1243—dc21   00–024861

ISBN: 10: 0–7619–9473–4 (US-HB)   10: 81–7036–948–7 (India-HB)
          13: 978–0–7619–9473–2 (US-HB)   13: 978–81–7036–948–6 (India-HB)
          10: 0–7619–9428–9 (US-PB)   10: 81–7036–912–6 (India-PB)
          13: 978–0–7619–9428–2 (US-PB)   13: 978–81–7036–912–7 (India-PB)

Typeset in 10/12 Times Roman.

Sage Production Team: Sumitra Srinivasan, N.K. Negi, and Santosh Rawat

CONTENTS

PART I: RETHINKING TRAINING

PART II: TRAINING POLICY AND RESOURCES

LIST OF EXHIBITS

LIST OF BOXES

LIST OF READINGS

PREFACE

...the audiences actually seem to concentrate better in bad weather.
—Actors' comment from the footboards of the
Globe Theatre, London, 1998.

In the mere three decades since *Training for Development* was first published,[1] training—the whole field—has pushed its boundaries far out, changed contours, and is now as open to all weathers as Shakespeare's Globe Theatre. If bad weather heightens concentration, then that is most needed.

Remapping that field will be a good start. But the next sea change may overtake the effort and shift boundaries and contours yet again, as the electronic revolution did and still does with its explosive spread of dispersed, individual learning opportunities across the globe: training on call, free of instructor, room, schedule. This alone should make remapping training a regular routine. Or, in a tempting alternative direction, maybe it has made most other training obsolete and fresh concentration on improving it quite unnecessary?

Such thought and impatience would be quite misleading and would only delay the needed effort. All simplicity vanishes as soon as a wonderful new training technology has to be meshed with purpose, place, and time—the three other key elements of training. The same goes for all advances in technology or method. And purpose it is— the task—that makes the storyline: effective training is in the service of task A in place B at this time C. Only from this does the rest then follow: the choices of actors, lines, props, style, scale, and speed of action, the sequences of scenes and sets—in short, the play itself, with its moral, and its direction and its strategy for getting there. That reality—complex, fluid, demanding, promising—is the field, all there is to work in and with.

And it is indeed this all-round reality that other major changes in training have addressed, be it a step or two at a time and from various

[1] Rolf P. Lynton and Udai Pareek, *Training for Development* (Homewood, Ill.: Irwin-Dorsey, 1967).

angles. Here are just some of the changes large enough to make waves and to have changed the field over these thirty years:

- From training individuals to training *teams* and on to including people in the *tiers* immediately above and below in the organization, and *inter-group* training;
- training links with *organizational consultation* (OD); both, and more, coalesce into *human resource development* (HRD);
- *socio-technical system designs* that put task requirements firmly in front: technical, economic and others along with people;
- as women, 'minorities', and immigrants from near and far gain public prominence and bring fresh approaches, strengths, and demands, *diversity training* starts and quickly spreads;
- with changes accelerating and increasingly complex, hopes shift from programming training people to developing all into a *'learning organization'* with a distinctive 'organisational culture' to maintain;
- training 'strategies' expand beyond the organization to include clients and suppliers, neighbors, public personages, others in the *'relevant environment'* along with those inside who are involved in the task: this expands the learning organization into a 'learning system'; and
- distinctive methodologies are developed for large-system training with focus on *'desirable futures'*.

Most telling for this new book, in all this changing, merging, and expanding, is that strategic concerns and decisions about training have moved into the boardroom. While trainers and training institutions continue improving training designs, methods, and materials and developing professional networks and institutions, issues of fitting their efforts into overall change strategies, funding, and organizational support—of scale, timing, best organizational fit, and also more basically of developing training capacity (e.g., in-house and what to look for outside)—are for policy-makers and change managers to deal with. So the book now has two publics, each with its distinctive points of view, functions, and responsibilities: 'different but related', as Fritz Roethlisberger of Hawthorne fame used to say. What is front stage for one readership is backdrop for the other, and vice-versa.

So clear has this division become, and so important, that we have therefore divided this new edition into two volumes, one for each public. Each volume is self-contained, including enough from the viewpoint of the other party to make sense of one's own. Reading the other volume as well would of course deepen that understanding and raise abilities to take others' view into account in actual practice.

This process of differentiation, of sifting out what is the primary responsibility of policy-makers and change managers from what belongs primarily to trainers and others in the training system, is so basic to good management that it is worth tracing in this present case. The prefaces of the earlier editions show it clearly.

SCALE AND COST

At first, cost consciousness was the outstanding overall policy and management concern, a concern that stands tall, perhaps taller, even now. Both macro- and micro-costs were clearly in view: the overall costs of training in national economies as well as costs for an individual training session—*total* costs, not only the direct, i.e., additional costs. The Preface to the first edition of *Training for Development* put it this way:

> organizations...are entitled to receive good value for their investment in training.
>
> A few sample figures can indicate the broad dimensions of what we are concerned about. American industry alone spends to the order of 3 billion dollars on formal training programs each year, i.e., a sum about equivalent to all American foreign aid. Investment in skills acquired through systematic training now accounts for over half of the expenditure on all formal education in the country. Six hundred million dollars are spent on management development programs alone. Total annual expenditure on training of all kinds is above 10 billion dollars. Professional membership of the American Society for Training and Development now exceeds 5,000. It was fifteen in 1943.
>
> India must have about 4,000 industrial training institutions alone and spends 75 to 100 million dollars a year on them. If the wages of participants for the time spent in training are added, as they should be to get at the whole cost of training, the total doubles to 150–200 million dollars. About 70–80 percent of Indians who live in villages by farming are served by other training programs and institutions. Reports mention 'training camps' each year for over 700,000 village leaders, for instance. Our estimate of expenditure on all kinds of training in India comes to about 6 billion dollars a year, i.e., the equivalent of 10 to 15 percent of the Fourth Plan outlay.

These figures, great as they are, do not upset us. Training is indeed required on a vast scale. But it must yield results more or less commensurate with the expenditure, and result in more and better output of goods, services and satisfaction.

Increases in effectiveness and reductions in cost must be achieved, if at all, by individual training programs and training sessions. There can hardly be a training session that costs less than $200 overall, or a training day that costs less than $1,000. A one month's program is a $25,000 product at least. Here then is the first question that 'consumers' of training ought to ask themselves: is *this* $25,000 product what they really want and need? Maybe they ought to get a new machine instead, or spend a similar amount toward reorganization. Do they need *this* training, not any other; for *this* person, not another? We simply cannot assume that this kind of question now gets raised.

If the answer to this question is affirmative, then quite simple costing makes another important point. The trainer's salary is a minor item in the total. The participants' time is the main expense. The table below sets out for easy reference the cost of that time for a session for participants earning various amounts and training in groups of various sizes. Since the trainer's part is the key to the results of training, it is good business to attract top-class people to this profession, to pay them well, and to establish work loads that allow time for adequate preparation of any session. No effort or expense is excessive to help develop their skills further and to ensure an institutional climate favorable to their use. The development of more effective trainers, training programs, and training institutions cannot be emphasized enough.

PARTICIPANTS' WAGES AND SALARIES DURING ONE TRAINING SESSION, ONE OF 100 SESSIONS PER MONTH

	Dollars			
One participant's pay per month 200	400	600	800	1,000
One participant's pay per session 2	4	6	8	10
All participants' pay per session				
10 participants 20	40	60	80	100
20 40	80	120	160	200
30 60	120	180	240	300
40 80	160	240	320	400
50 100	200	300	400	500

These themes and their importance and implications remained the same for the second edition twenty years later, but scale and costs had multiplied at least by five. From the Preface to the second edition of *Training for Development*:

Most evident is the escalation of scale. Training and retraining is going on in many more institutions and in many more connections than before—in new technologies, of course, from computer operating and servicing to hang-gliding; also of women in management, woodsmen in social forestry, unemployed to be resettled, black youths, the physically handicapped, professional athletes, post-Vatican II clergy, program administrators, and armies in the space age. Prime Minister of India, Rajiv Gandhi, has instituted weeklong residential in-service training programs for all officers of the Indian Administrative Service and also for ministers; twenty-five institutions provide these programs to all parts of the subcontinent. In 1967 we noted that the membership of the American Society for Training and Development had grown from fifteen in 1943 to over 5,000 twenty years later. The Indian Society for Training and Development (ISTD), founded in 1969, now has 220 institutional and 1,700 individual members, and a second national network started in 1985 for Human Resources Development. With almost every mail we receive announcements of regular and new training programs; the dailies, weeklies, and television advertise still more. Even small market towns have institutes for training in English and secretarial services, and everywhere there are institutes for working with computers. The US Agency for International Development earmarks $150 million a year for technical assistance to management training alone. The health services projects on which we are currently working envisage training for over 200,000 more nurses in Indonesia and 48,000 field staff in just four of India's twenty-five states. Training overall must have at least doubled in scale in these twenty years, in number of people going for training, size of training facilities and staff, and costs of training. That would mean that the $10 billion spent on training in the US in 1967 has now come close to $90 billion in today's currency and India's estimated $6 billion then to about $45 billion.

This is a massive enterprise, and its continuing escalation should be proof that training (or at least most of it) results in notably improved performances by individuals and organizations, indeed by whole sectors and governments. And this ought to be so most of all in developing countries, i.e., in economies with the tightest budgets and the longest way to go. Training would then be a success story and its contribution real and tangible, justifying the expenditure on it to date and its trajectory into the future.

What evidence we see in this direction, however, continues to be slight and sporadic. Given the massive expenditure on training, surprisingly little determined effort is directed toward tracing it, let alone making training solid and reliable. Only here and there do we see instances where training has clearly resulted in improved performance at work; those in which improvements accord with predetermined goals which were planned into training programs furnish examples throughout this book. They point to the feasibility and promise of good training, but simultaneously reveal the vast reality of its absence. Most of the programs we have seen and know about make little or no difference to performance at work. Indeed, their plans and designs were not really of a quality to improve praxis; yet they were funded and continue to be funded.

Users of extramural programs, who are dissatisfied with one program, usually shop around for another for their participants; only rarely do they use more rigorous criteria in choosing one program over another. Hardly ever do they stop sending participants altogether. So training enterprises also go on and on. If one training program is discontinued, another usually takes its place. Only very rarely does a training establishment close its doors. One large Indian company was such an exception.

Once in the forefront of the training movement, this company discontinued all management training and closed its department. Now it selects and promotes managers strictly on the basis of their past performance with the company or, if such personnel are new, during limited probationary periods; training and educational qualifications no longer count in promotion. In the US, dissatisfaction with what new graduates of colleges and universities know and can do has led large companies and associations to set up their own institutions to such an extent that funding of these 'proprietary institutions of higher education' now exceeds funding for state universities. But direct control over preparatory work does not guarantee the outcome either and, furthermore, is fraught with intrinsic pitfalls.

As things are, dissatisfaction with training and the scale of training efforts are both increasing side by side, but training seems unaffected by its partner. Like a juggernaut, training just rolls on.

In the ten years since the second edition (1990), the figures have at least doubled again. The themes remain the same, and they will permeate this volume.

How to Take Hold

That second preface then went on to identify seven 'holds' that people could use to wrestle with the issues of making training worth its great cost. Of those seven, four are really up to policy-makers and change managers to use: *their* decisions must set the stage. They may draw on advice from trainers and others, discuss, even collaborate in taking decisions jointly. But theirs is the responsibility. Those four are: making training fit change strategy; outcome evaluation;

organizational readiness and support for training; and ensuring good fit of training with organizational and wider cultures.

Re: Strategy

Trainers and funders have become quite inordinately preoccupied with curriculum content, program design, training methods and materials, and other details—anything, it seems, rather than face such broader basic issues as purpose, options for achieving it, and a good fit with the wider organizational and social contexts that must first support the training and then the developments training is expected to promote. This premature, misplaced preoccupation reduces to chance any relevance and usefulness training may have. All that it guarantees is high entertainment value.

We are particularly distressed by the apparently ubiquitous one- or two-day workshops in management, supervision, community involvement, and other people-centered topics. They are highly advertised, and even at fees of $200 and more per day (plus travel and living) attract an apparently unending stream of participants backed by organizations. If such short programs affect participants at all (and enrollment lists show that many participants repeatedly attend programs with similar titles), they are far more likely to strengthen the participants' defenses against human understanding and encounters than lead to useful learning.

Re: Evaluation

Better evaluation could check the perversions, ineffectiveness, and excessive costs of many training programs. The clients of training, work organizations, and public funders are in the best position to take hold of training from that angle and can be coached to do so effectively. The two most telling moves for measuring the effectiveness of training are, first, to help them institute work-based evaluation well after participants have returned from training and, second, to establish the *total* cost of training instead of only the direct training costs or fee payments. Total training costs would include the participants' ongoing salaries as well as their travel, stay, and meals, and also the costs of replacing them, extra organizational costs, and overheads during training. Such realistic costing yields figures at least twice those now commonly used and can translate quite quickly into client insistence on more effective training.

Happily, many countries are now sufficiently far along in staffing their civil service following independence to be able to look at training far more critically and to insist increasingly on adequate value for training funds.

Properly used, evaluation can be a second promising hold on training, alternating with a firmer grip on strategy.

Re: Organizational Readiness and Support

Where these are lacking or deficient, training makes little or no difference, certainly not for long, except to increase the frustration of the best participants and to stimulate them to leave for situations where competence is valued more. In this larger picture, the quality of training itself is secondary. Moreover, more is known about how to achieve it than how to assess organizational readiness and support and, beyond assessing, to ensure them.

Re: Fit with Cultural Contexts

Besides urging *sensitivity to local cultural contexts,* it is prescriptive in just one respect: to engage actively with the cultural environment relevant to the task in the expectation that organizational development and the training of people are channels for also *developing the culture.* This realization is similar to that recorded only twenty or thirty years ago, namely, that organizations need not regard their environments as fixed, to be taken into account and adjusted to, but rather to be actively interacted with for mutual adjustment and development in tandem. As this realization widens to now encompass the cultural context, it has very practical consequences for training and its organization.

Except for altering their order, these four issues have chapters in this volume: the cultural context first, in Chapter 2; strategy in Chapter 4; outcome evaluation and system-wide support for training (together) in Chapter 7.

CONCEPTS AND TERMS UPDATED

Clearer differentiation of responsibilities and of practice calls also for distinctive terms. By the time of the second edition we had run up against this:

Our practical experiences with 'taking hold' of training over the years—through stretching the perceptions of it by clients and, when possible, by trainers and through pushing forward more precise, exacting measures for its effectiveness and economy—stretch the language we need to use beyond what is commonly used in and about training. All the particular 'holds' interrelate training more directly and actively with wider 'system' contexts than the earlier book did: with participants including in that term the increasingly large number of independently motivated learners using varieties of public media and self-study; with work organizations and public funders of training and development; and, wider still, with broad cultural dimensions which training has to reflect if it is to be effective but which it also in turn shapes. The earlier edition had this broad framework too, but to a much lesser extent than this, whereas now we shift the focus from training activities *per se* to the systemic interconnections and hold it there. This calls for systems language, and we will use as much of it as will clarify our purpose—as craftspeople at work, in short, not as discussants in the ongoing elaboration of systems science itself.

In our eagerness now to distinguish the part policy-makers and change managers have from that of trainers and others in the training establishment, we will now cut through a complication which we only acknowledged, but did not resolve, in the second edition. There we had used 'training system' for 'the whole range of training resources to which any particular set of work organizations and participants have access to meet their needs, or could have access to if they knew of their existence and if the resources were organized enough in actuality'. In this edition, for the system from the *clients'* perspective, we will use 'training resources system' (TRS). And we will use 'training system' for the institutions, associations, and networks of the trainers themselves, *their* professional support system responsive to *their* perspective. The use, development, and maintenance of training systems is matter for Volume Two, but in two connections that professional 'training system' will also appear in this volume. One is as partner/informant/consultant available to policy-makers and change managers for reaching the decisions for which they are responsible; it is most important that trainers then speak clearly from their professional point of view and that their partners expect them to do so. The other, more limited but also quite essential, is the recognition by policy-makers and change managers that the 'training system' needs and deserves their systematic encouragement and support, including financial support; if that falls short, training capacity will fall short too.

OVERALL STRUCTURE OF THE BOOK

With the division of this book into two volumes, we are again able to include readings following the chapters; our growing attention to systems had crowded readings out of the second edition.[2] The text is therefore structured similar to the first edition.

To make the book directly useful...we have included many descriptions of experiences, ours and colleagues', in various institutions; research findings in summary; and additional readings. This material is set off from the continuing text in various ways. Descriptions that directly illustrate the main text and can be read as part of it are indented, for easy reference or omission, whichever the reader prefers. Numerical data are set out as 'tables'. 'Exhibits' contain conceptual material or sample forms and other aids that enable the reader to try out some idea mentioned in the text. Finally, there are two kinds of 'readings'. One kind consists of summarized research findings on some points. To avoid unbalancing the main text, they are set out in separate 'boxes' and are only referred to in the text. The other readings are longer and follow the appropriate chapter. They go into more detail in various matters than we want to include in the text of this book. Some offer a different approach or point of view than ours.

To facilitate reference to these different kinds of data, each chapter has a detailed contents sheet.

The last paragraph of the Preface to the first edition of *Training for Development* still holds good thirty years later. Hope never dies!

What has impressed us most throughout the process of consultation with colleagues and collection of data is the near unanimity of concern that training as now practiced needs to shift gear in a major way. The consensus seems to be that there is enough dissatisfaction and also enough competence and endeavor to make significant progress in practice.

Rolf P. Lynton
Chapel Hill
North Carolina
USA

Udai Pareek
Jaipur
Rajasthan
India

[2.] A separate volume of readings—selected and annotated—resulted: *Facilitating Development: Readings for Trainers, Consultants and Policy-makers* (New Delhi: Sage Publications, 1992).

Part I

RETHINKING TRAINING

1

STRATEGIC THRUSTS:
THE NEW DIMENSION OF TRAINING

Repositioning Training

Seamy Alternatives

Assumptions about Training: Two Alternative Sets
    Knowledge↔Competence
    Training↔Learning
    Competence↔Actual Practice
    Responsibility for Training

Change with Training or Change Through Force

Increasing Employment and Organizational Performance

Exhibits
1.1 Assumptions Underlying Two Concepts of Training

Readings
1.1 The Changed Nature of Change and the Response of the HRD Professional

---

In a dynamic economy, where technological changes and market shifts are forcing lay-offs of some people even as other jobs are being created, the key is to equip workers (at all levels) with needed skills—and then link them efficiently to the vacancies.

...But [this] is one of the hardest things to get right. It requires cooperation of business and labor and three levels of government—and finding the right mix of flexibility and accountability for everyone involved.

—David Broder

From our current files of consulting assignments, field visits and reports from around the globe come these samples of sea-changes in tasks and settings, and prospects of unending more to come. They show the work and social scenes that policy-makers and change managers now have to deal with.

1. A large machine hall, not new, but obviously well-appointed and tended. Mostly automated technology, and more in the aisles to install.

2. Across Europe and all its many differences, unemployment among work entrants without vocational training is double that of entrants with training.

3. In several booming US cities with unemployment below 2 percent, 40 percent of young African-Americans are out of work. They hang out in the street, like with like, are the highest risks for drugs and drink, with violence next. A year or two and a conviction or two, and they are 'hard core unemployed: unemployable'.

4. More and more women, now 45 percent of the labor force overall, work part-time or on home-based and contractual arrangements so that they can control their time. To organizational and public issues they bring fresh views and approaches and make them count. In the 1997 local elections in Maharashtra, India, eighteen villages elected all-women local councils.

5. Each Monday morning, all nurses in state service in a low-income state in USA are on interactive TV to stay abreast with advances in pharmacology and other treatment regimen.

6. A nation-wide packing and shipping company sends all new workers to its headquarter city for training for 'as long each takes to become fully competent—one to three months'.

7. Programmers, in long rows of individual cubicles, work in project teams that are rapidly made up, dissolved, and composed afresh as the company accepts and finishes contracts. No programmer moves; team working is all by e-mail.

8. 'Turn-over? We lose one-third of our managers every year—we count on that and plan for it. We no sooner train them than they leave. This is a very competitive business.'

9. The computer has turned relationships upside down. Between generations, in the first place: now it is the young, the most recently trained, who have essential expertise and authority, and they keep updating their advantage. When fathers, uncles, and other seniors block the way, sons leave for new, well-paid positions elsewhere. Or they set up their own independent enterprises, many home-based (and thus also tax-sheltered).

10. California, USA, Spring 1998. In a regular high fee, one-week 'senior executive challenge' program, just one out of four participants were Americans working with American organizations in America; the rest came from all over the globe.

11. 'A quarter of expatriate staff leave in the first year…they—or their families—just can't make it. They insist on going back, even if it means losing their jobs. The cost of bringing them, having them here (when they are least productive) and then returning them is *enormous*. All waste! And the replacement may be no better.'

12. Every two to three years, NIIT, a leading information technology company in India, has changed its organizational structure to stay abreast with changing technologies, the exploding market for its products, scarcities of skilled personnel, and the successive deregulation of foreign imports and capital investment. 'What *we* need is a quite new culture—for the *whole* organization!'

Training individuals, the dominant perspective on training even three decades ago, has no chance to encompass opportunities and headaches like these, and training teams, the next step on, gets not much closer. Organizational health, no less than individual livelihoods, now requires a handful of partners to visualize training of a different order: a major resource for whole systems in constant change. And translating that vision into 'the right mix of flexibility and accountability,… [is then still] one of the hardest things to get right.'

All around the world now, settings like these, complex and ever-changing, define the policy-makers' task of choreographing training to best advantage. They set the stage and compose the plays, and change managers produce and direct the trainer-actors. At a moment's notice new conditions can intrude and dominate anywhere: none now distinguish the so-called developed countries from the developing ones. For the record, six of the twelve pointers stated earlier come from our practice in India (Nos 1, 6 to 9, and 12) and No. 11 from joint ventures in China. Distinctively local traditions are eroding fast even in villages and small towns; TV and computer training centers are everywhere. With quite remarkable uniformity, young people are preparing themselves for life and work in the computer age.

In two-day seminars with policy-makers, which we organized in north and south India in late 1997 specifically to test our impression of global similarities, these were the words of greatest frequency and weight: training is to be comprehensive, integrated, for line managers to 'own', futuristic; sensitive to information technology, changing customer preferences, the global environment, and cross-cultural differences; long-term, value-oriented, to build organizational culture; to include networking—'to keep up'—and ongoing recording of experience, to include institutional memory and contextual analysis.

REPOSITIONING TRAINING

With these concerns, to *position* training better has become the most important and urgent task. Lest this harsh terminology suggest only factories and output graphs, we mean settings and tasks for people in all kinds of settings and roles—'high' and 'low', at home, in neighborhoods, and larger public affairs, even alone for individual self-improvement—all, as long as the task is 'set'. Focused intentionality and the use it is meant for planned and prepared in advance makes training different from education.

For positioning training better, i.e., for ensuring its best possible fit with ongoing change strategies, policy-makers and change managers set the specifications that training is to achieve and also the limits to time, numbers, costs, and other considerations to suit. Managing this best fit over time is not a mere one-way process of accommodation, as if the organizational and wider environments were made up of more or less fixed imperatives. It will be well to use change strategies—and quite specifically their training component—to intervene and change the environment. The eager wishes to change organizational culture, to improve inter-cultural relations, and to develop change strategies for 'desirable futures' reflect this broader determination.

SEAMY ALTERNATIVES

Where policy-makers give no clear lead and change managers fail to direct, organizations fill the ever expanding training apparatus with people, but do so without enthusiasm. Like a tax training is levied on the willing and unwilling alike. In fact, some countries have made it a tax, or at least an expenditure strongly encouraged. French law, for example, requires factories in some industries to spend a fixed percentage of their budget on personnel training or forfeit any unspent amount in taxes; the purpose behind this policy is the equitable spread of the costs of upgrading the workforce in general.

Dissatisfaction with training as it is growing and most notably at the working level where the benefits of training should stand out most clearly. It shows in many ways: in reluctance to send the most promising people for training, for instance, and in inadequate use of personnel after training. With disillusionment mounting in the midst of expansion, training has entered a dangerous phase in its development. One minute it is overloaded, saddled with expectations it cannot possibly meet; the next (or next door) it is utterly disparaged and undermined. Such extreme swings of opinion usually denote impatience and lack of skill. This is no less true in the case of training than in other endeavors. An inexperienced operator on a machine uses movements that are too large and tiring. A small child alternately runs or sits before 'just' walking. A new teacher speaks too loudly or whispers before settling into an appropriate speaking volume. The extreme views on training are analogous. In sober fact, training is neither a panacea for all ills nor is it a waste of time. What is required most of all is for policy-makers and managers to use their divine sense of impatience for acquiring insight into what training can or cannot do, and set the stage for trainers to design and carry out training effectively and economically. In short, to take a good sharp look.

This searchlight of inquiry may make the task and its challenges stand out too starkly, too simply. It seems a risk worth taking in order to achieve the greatest possible clarity. The reader's own experience will be the best guard against oversimplification. Using experiences in India, Indonesia, and other rapidly developing countries has this same advantage too, at similar risk. The contribution that training can make to development is needed in such countries so acutely and so obviously. At the same time, the limited resources available in these countries make this contribution hard to come by. These lines are sharply drawn: on the one hand, no promise can be ignored; on the other, no waste is permissible.

The point about waste may also help readers who are inclined to fret with impatience when clarification of an issue requires slow, meticulous attention. Why bother? First, of course, because all life is lived minute-by-minute and it is the minutes in succession that hold all the potential there is for good and ill. Second, when impatience surfaces, it may also help to remember the high cost of training. Eight hundred dollars per training hour is common, also in poverty-stricken Asia and Africa. The very best use of that hour is worth meticulous attention, even on this score alone.

ASSUMPTIONS ABOUT TRAINING: TWO ALTERNATIVE SETS

All 'graduations' in human development mean the abandonment of a familiar position,...all growth must come to terms with this fact.
—Erik Erikson

The way training is too often set up, even now, is something like this: Pressure to improve performance in some sector, say health services or agriculture, builds up. Policy decisions are taken to give existing staff 'some more' training and to add more staff. The matter is urgent. (In developing countries things are always behind hand by definition and hence urgent.) The first training course has to start without delay. Its length is roughed out. The syllabus is developed quickly at the desk and discussed with other officers down the corridor. It ensures that the subject 'gets covered'. The 'subject' fans out as its application is considered and as more and more people want to contribute to planning the course. Soon the syllabus is overfilled. Trainers are told to follow it strictly; otherwise they could not 'get through it'.

Notices go out to agencies to send staff to the first course. The notice may be short, but the agencies feel obliged to send their quota of participants. Qualifications are minimal: a certain academic standard and so many years of experience. The experience qualification is loosened when necessary so that the course is sure to be full.

The course starts. Lecturing seems almost the only way to 'get through'. Trainers console themselves with the thought that participants will at least be 'exposed' to the subject, somewhat 'oriented'. As soon as the first batch leaves, the next batch arrives. There are so many people to train and time is so short. After the first round or two, the syllabus is standardized. Thus, a new training program is established and standardized across provinces or the whole system.

The assumptions underlying this kind of process are usually not stated. There is 'no time'. There is also little inclination to touch matters that look unmanageable and may be unsettling, either to those responsible for the course or to those who will decide about sending people to it, or to both. But the underlying assumptions can be stated and checked against experience, and more useful assumptions could be developed. We will therefore start with the assumptions with which people usually approach training.

Exhibit 1.1 presents four, and matches them with four much more useful ones. Each four make a set; they hang together. So we include even the two about individual learning and the learner/trainer transactions that belong more particularly in the companion volume on the training process itself (and will be discussed more fully there). Then, too, the very first assumption, about how knowledge relates to action, continues to confuse many policy-makers and managers.

Exhibit 1.1
ASSUMPTIONS UNDERLYING TWO CONCEPTS OF TRAINING

1. Participants' acquisition of knowledge means greater competence.	1. Motivation and skills lead to improved practice. Competence grows through practice.
2. Participants learn what trainers teach. Learning is a simple function of the capacity of participants to take in and the ability of trainers to teach.	2. Learning is a complex function. Participants' motivation and use of training varies with support in the organization.
3. Individual improvement leads to improvement in the organization.	3. Improvement in practice is a complex function of individual learning, the norms of the working group, and the general climate of the organization. Efficiency and individual learning, if unused, lead to frustration.
4. Training is the responsibility of the training establishment. It begins and ends with the specific program.	4. Training involves three partners: the organization, the participant, and the training establishment. It encompasses a preparatory, pretraining phase, a training phase, and a subsequent, posttraining phase. All phases are essential.

To keep things simple we will discuss the assumptions in the language of just one setting—that of business and industry—leaving it to the reader to transpose it into their settings. In like circumstances later in the book, we will use the language of another setting.

Knowledge ↔ Competence

It is strange how something quite clear in staff selection gets quite ignored when it comes to training. Often, the very same managers who will only consider recruiting applicants with prior work experience, even for technical positions, say in agriculture or engineering, let knowledge-gathering stand for training. Maybe personal memories from school and student days confuse things here. While education is primarily concerned with unveiling the world to students and enabling them to choose their interests, lifestyles, and careers, training is for acquiring new competencies or enhancing existing ones. And competency relates to effectiveness on a task and on enhancing performance of it in the participant's role in the organization.

Training ↔ Learning

Learning is a kind of action, and like other kinds of action, depends on many things. What is taught is only one of them. So the connection between what trainers teach and what participants learn is at best indirect and partial. To assume that teaching and learning are related simply, as cause and effect, has an inherent defect: it equates the trainers' viewpoint from which they teach with the participants' viewpoint from which they learn. As trainers and participants work together, they may understand each other's viewpoints better and take them into account. But to proceed on the assumption that their viewpoints are identical is folly.

What then explains the continuing prevalence of so patently unrealistic an assumption in most training? Very likely, personal more that intellectual difficulties are involved. Indeed, trainers seem to grasp intellectually the principle that training must start from 'where the participants are'. Yet, many take no action to find this starting point, to ascertain what participants already see and understand. They seem reluctant to establish such a premise.

Competence ↔ Actual Practice

This connection, too, is not direct; bitter experience aplenty has alerted all concerned that participants returning from training often find their new capabilities ignored, even resented. They look for support and find instead indifference or opposition. Doubts then assail them about the usefulness of the training. Enthusiasm wanes. Soon they accept their colleagues' advice to 'forget it'. And so, few more have been trained only to suffer disappointment and frustration. Next time they will know better than to invest so much of themselves in new initiatives and developments.

The simple linking of individual training and effective action ignores the manifold problems of introducing and sustaining change in an organization. Putting an individual's competence to use depends on a number of people and often on additional resources. It calls for the encouragement and support of a receptive organization.

In the organizational approach, training should commence with a set of organizational questions. Instead of asking what X or Y needs to learn in order to carry out a new activity, the first training question should be addressed to all involved in the projected change. What do they, given their different functions and different positions in the organization, have to do differently, together? What, therefore, do they have to learn for which training is needed not only individually but also collectively? These questions concern those who collaborate directly on the task and also those who sanction new developments and provide new services and organizational support. These much more encompassing questions then lead to a systems approach to training.

The systems approach often involves training minimum concentrations of staff at several levels of the organization; the provision of supportive follow-up services from the original trainers, consultants, and other resources for a considerable period; and the allocation of resources within the working organization to sustain the change strategy at various stages in process. Instead of thinking in terms of someone's participation in this or that training program, this approach leads to training strategies that include pretraining and posttraining phases, and also foresees further training events related to *career* plans. Taking a longer view, this approach tries to deal with the entire network of factors that determines an organization's readiness for further development. What is required is not an occasional change, but change on a continuing basis, more or less, in interaction with a changing environment. In such an ongoing process, the organization is both a recipient and a contributor.

Yet, even with this approach, it is useful to bear in mind that a prickly problem, a real uncertainty, remains. The gap between what trainers teach and what participants learn (Assumption #2 in Exhibit 1.1) can lead to unintended consequences. And these consequences may work to the disadvantage of the organization. One that has staggered many a manager is when an engineer decides to leave the organization soon after returning from a training program. The engineer may have come across a more promising opening in another company while taking the course; or the course may have stimulated entrepreneurial thoughts and now the engineer wants to become self-employed. For reasons such as these some managers refuse to send staff for outside training. They are afraid of losing them or, alternatively, having them return to insist on unsettling changes for which the organization is not ready. Timing training in relation to an organization's needs and opportunities, and exercising discretion in the selection of participants, are important ways of balancing individual growth and organizational needs; but they do not mesh automatically or necessarily, and it is useless pretending they do.

Often managers take a more positive view of the unintended consequences of training. If a member of their staff has gotten more from training than expected, so much the better. Personal growth is a good thing. These managers may or may not be aware that their generally positive attitude toward people and personal development helps to make the organization a good place in which to work. Their attitude elicits initiative and free application from the staff and provides work satisfaction that staff members would loose by leaving. It makes for the kind of organization which, if some leave, others will join.

The same positive policy can be deliberate. It can be derived from the rapidly changing work to be done, notably in developing countries, and the speed with which new technologies, management methods, markets, and so forth crowd the organization. Staff cannot realistically be trained for such changes one by one. It is more fruitful for managers to see their task as one of fostering employees who are generally inventive and receptive, aware and thoroughly alive, not just now and then, but habitually. Training, unintended consequences included, will then be seen by policy-makers and managers as a means of achieving this goal.

Responsibility for Training

To invest trainers with full—or even primary—responsibility for training can only be unrealistic. The misunderstanding now protects training systems from the demands for more effective training that organizations and participants could rightly make; to further confuse the issue, it also protects organizations from demands that trainers and their systems could rightly make for clear training goals, carefully selected participants, and organizational support for the improvements to be achieved through training. It is a kind of collusion.

Participants, their organizations and trainers are all partners in the training effort. To be effective, their collaboration should start with defining training goals and strategies. After training, collaboration should continue with follow-up services from the training system and support for innovations from the organization.

CHANGE WITH TRAINING OR CHANGE THROUGH FORCE

Alongside the quartet of assumptions that inspires much current training, we have proposed an alternative quartet (Exhibit 1.1). The new quartet takes into account more adequately our experience and seems therefore a better basis on which to proceed. It calls for far more thought and rigor than the first set and requires careful consideration of expectations, needs, relationships, and costs. This initial investment of care and attention is very taxing. Organizations are entitled to ask whether training is worth the effort.

Most unfortunately, the electronic revolution and its uniquely fast spread of individual learning opportunities to all corners of the globe have clouded this question once again: maybe the effort is no longer necessary, or at least not *this* much effort. But however sophisticated and widely available electronics and 'distance learning' have so wonderfully made the acquisition of knowledge, that is still all it is. Knowledge, however enhanced, still remains only randomly connected to heightened competence in practice and less directly still to enhanced performance in the organization.

And there is a more basic attack still. Is training, *any* training, really necessary? Surely, similar ends can be attained without training and achieved with greater expedition, certainty, and economy by management simply 'doing its job', parents 'doing their duty' by their children, teachers 'teaching', and community leaders 'leading'? Maybe what is really required is that people in positions of authority *exercise* their authority; that is, ensure that their views *are* implemented. They are in a position to know what is necessary. They ought to insist on it—kindly, of course, listen to objections, make adjustments where possible, consult, 'take people along', 'get them to do' willingly what the authorities have decided while giving the impression that the decision is 'really their own'.

The many phrases used in singing this familiar tune reveal how out of fashion it is, but also how very much present; unmasked, this is the theme of force. Its antecedents and personal implications deserve a brief closer look. Force, in fact, is the primary moving power of traditional relationships, and often comes readily to hand even today. Its success has been monumental. Cathedrals and temples, massive forts, great old roads and water systems, even that timeless monument to a loving relationship, the Taj Mahal, all were built, details aside, by a few who imposed their will on thousands by a personal combination of kindness and cruelty. India at the height of her glory and power centuries ago was characterized by relationships of force. Likewise, other countries. If force, authority, was productive then, why should it not serve now? Why not train just a few masters to get work done through force and manipulation exercised on servants by the string of up-to-date phrases for this very phenomenon. Moreover, only a glance across some frontiers reveals that large-scale changes are being accomplished through force also today.

Many people impatiently advocate force and even use it, openly or camouflaged. In truth, resorting to force to achieve better action tempts us all in our heart of hearts. We may call it 'authority' or some other nice word. Perhaps right here, embedded deep down, is the actual source from which genuine opposition to training or action flows. And facile approval, excessive expectations, and kind words for training are simply varied manifestations of the self-same opposition.

Opposition, then, may be deep-rooted and stay with us. But it is not founded on the relative efficacy of training compared with force as a means for achieving change and it stands no chance at all to keep change going as modern developments demand. At best, force engenders action limited to a given occasion, and often limited to the actual presence of a powerful supervisor.

Training, on the other hand, leads to change that can be kept up, to self-motivation, and to further improvement through onward practice. In short, although force may result in an action, and repeated force in repeated action, only training can lead to sustained, self-generating development. Training, not force, promises what is essential to modern technologies and economic systems: flexibility in action through understanding and confidence; inventiveness, initiative, and ability to make decisions; and respect for the contributions of other and readiness to collaborate with them.

Training is therefore properly part of the grand march toward greater equality between people, toward more widespread opportunities, participation, involvement, and rising expectations. However stumbling the progress, these are milestones along a clear path in all spheres of new life. The preference for force is understandable. Those who subscribe to it would *apply* force, not act under it; their real opposition is not to training, but to the kinds of development training seeks to foster. In a training-oriented regime the subscribers to force would have to share power with others or, more likely, lose it, and thus forego their positions in society.

As a consequence of training for development some people therefore stand to lose. They have to reorient themselves toward a new kind of society, one that is developed and maintained through hard work in partnership with many others. Only then will they be able to discard the naive attractions of force. Others are caught in their life history, such as the child who submitted to a parent's authority, and then repeats the pattern of parental authority on the next generation. The new society would cheat such individuals of a prospect in which they have much invested. Still others are willing to pay the price of force as long as it provides order, neatness, and predictability in their world. That they cling to this promise even when it starts to fray reveals the depth of their fears—fear of an unknown world ahead, with familiar landmarks gone and long hard-earned experience perhaps irrelevant; people, whose trustworthiness engenders skepticism.

The case for training stands firm. It has deep roots and is broadly based. The present inadequacies of training may be glaring, but they can be examined and removed, and real progress can be made in action.

INCREASING EMPLOYMENT
AND ORGANIZATIONAL PERFORMANCE

Training is emerging as central to new thrusts for ensuring high employment and also high organizational performance—both together. In Europe, 15 member states of the European Union agreed at their 'job summit' in November 1997 to improve their training programs over the next five years so that all young people out of work for six months and anyone out of work for a year or more, have access to a training scheme for helping them back into the labor market. Studies had found that young people with vocational training were only half as likely to be out of work as school leavers without any and that this ratio held for all countries. Denmark and Sweden were already putting as much public funds into 'active' measures like training and counseling as into the 'passive' payment of unemployment benefits. 'Training, the Competitive Edge' headlined an advertisement in the *New York Times* (September 29, 1987) by a multinational high-tech company claiming big gains from intensively training its employees for new technologies.

For training to play this pivotal role in achieving high employment and high performance together calls for hard rethinking and reworking of conventional approaches. High on the agenda for trainers and their whole establishment to work out afresh is how people can develop needed competencies in much larger numbers and across ever greater diversities of background, preparation, and learning capacities. The other volume, specifically for *them*, will focus on their whole agenda.

Repositioning training within organizational change strategies is the primary agenda for policy-makers and managers and the number one focus of this volume. Contrasted with the 'fragmented' (traditional) and the 'formalised' (mechanistic) approaches, is this 'focused' approach. We will share this approach and these terms for it.

Reading 1.1

The Changed Nature of Change and the Response of the HRD Professional

DAVID KIEL*

The Evolution of Change

It appears that the HRD field has evolved through four stages, each building on, including, but gradually supplanting the others and subtly shaping the action of practitioners in the field. We are in the middle of the fourth major stage which entails a major paradigm shift. This has broad and profound implications for training and development practitioners.

The first phase (roughly 1940–1960), 'the classical period', cannot be understood without reference to the scientific management theories of Frederick Taylor and the classic formulations of bureaucracy by Weber. This precursor to the modern era of HRD was based on mechanistic assumptions and engineering models and culminated in the famous Hawthorne experiments. In the decades that followed, social psychology and education replaced engineering as the disciplines that were most likely to lead to improvements in human productivity and satisfaction, yet the emphasis on isolating and manipulating variables within the organization remained.

Following the work of Kurt Lewin, the 'force-field of variables' affecting performance was analyzed and adjusted. Individual behaviors and group norms were 'unfrozen', 'changed', and 'refrozen'. Maslow, Hertzberg, and McClelland alerted us to the 'factors' or 'motives' or 'needs' to be addressed. Bion, Bales, Bennis, Shephard, and others helped us understand how small groups could be powerful vehicles for behavior change.

Within these frameworks, the scope of change was mostly aspects of individual behaviors and attitudes within organizational subsystems. The organizations themselves were seen as relatively stable. The organizational environments were not considered important or were treated as homogeneous and stable.

The next phase (1960–1970) saw the birth and growth of OD. Spurred on by the application of group techniques to organizations and large infusions of funds by such corporate giants as EXXON and AT&T, training and development practitioners expanded the scope of the changes they were willing to undertake from subsets of the organizations to total systems. The methods were psychologically based, prescriptive, and had a 'one size fits

* Special contribution (1999).

all' quality (e.g., GRID OD, Rensis Likert's System IV, Chris Argyris Pattern B, David McGregor Theory Y.) In these approaches, for the most part, organizations were considered to be operating in homogeneous environments and change was seen to be driven by the needs for growth and development of individuals, frustrated by hierarchy and mechanistic norms.

The decade 1970 to 1980 replaced these 'one best way' approaches with contingency models and recognition of the external environment. First, the implications for work of the socio-technical theorists like Eric Trist and his colleagues at the Tavistock Institute gained more acceptance. Lawrence and Lorsches showed that environments were not homogeneous but discrete and that different organizational structures and norms were needed to match organizational subsystems with their specialized environments. As the post-war hegemony of American business began to fail in the face of international competition, particularly from the Japanese, economic performance replaced human development as a major value as TQM overtook OD as the strategy of choice for organizational improvement.

Situational leadership replaced the managerial grid as a leading theory. Strategic planning gained currency. Early strategic planning models assumed the future could be assessed with relative certainty and that the organization should be changed in fundamental ways (e.g., products, structure, markets, culture) to match up better with the predicted environment.

The Fourth Wave: The Learning Organization Paradigm

By 1980, things began to shift again, ushering in the current era. Environments of organizations were seen as changing, but now changing much more rapidly and, more importantly, in unpredictable ways. The word frequently used to describe organizational environments during the current period is 'turbulent'. Webster defines turbulence as 'violently agitated or disturbed, stormy, causing unrest, unruly....' Some, like Tom Peters and Meg Wheatly, would argue we are no longer dealing with change, but chaos. The hopeful response to this terrifying analysis of current conditions was and is the Learning Organization.

Arie Geus, corporate planner for Shell Oil, writing in the *Harvard Business Review* (March–April, 1988) puts it this way (after noting that fully one-third of the FORTUNE 500 companies in 1970 had disappeared by 1983): '...high level, effective, and continuous institutional learning and ensuring corporate change are (considered) prerequisites for corporate success (at Shell)....' Articles by Craig Lundberg ('On Organizational Learning'), and two books, Peter Senge's *The Fifth Discipline* and *Organizational Learning* by Chris Argyris and Donald Schon, summarize most of the key ideas in the paradigm, which articulates ways that organizations may learn quickly enough to adapt in turbulent environments.

The Learning Organization Paradigm has a number of major tenets:

1. *Responding to Partial Understanding.* Human systems are too complex for any one person to understand. Excessive reliance on a linear approach to strategic planning can lead to serious planning errors. Treating uncertainty as the reality can lead to adaptive strategies such as 'gaming out future scenarios' and planning for contingencies.

2. *Appreciating Complexity.* Cause and effect are not closely related in time and space. 'Effects' often take a long time to happen and may show themselves far away. Probing deeply into the organization's situation, history, and dynamics can produce a more profound understanding of the causal change that determines long-term performance.

3. *Constant Collaboration.* Because change results in a multitude of planned and unplanned results, most of which are beyond our abilities to predict, people need to share information continuously. In the learning organization, teams need to be able to talk about complexity, to think insightfully about complex issues, and to develop the ability for innovative, coordinated action based on in-depth understanding of the situation with all of its uncertainty.

4. *Learning to Create the Future.* Creating the future requires that organizations be able to develop shared visions among their members, and to implement their visions. The ability to translate these visions to specific action-learning experiments in the service of the organization's purpose is both an important skill that needs to be widely developed and a function of the organization's environment.

5. *Mastering Personal Excellence.* A new kind of leader is needed to respond to the challenge of change: one who adopts a systems view, can create a personal vision, and can know and understand other people's visions. Much of what he recommends is based on developing a truly profound capacity for listening, understanding, and communicating.

6. *Experimenting Continuously and Learning How to Learn.* The final aspect of the Learning Organization is continuous experimentation. This requires an organizational culture which favors unbiased commitment to knowledge, skills in communication, development of shared visions, and efficiency in execution. Effective organizations and managers are self-conscious and reflective about the way they learn and problem-solve, constantly seeking to improve the social processes as well as technical processes.

The Learning Organizational Model: 15 Implications for HRD Practice

There are a number of areas in which the Learning Organization Paradigm can be applied to improve current HRD practice in the year 2000 and beyond.

1. *Fostering Acceptance and Understanding of Unending Change.* HRD practitioners can help managers and the rank-and-file organization members understand the conditions in society, in industry, and in the organization so

that they will have more understanding and acceptance of the business necessity of rapid and continuous change.

2. *Developing a Culture of Continuous Improvement and Continuous Learning.* Establishing a culture of continuous improvement involves accepting the fact that learning at all levels and all functions is a critical organizational process. But HRD practitioners should go beyond the installation of a particular quality effort which is essentially a third wave approach. They should add a fourth wave component: ways that managers and employees can be self-conscious about how the learning that leads to organizational improvement at every level occurs, and assist organization members to become and see themselves as increasingly more effective, self-reliant, and cooperative learners.

3. *For Strategic Planning at All Levels.* The Learning Organization model suggests that strategic planning concepts should not be reserved for the highest level of management alone. In an organization that is facing demands for continuous improvement and a turbulent environment, the unit managers need to plan strategically as well, and all levels of management need to share their maps of the future. All employees, as well, need to be encouraged to think strategically about their own futures.

4. *Structuring the Organization to Enhance Adaptive Potential.* Units responding to turbulent environmental sectors need autonomy to plan and implement rapid changes. Managers will need to understand the importance of linking and liaison roles, and of working in a project mode in cross-functional and vertical teams. In addition, units that deal with different environments must be horizontally linked to insure consistent direction. Lack of change management roles at the top levels limits the capacity of the organization to search out the environment and plan new responses.

5. *Creating New Communications Networks.* The inter-personal barriers that go with differences in rank and status are even more dysfunctional in the current climate than in previous years. An all-to-all communication network for a specific task or function is usually more useful than a hierarchical-go-through-channels approach. HRD leaders should therefore develop programs that bring people together across levels and functions to share information and develop the working relationships and networks which will facilitate adaptation and learning.

6. *Creating Organizational Capacity for Anticipating and Responding to Change.* Coordination will be achieved by helping everyone understand the big picture, structuring rewards for team work, and inculcating the win-win conflict resolution throughout the organization. HRD professionals also need to help managers learn how to support, protect, and encourage their employees involved in non-traditional structures such as matrix, cross-functional, and vertical teams, and project management efforts.

7. *Helping Executives Select and Sponsor Desirable Changes.* Top managers may also be 'change stiflers' by their controlling approach to bringing about

organizational change. Similarly, top executives often neglect their own role in making changes. They may feel that mandating change is their role and that change takes place below them. They may tend to neglect their roles in leading, supporting, and, most importantly, living the values they are espousing for their organization. The consequence is that core changes essential to the organization's competitiveness may be only partially implemented, or even resisted.

Hard hitting educational programs that help executives look at their own behaviors in conceptualizing, mandating, and sponsoring organizational changes may help minimize turbulence from misdirected change efforts. Such programs would include studies of patterns of ineffective change, models of effective and ineffective executive change leadership behavior, change management assessment centers and simulations, and personal feedback skills.

8. *Improving Change Tactics for Executives and Managers.* Some things stay the same. The key to both learning and change is participation. Managerial skill in involving employees in the assessment, planning, and implementation of change still appears to be critical to effective innovation at the core productive level of the organization. Change managers need skills in needs analysis, impact assessment, and implementation planning. They also need to be able to talk honestly, sensitively, and persuasively about change. They need to be able to choose the right mix of negotiation, education, persuasion, and imposition. They need to know how to pilot efforts, listen systemically, and adjust action-experiments. Not surprisingly, educational programs which assist managers in actually carrying out experiments and learning from experiences in managing changes seem to have more impact that those which rely on concepts and approaches alone.

9. *Updating Team Development Concepts.* The nature of team development is evolving from a purely relationship building and group maintenance process to a process that explicitly helps groups identify and manage change in their environment. Team building should be an opportunity for team members to assimilate and adapt to change on a continuous basis, to increase skills for team learning and adaptation, and to acknowledge and deal openly and constructively with the feelings and dynamics attendant to rapid organizational changes. This means that teams need time together to set goals, plan, organize, and implement. They also need time together to process what is happening to them, express their feelings about it, and support one another through the process of constant adaptation.

10. *Changing How We Train Managers to Get the Job Done.* In dealing with task performance, managers need to learn how to identify realistic goals and time frames given the constant change and shift. They need to learn what signals to pay attention to and what to ignore. They need to learn how to juggle schedules, resources, and assignments in order to respond to inevitable crisis situations and to plan for various contingencies.

The manager in the changing environment may have to play a 'buffer role', spending more of his/her time sorting out, negotiating, and 'warding off' or 'pacing' externally imposed changes in order to protect the staff's ability to work. This role also requires the ability to negotiate with upper managers and peers about how and when change is implemented in their areas.

Finally, on the relationship side of management, the ability to manage group awareness, acceptance, and adjustment to change, and the ability to support, counsel, and redirect individuals whose roles are most deeply affected by change now becomes very significant.

11. *Helping Individuals Cope with Frequent Reassignments and Role Changes.* Managers in organizations going through major changes are often forced to cope with frequent reassignments and changes in reporting relationships, roles, and job descriptions. These factors create uncertainty in the career development realm as well. In development planning with subordinates, managers have to be adept in mapping out alternative paths for employees, stressing the continuous development of skills that may become critical for the organization in the future as well as for their continued marketability, and helping employees adjust to these short-term assignments and transitions.

HRD programs that help individuals cope with frequent assignment and reporting relationship changes will reduce transition costs and improve organizational morale (e.g., how to enter a new group, how to exit effectively, and maintaining personal networks across distance). Teaching managers to assist employees making these transitions will strengthen managerial effectiveness and subordinate–superior relationships.

12. *Strengthening the Career Development System.* Effective career development efforts play a major role in helping organizations manage change. Building change management capacities and skills into selection and advancement criteria for succession planning helps the organization assure that job incumbents can effectively adapt to changing circumstances.

Above all, employees need to be empowered and motivated by a personal vision with meaningful commitments that go beyond a specific role or job. HRD staff will need to create programs that help employees develop and maintain their own visions within and beyond the boundaries of the company.

Individuals in rapidly changing organizations also may need new career maps based on a succession of skills and experiences rather than positions, and may need to develop improved skills at networking and pro-active management of their careers. Mentoring in a turbulent environment will change as well. Senior managers cannot be so sure as to the paths toward organizational advancement and thus need to be more tentative in their advice while at the same time adopting a collaborative rather than a paternal/maternal stance with those they mentor.

13. *Establishing Effective Support Systems.* Major organizational change always creates gains and losses. It has become widely known that groups go

through stages analogous to grief responses when coping with loss and major change. Losses must be acknowledged and grieved, or emotional blockage may occur leading to greater resistance to change, increased burnout, and ineffective implementation. However, most organizations are still unable, to respond to emotional issues among staff, or to fully understand the human dynamics underlying major changes.

HRD programs that help organizational leaders and followers understand and accept the emotional dynamics that accompany change processes and provide ways to help individuals and groups deal with their feelings about change will enable the organization to adapt with less unconscious sabotage, employee burnout, and subtle resistance.

14. *Providing Organizational Support for Individual Coping.* Organizations can support employees' ability to cope with change by helping them develop their creative thinking and stress management skills, providing opportunities to develop a personal vision and plan, learn conflict resolution skills, and by providing an environment that recognizes family needs. Organizational policies (e.g., job sharing, flexi-time, day care) that help reduce conflicts between work and family roles for employees may relieve stress that indirectly could impact organizational change efforts. Finally, organizations undergoing major changes, such as downsizing may need to explore extraordinary programs such as support groups for 'survivors', as well as outplacement and other supports for those laid off.

15. *Acknowledging and Responding to the New Diversity and the New Globalism.* The workforce is becoming more and more diverse in the US, a trend that will only accelerate in the next century. Companies are becoming more international in ownership and composition as well. Taking time to understand, appreciate, and celebrate difference is an important first step for any organization. Once all feel valued, they can then engage in dialogue about how to integrate their differences in a way that advances the work of the organization. In the new era of constant change, Steven Covey's dictum for individuals works as well for the organization–individual interface: 'Seek to understand, then to be understood'.

Conclusion: The Fourth Wave is Here, the HRD Professional Must Respond

Our understanding of the nature of change has evolved rapidly over the past four decades of HRD practice in organizations. Change has gone from a single topic within the human resource development field to become the environment with which all of the activities of the field take place. Much of the work of human resource development in the first decade of the 21st century will be to recalibrate our practices to take this fact into account. The classic topics that training and development professionals concern themselves with— leadership development, planning, conflict resolution, team building, career development, and so on—must be reconceptualized and practice reconfigured to reflect the new realities.

This is a tremendous challenge and opportunity for HRD professionals for several reasons. Our clients, like ourselves, may still be caught up in first wave, second wave, or third wave thinking. Like ourselves, even if our thinking has evolved to match the times, the needed skill development may yet be lagging. Organizational structures and practices may be even slower to evolve. At the same time demands for effective change management escalate as competitive pressures continue to mount.

There is no easy answer, but surely the right direction is continued dialogue within the profession, and between HRD staff and their clients—all leading to thoughtful experimentation in the service of responding effectively to the changed nature of change.

2

ASSESSING CONTEXTS AND
OPPORTUNITIES FOR CHANGE

In an age when most directors take a broad, high concept approach...,
Barton is going in the opposite direction by forcing modern actors to
engage more deeply with the text.... What he does is to offer the actors
a practical method for understanding clues that are buried in the text.

—John Lahr

...what is living derives from the continuous interaction of an organism...with his entire world. To neglect the environment is just as bad an error as to forget the organism in which its forces are momentarily concentrated.

—Lewis Mumford

We must lead men to the particulars themselves, ...to lay their notions by and...familiarize themselves with the facts.

—Francis Bacon

Positioning training better in strategies for change requires fresh attention to contextual factors—fresh, new, pro-active kinds—and happily also quite manageable attention. Most directly it is the people factors that affect training, just as changes in technology, finance, competitors, the economy, and rules and regulations most directly affect investment decisions, and climate, water, and soil conditions affect farming. But, as all know who look for practical guidance, one factor cannot be understood without the others, but—and this is the dismay—the connections become a maze very quickly, impossible to make sense of at first glance, never mind act on; so, better stick to dealing with what is at hand.

To help sort what factors and connections matter from others that matter less and which matter now from some others that can come later is our purpose in this chapter. Like John Barton on the stage for Shakespeare, we too want to 'offer the actors a practical method for understanding clues that are buried in the text'. And a crucial step beyond understanding, we are especially interested in identifying clues to use for taking action in the environment and so helping policy-makers and change managers forego the time-honored passive stance toward the environment—waiting for things to happen which then is weathered as best one may—in favor of actively looking for opportunities to anticipate developments, and even to create them.

That is clearly what several enterprises have done which we used (at the beginning of Chapter 1) to illustrate the wide range of recent major changes in training, in locations as far flung and disparate as a mammoth engineering plant in North India and a dispersed health system in a low-income state in USA. Part of the learning will come from finding the clues right there, among the experiences on the ground. Recent organizational theory holds others; it is sobering and suggestive that concrete, factual attention to the environment entered major research agenda and professional journals only forty years ago.

CULTURES OF HIGH-COST NEGLECT

Shifting to broad enough appreciation for action is crucial and urgent. Even in slow-changing times and places, close to exclusive concentration on one's own immediate in-house affairs is hopeless. It condemns any enterprise to bumping along from crisis to crisis, which then jerk it into catching up, each to that present, till the last crisis finishes it off; this, basically, is the story of two-thirds of new enterprises that fail even in those times and places. Now, with changes escalating and speeding worldwide, neglect for contextual factors disables fast.

One question remains before we can focus usefully on examining 'the text'. If the certain consequences of neglect are so utterly dismal, what then explains that this neglect continues to be so widespread that we can quote prominent personages drawn from a wide range of occupations and eras, all weighing against the very same temptation to avert the eye and turn away? We ourselves certainly see 'most directors (preferring to) take a broad, high concept approach', to 'neglect the environment', and, like their ancestors four centuries ago, to settle for 'notions' away from the apparently pressing but also intolerable need to 'familiarize themselves with the facts'. Complexity alone, however great and apparently intractable, cannot explain so stubborn a suicidal attachment. For intellectual clarification to have a chance, the underlying hindrances need surfacing first and to be recognized.

The helplessness that the traditional wait-and-see stance incorporates and also signifies echoes conditions present as well as past, some deeply personal. Readiest to be recognized as outdated in most (but by no means all) places is the realistic dependence of farmers on the weather and its vagaries. Debatable issues aside, of mankind's responsibilities for climatic changes, to treat contextual factors generally as if they were uncontrollable like climatic ones is clearly inappropriate for most of us.

More understandable and seriously hindering are the many people in mid-career, with the ingrained habits of wait-and-see which they learned as a child, continued as obedient son (or even more consistently as obedient daughter or daughter-in-law), who wait to be told what to do and, often, what to think. So general was this stance among the mid-career executives and community leaders who came to the Aloka international training center in the 1950s from twenty-six countries, that we shifted the most personal part of the program there to psychoanalytically-based methods, for the very reason that they highlighted best for working-level resolution the quite elemental issues of dependencies in growing up. Unrecognized, they immobilized even these young leaders chosen for proven abilities and promise and hid from them clues to opportunities for action open to them that were obvious to others. Now, forty years on, strong competition in expanding economies for engineers, information technologists, doctors, managers, public administrators, and other young professionals accounts only in part for the proliferation of one-person professional offices and high mobility everywhere. Getting away from paternal control and from enterprises run on traditional hierarchical lines figure large in many people's decisions we know. Their decision to strike out on their own only looks like a good step. As long as the personal issues of dependencies and control remain unresolved, they visit them unwittingly on other people; hence so little colleagueship and sharing and so much angry in-fighting, also in institutions. They remain blind as before to forces in the environment, except to opportunities that offer the most immediate and blatantly personal advance—in some hierarchy in current favor.

Too eager copying of others often masks the same set of dependencies in yet another fashion. It sidelines sound habits of keeping informed and fitting new understandings into one's practice and settings, of driving to keep up with the latest information about what others are doing, irrespective of differences in contexts. For addicts to copying, the prominence of speakers and enterprises that show success attract most, even if they are in a far away place in contexts widely and patently different from one's own. Quality circles in Japan, organizational downsizing in the US, and joint labor management bodies in Germany are major examples on their busy agenda. Copying mindless of context is chancy at best, and often leads only to dead ends, and it certainly postpones further the essential personal and organizational work of finding and using opportunities to change in the actual situations as they are and as they are developing. Town planner Lewis Mumford, continuing the quote at the head of this chapter, sees this and the other failures and enduring temptations as 'a disguise for laziness and psychological incompetence'.

Whatever function they serve for people and organizations mobilizing them, all of this crowded, far flung shifting scene—of temptations, trends, successes, distortions, delays—is of course part of the environment for policy and change on which we are focusing this chapter. What all to take into account, for any particular purpose in its particular setting and ways to do that, now move to the forefront. Having a map (or maps) for entering that complex territory, and the priorities, sequences and other guides for pacing the effort can be very useful. Pareek's paradigm in Box 2.1 maps the major components and their conceptual relationships. For trainers we see four fresh scenarios and describe them in the companion volume.[1] For policy-makers and change managers we see a two-step sequence as most useful—the first deliberately to reduce complexity by limiting the environment to take into account; the second to indicate five priority areas within that relevant environment for policy-makers and change managers to take into account for sure.

Box 2.1

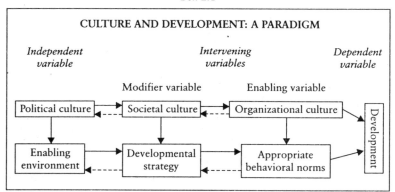

SOURCE: Udai Pareek, "Culture and Development: The Case of Indonesia" in D. Sinha and H.S.R. Kao (eds)' *Social Values and Development: Asian Perspectives* New Delhi: Sage Publications, 1988), p. 177.

THE RELEVANT ENVIRONMENT

The working notion of good enough is a firm way to avoid feeling overwhelmed by fast changing and ever more complex environments

[1] Chapter 8.

and, since it seems pointless to invest the energies, doing nothing to understand and act in it. The practical questions are just two: 1. granted that everything is indeed connected with everything else, what all really matters to this particular enterprise; and 2. how is this part of the environment that matters in my affairs best understood to cope and interact with.

Scope and Boundaries

The most useful process we know for drawing the line between what to include and what not starts with highlighting the overall purpose, mission, and task of the enterprise (or part) for which change—and therefore training—is envisaged (along with other inputs). The parties needed to get the task accomplished, outside the immediate circle of those actually carrying it out, make up the relevant environment. Most obvious to include are suppliers of parts and services that go into the enterprise and also clients to whom the outputs go. Less obvious, but also important to include, are the financiers of the effort, the families and wider communities whose standards of diligence and quality the actors bring to it, public agencies that regulate it, competitors for the same clients, and wellwishers. The sheer practicalities of the inclusion/exclusion decision deserve emphasis: whoever, individual, department or agency, near and far, *in fact* influences task performance or is pretty directly affected by it is included. So, for work with a youngster in difficulty the relevant environment would probably include parents and siblings and often a grandmother or grandfather, a neighbor and teacher or two, his/her pastor, a local agency, and certainly some peers. For change in the department of a plant or a store, it would include decision-makers and funders of the intended change, other departments and services whose inputs and/or receptions would be affected by it, maintenance and administrative services inside the organization, and also customers, suppliers, often a neighborhood or two, and agencies outside.

Organizational boundaries do not distinguish what is practically needed here. The inclusions need to be worked out specifically for the purpose, and some will clarify only as the overall task gets under way and actually shows up what is well identified as the 'causal texture of the environment'. This readiness to learn from experience and to adjust is extra important when aiming change strategies at long-term futures in environments that can only be roughly foreseen.

The mission of a new professional school (in a State university in USA in the mid-seventies) involved many other professional, academic and administrative bodies on the campus and also a dozen State agencies and selected communities off-campus. The total number of relationships to build and maintain from the start came to 97 and this grew to 132 in the first six months' working that was heavy on outreach. About two-thirds were with identified persons or key office-holders.

Drawing that many parties in and focussing them on the mission was a formidable venture but not an infinite one. It had clarity and boundaries, and was made manageable by dividing responsibilities for it within the school. That delegation then called for developing mechanisms in the school for integrating the parts and for developing overall policies and strategies for the school's environment as a whole.

Dominant Characteristics

From work with a wide variety of organizations and using system theory as it was then fast developing, Fred Emery and Eric Trist mapped a four-fold typology of major environmental states in ascending order of the system connectedness that they required.

1. The traditional, slow-changing environments that can still be found in isolated, usually small farm areas, are of the first order: 'placid, randomized' is the characterization. Immediate awareness and day-to-day local action is all that is required there.

2. In environments of the second type, all is still placid but goals and obstacles to change are in clusters. With that, understanding the environment and developing strategies, for positioning oneself in it well and developing that distinctive niche, become essential. Under these conditions, organizations become larger, hierarchical, and centralize control.

3. The next more complex type has several similar organizations in the same environment competing for the same resources, customers, and goodwill. Anticipating what others will do, influencing it, and reacting quickly to what they do do complicates matters greatly. Organizational capacity for foresight and flexibility are important here and call for highly sensitive contact points with the environment. Readiness to collaborate, with other enterprises, interest groups, and government agencies may be important.

4. In type four, changes arise not merely in and between organizations in the same environment but the environment itself has

become turbulent and largely unpredictable. Action decisions of very large organizations and powerful interest groups, legislation and regulation, social unrest, and the escalating responses to them within organizations and in the environment make high uncertainty a permanent condition.

Exhibit 2.1 summarizes the four types of causal textures in environments, so that readers can position themselves and their organizations and interests suitably and can also see some practical implications for managing to live and work well in and with their environment.

Exhibit 2.1
THE CAUSAL TEXTURE OF ORGANIZATIONAL ENVIRONMENTS:
FOUR TYPES

Characteristic features	Best strategy	Best tactic
1. Slow-changing: 'placid, randomized'	Strategy and tactic are same: do best on local basis; learn by trial and error	
2. Still placid but 'clustered'	Optimize position; develop distinct niche in field	Know environment; enlarge organization and centralize control
3. Similar organizations in same field: 'disturbed, reactive'	Build capacity and power; develop environmental startegy that includes competitors, interest groups, and government agencies	Prize information; operational-type centralized control for highly flexible responses; absorb, collorate, overpower
4. Turbulent, unpredictable environment	Long-range; highlight metagoals and shared values *for all in field*; reduce uncertainty; prize R&D	Collapse hierarchies and open system boundaries; overlap memberships; prize information giving and receiving

While all four kinds of environments in this typology exist in all parts of the globe, the trend is strongly toward No. 4, the most complex and 'turbulent field'. Unhappily, moving from one to the other is not a smooth progression. The complexity and turbulence of No. 4 in particular is a quantum jump beyond No. 3, with the result that effective ways of working well with the less complex and disturbed No. 3 does not guide and certainly not escalate well to the different orders of complexity and lasting turbulence of No. 4. There is real danger in fact that effectiveness in No. 3 hides the emergence of the new conditions and postpones radically new preparation for them, some amounting to reversing course, and so gets solidly in the way of effective coping with the new conditions.

FIVE AREAS FOR SPECIAL ATTENTION

In this environment then, relevant to organizational purpose and itself having characteristic features which favor some strategies and tactics over others, five areas deserve special attention for developing training policy. They are: the organizational culture and the culture of the local environment, each as it is: the human resource management system in which training is to fit; emerging trends in organizational thinking far and wide and the future for which the intended changes—and the training for them—are to prepare; the likely future but also the future 'if I could have my wishes'. The gap between these two futures is the scope for developing strategic values and sustained system-wide action.

1. Choosing Best Opportunities for Change

Organizational culture is a useful term for choosing the best opportunities in an existing situation and also when setting out to create a new one—but only if we can both enlarge and also concentrate its common usage. We need to enlarge it beyond the formal corporate and institution settings for which it is most used, so that it can also accommodate the larger fabric of essential connections the intended developmental tasks must make in the relevant environment; 'system culture' would serve us better for that larger area (if we could make it stick). That substitution would also remind us that our concern here is not with formal, legal entities as a whole—a state agency or a private company or a school or a neighborhood—but with systems tailor-made for a particular change-task and a particular environment and culture to make it in. Box 2.2 shows the culture of a whole army stifling officer recruitment, even at enormous risks and against well-publicised policies to the contrary, and also the wide differences between army units. The task-system is often only part of an organization—a department, say, or a block in a city—with boundaries that would straddle the lines on an organization chart and would commonly include parties outside the organization's boundaries altogether.

Box 2.2

ORGANIZATIONAL CULTURE AND DIFFERENCES BETWEEN UNITS

In the first four months of the experimental board the supply of candidates in the country as a whole was barely one-third of what was needed and in the catchment area of the board itself it was even less. A survey was made of the sources of candidates in a command area with the startling result that their numbers were absurdly small from the majority of units. Over two-thirds of the 700 independent units (Lieutenant Colonel or Major commands) provided no candidates in a 15-week period and 14 percent only one candidate, the proportion of units then decreasing as the number of candidates increased. The accepted, though tacit, convention was not to put candidates forward. Further analysis showed that the nearer a unit was to going overseas to take up a role in combat, the smaller the number of candidates it produced; the larger the unit, the smaller the proportion of candidates; and, the more candidates a unit sent to a selection board, the higher the proportion accepted (A.T.M., Wilson, 1951). Furthermore, units producing most officers usually had internal institutions to discover such candidates.

SOURCE: Eric Trist and Hugh Murray, *The Social Engagement of Social Science: A Tavistock Anthology* (University of Pennsylvania Press, 1990), Vol. 1, p. 58. Every effort has been made to trace the copyright holder(s). In the absence of a reply, permission has been assumed.

The culture of *this* task-environment system is the part of the field where all forces concentrate most powerfully and determine opportunities for change. With new enterprises this is most glaring, and most of all with those born of dissatisfaction with how things continued to be done elsewhere in an existing culture; having given up on it, these set forth to fashion something better on their own. Enterprises that succeed have composed their systems and manage themselves well; always and everywhere there are twice as many that have died for failing at exactly these essential tasks.

Success experiences, i.e., change opportunities in hindsight, actually abound in the wider cultures of whole organizations, cities, provinces, countries, and regions, even as they now exist. Averages hide them with flattening out the variances. It is the variances that tell of opportunities for change well taken. Several examples figured in the illustrative list at the beginning of Chapter 1 of striking changes in the settings for training in recent decades. Opportunities abound in systems of all sizes.

So, in South Asia, Singapore's high technology urban culture is quite different from Burma's. In the largely slow-changing South of the USA where women are still commonly thought of for grace and children at home rather than smartly in professional and business careers, all three leading universities in the Research Triangle have women presidents. In the same India, Kerala has several times higher literacy (and other) rates than Rajasthan. Within Kerala, with the same State-wide policies and support and cultural traditions, some cities show development well ahead of others and some parts of the same city stand out again. The same is true inside the same company: one plant, and one or two departments within that plant, develop ahead of others and, in time, become known for that throughout the organisation. They have a culture open to change, even thrive on it.

In actual practice, then, choosing best opportunities for launching a change strategy is a matter of practicalities: such as, determining the readiness there is for the idea (or how it can be stimulated and mobilized) and what impacts its implementation would have on people now living and working there. For the onward dialogue between key partners the range of extra resources that could be allocated to the effort, the initiatives and controls it would call for, and who the key figures could be often become important parameters. Here, some detailed arrangements would promote it; there, others get in the way. Prospects clarify with successive steps. The people immersed or closest to the prospective task-in-its-environment are expert guides to where, how and how fast, and by whom first a start might best be made and then best unfolded. They know what is really possible there, obstacles and all, and how to prepare the ground. If policy-makers and managers did choose that setting, the local people would have to become the most active participants in any case, so involving them early on is good strategy.

For local people to speak up and engage themselves fully would be strangely new in many settings, to them and to others, and probably suspect at first. This is most common where policies and instructions have habitually been made at the top and passed down, so that part-ners-to-be have a long experience of distance and stand-off and doubt that will now change. Even in unpromising settings, however, change opportunities exist here and there; they can be surfaced and effective beginnings made.

In our work with the Indonesian Ministry of Health (1981–86), to help it decentralise much decision-making to its provincial and district offices, we started our part by setting out this intent, its likely practical implica-tions, and also the considerable efforts participation would require at the various levels of the national system. This picture the Ministry then sent out to the provinces and encouraged them in turn to publicise in the districts. Applications to take part came quickly, welcoming the initiative. They covered enough settings for reaching firm decisions to start building the additional capacity and decentralising decisions in three named provinces, the patterns of concentrated District-level efforts in each, and also the sequence is which further provinces would be involved.

2. The Surrounding Wider Culture

Practical too is to choose and position change efforts where they can draw most readily on supportive elements in the wider culture, of an organization or an inner city as a whole, or of yet larger systems up to regional and global levels.

> Notable for our work in Indonesia were widespread traditions of community-wide decision-making, collaborative working and firm commitments to one another, and active participation by all in voluntary work. Proceeding only after concensus had been reached was customary; it is a slow and thorough method that leads to reliable agreements and leaves no scars. Family planning programs were spreading singularly fast with these traditions which served also for monitoring and making local adjustments in the program. So we highlighted the same traditions in renewing the health services.
>
> For work in China a consultant advises high mindfulness for personal relationships (Box 2.3).

Cultural considerations need not be tied to place; migrations have spread them and inserted pockets of innovative readiness into most areas and kinds of enterprise. Where migrants settle as a community, the traditions they bring may last long and may even have been heightened in the moving and in settling in strange places. Strangers in the system therefore deserve special attention when preparing for change.

> Punjabis displaced from ancestral lands in India and Pakistan, Jewish professionals, second (and later) sons of landowners where they cannot inherit property and therefore need to move and strike out on their own, figure large in developing fresh enterprises and innovative components. Major theories and whole sets of training institutions have taken off from these migrant cultures.[2] Displaced from ancestral property and careers,

[2] For theories, see, e.g., Everett Hagen, *On the Theory of Social Change* (Illinois: The Dorsey Press, 1963).

Box 2.3

GUIDE TO USING *GUANXI*

Introductions: Use knowledge of relationships to improve your own network. Remember the importance of having someone introduce you to a Chinese rather than walking up and introducing yourself.

Be personal: Take the time to become familiar with any Chinese with whom you want to interact. Jumping into business discussions without introductory small-talk is impolite. Your conversation partner wants to know what kind of person you are, and if already acquainted, he wants to get a feel for your current state. These informal chats can include information valuable to your ongoing business discussions.

Map relationships: Be smart about mapping relationships. Make friends with second- and third-tier people in an organization, not only top-level staff. In politics, be aware that the structures are rarely clear. The person apparently in charge may not have the internal pull to accomplish what you want. Do some background investigation and pursue relationships in different organizations simultaneously.

Maintenance: Remember that *guanxi* must be watered, like a plant. That is what distinguishes it from bribery. Chinese say that managing their close relationships is a part-time job. Friends see or at least hear from each other regularly. You must invest time and thought in your *guanxi*. It is like a bank account, into which you must pay before you can withdraw.

Give and take: Always remember to return the help that you have received from your Chinese friends. Do not be so rigid in your approach that you preclude getting a better deal than you originally planned. And do not forget to call in help when you have done favours for others.

SOURCE: Nandani Lynton, "Playing the *Guanxi* Game" in *China Staff*, May 1998, pp 20–24.

these migrant populations are characteristically eager, versatile, persistent and often very able to regain their accustomed standards of living in fresh ways.

When he looked to develop a new cadre of diplomats for the post-World War II era, Generalissimo Stalin by-passed the usual sources for possible recruits and specifically identified instead aero-engineers with particular backgrounds and reputations. This is how one future ambassador and Party Secretary described this cultural thinking of a top policy-maker.[3]

At one of the Politburo sessions in the summer of 1944, after discussing the successful offensive of the Soviet Army at the front, Stalin had suddenly changed the subject and started talking about the necessity to prepare new diplomatic cadres because Hitler would soon be defeated and Soviet diplomacy had to be ready for the rapid revival of foreign affairs. New ties would be established with many states, and would also be necessary to solve a lot of postwar problems. In short, the Soviet Union would very soon need a large and fully qualified diplomatic corps. Even though it was the peak of the war and almost all of the young men had been called up by the armed forces, Stalin told Molotov that a diplomatic school had to be established at once.

"But where shall we get students?" Molotov asked Stalin. "Especially those who have studied liberal arts and languages?" Stalin replied that it was not necessary to find candidates educated in the humanities; they could learn that later. Right now, he said, the Foreign Ministry could take young engineers from defence plants. He said to be sure to choose those who got along well with workers. "Both engineers and workers are leading a very hard life; they receive only 700 grams of black bread, and many of them practically live at the plants and don't see their families for days." Stalin reasoned that if a young engineer manages to handle the difficult day-to-day problems and conflicts that were inevitable in those hard times, and the workers still respected him, he was a real diplomat or at least had the necessary abilities to become one.

And indeed our first class of close to fifty students consisted of young engineers, mostly from the aircraft industry. Before the war the aircraft institutes had been considered the nation's most prestigious, and the majority of ambitious young people tried for admission. This was what we called the "Stalin enrollment" to diplomacy, although hardly anyone knew about it at the time. Moreover, Stalin had deeper motives. Having got rid of the old generation of diplomats in the purges just before the war, he wanted to be sure that the old ways of thinking would not return....

Like me, most of the new people were technicians who were in no way affected by the old ways of thinking. We did not feel particularly vulnerable to Stalin's excesses, about which we knew only vaguely at the time. All of my family were ordinary people, and we did not have a single intellectual except my uncle, who was a professor of mathematics anyway.

---

[3] Anatoly Dobrynin, *In Confidence* (New York: Times Books/Random House, 1995), pp. 15–16.

Preparing change-tasks is the explicit mission of research and development units and outsiders usually expect, or at least accept, that R&D develop quite distinct cultures appropriate to that task. Training partakes of a similar aura and tolerance for difference. Problems come with transferring changes developed in the R&D (or the training culture) to operating systems that are meant to use the results. This may be best done with intermediary mechanisms to link them. Well-functioning linkage mechanisms have yet a another set of characteristics, a third culture. Small is best—let's say two members from each system, no decision-makers, indeed no reference to status, age, etc., in the home˘system. Taking the middle position between R&D and the relevant operating system on orientations to goals, time, inter-personal relations, and structure, they keep the focus steadily on the integrative task, solving problems along the way, and gain satisfaction from succeeding in this exacting and essential task as a group. Conflict resolution and flexibility are particularly important norms in this culture.[4]

3. Dominant Themes in Organizational Thinking

Flexibility, initiatives from many places, collapsing hierarchies to three or four levels, project teams and group rewards, mobilizing resources best for task performance over the long haul, visualizing outcomes and directions for development and doing whatever it takes to solve problems along the way, surfacing and resolving conflicts along the way—all echo the values and norms we have just described for effective linkage mechanisms. Policy-makers need these to do their particular task of innovating and getting innovations used to effect actual change. Worldwide thinking about organizations tends strongly in these very same directions. Boxes 2.4 and 5 summarize socio-technical thinking.

No marked increases in human kindness or grace of disposition and deportment are evident to explain this growing confluence. It is *most* tasks and those most characteristic of this era—their escalating complexity, changeability, and high interdependence with their envi-

[4] For fuller descriptions, analyses, and examples, the seminal work is Paul R. Lawrence and Jay W. Lorsch, *Organisation and Environment: Managing Differentiation and Integration* (Boston: School of Business Administration, Harvard University, 1967). For an overview and summary of several researches, see Rolf P. Lynton, "Linking an Innovative Sub-system into the System", *Administrative Science Quarterly*, Vol. 14 (1969), pp 398–416.

Box 2.4

SOCIO-TECHNICAL SYSTEMS THINKING

Considering enterprises as 'open socio-technical systems', helps to provide a more realistic picture of how they are both influenced by, and able to, act back on, their environment. It points in particular to the various ways in which enterprises are enabled by their structural and functional characteristics ('system constants') to cope with the 'lacks' and 'gluts' in their available environment. Unlike mechanical and other inanimate systems, they possess the property of 'equi-finality'; they may achieve a steady state from differing initial conditions and in differing ways. Thus in coping by internal changes they are not limited to simple quantitative change and increased uniformity but may, and usually do, elaborate new structures and take on new functions...

Inherent in the socio-technical approach is the notion that the attainment of optimum conditions in any one dimension does not necessarily result in a set of conditions optimum for the system as a whole. If the structures of the various dimensions are not consistent, interference will occur, leading to a state of disequilibrium, so that achievement of the overall goal will to some degree be endangered and in the limit made impossible. The optimization of the whole tends to require a less than optimum state for each separate dimension.... This approach does not imply that in all circumstances a detailed study of all three dimensions must be carried out. It does, however, underline the importance, when any aspect of a production system is examined, of taking into account the manner and extent of its interdependence with the other dimensions.

SOURCE: Eric L. Trist, Murray Higgin and Pollock, *Organizational Choice* (London: Tavistock Publications, 1963), pp 6–7.

ronments—that explains it, and that task-environments are also so instantly and continuously interconnected around the globe. The financial throes that started in East and South Asian countries in mid-1998 and threatened major countries on other continents with similar collapse only weeks later epitomises this. Also, on the more cheerful side, does the explosively expanding electronic information network, with people everywhere joining it or preparing to join it. For clarifying the values that these developments imply and most certainly need anchoring in, and for spreading and strengthening the capacities of people individually and in families and in larger systems of all kinds, training is then in the mainstream for this era. It may in fact have a pivotal role to play in keeping pace with this restless transformation and even anticipate and move ahead of it with timely preparation. We will turn in the next chapter to the policy and managerial practicalities for supporting training in this crucial function.

Box 2.5

SOCIO-TECHNICAL THEORY: SEVEN PROPOSITIONS

...In practice, working toward the joint optimization of the social and techno-logical systems of an organization is a complex process that requires a thor-ough understanding of: (1) the social processes that occur in organizations and the variety of theories and methods that exist to make more efficient use of human resources; (2) the technological process used by the organization and the constraints that it places on the design and operation of the social system; (3) the theory of open systems, because no two organizations are exactly alike or faced with the same environmental demands; and (4) the mechanics of change, both in the execution of the initial socio-technical system design and in provision for the continual adaptation of the organization to new environ-mental demands.

...Socio-technical theory has evolved into a set of fairly stable and recogniz-able propositions. These specify: (1) that the design of the organization must fit its goals; (2) that employees must be actively involved in designing the structure of the organization; (3) that variances in production or service must be controlled as close to their source as possible; (4) that subsystems must be designed around relatively whole and recognizable tasks; (5) that support sys-tems must be congruent with the design of the organization; (6) that a high quality of work life should be provided; and (7) that changes should continue to be made as necessary to meet environmental demands.

SOURCE: William A. Pasmore and John J. Shirwood, *Socio-technical Systems: A Sourcebook* (San Diego: University Associates, 1978), pp 3–5.

4. Human Resources Development (HRD)

The rapid spread and prominence of HRD clearly signals the high and pervasive importance newly accorded to the people component in well-organized enterprises in virtually all fields. It points to the same dramatic changes in new era tasks and environments that we have highlighted. However, in projecting itself as the leading con-cept for dealing with all people aspects, comprehensively and in an integrated manner, HRD has also taken on all the traditional per-sonnel functions accumulated from the more settled and hierachic-ally controlled times, e.g., salary and benefit structures, formal search, hiring and firing processes, rules and regulations, grievances and union negotiations, insurances, and outside arbitration of disputes. This combination makes for an awkward mix of orientations within HRD and for projecting a vague image in public. Organizations are busy experimenting and learning how best to combine the creative with the routine sides of HRD. Many, meanwhile, have advanced HRD in the system to give it more prominence, increasingly with direct representation on the board.

For training, HRD is an additional interface. How much of the traditional personnel culture training has to accommodate is a live issue. Many systems prefer to link training more directly and closely with the operating systems in direct line for using its results, find ways of keeping it formally in the realm of HRD and also very autonomous. Training budgets, for instance, receive separate consideration or, in an alternative that is gaining ground along with developing cost centers, operating managers include estimated training costs for their purposes in their own operating budgets.

5. Desired Futures

Differing from the other four areas for special attention, each a segment of the current environment, this fifth context integrates all for a specified time in the future, say ten years ahead, and, as a first step, produces a vision that organized change efforts can then be directed to bring about. This is a realistic vision, not abstract or ideal; it tunes into a future that is quite clearly in the making already now.

Invariably identified on mind maps of 'the future already with us' are fast(er) changes in technology; a more highly educated workforce; more independent, high-expectation young people; higher status and employment of women; rising populations in poorer countries and increasing proportions of old people in all; rapidly growing large cities and megalopolises with highly diverse populations; the gap between rich and poor widening still further—so also more social divisiveness, high conflict, violence, and difficulties in public services and governance generally; widespread loneliness and fundamentalist movements; organizational downsizing leading to sudden spurts in unemployment, even in the midst of general economic growth (that growth being largely in the low-paying service sector); global interdependence—so instantaneous exchanges of knowledge; and a global sense of uncertainty, tempting individuals to safeguard narrow self-interest.

Along with general societal features like these, a mind map of the causal texture of the relevant environment in the agreed future of ten-plus years ahead also includes quite specific local and within-organization features. Policy-makers and managers can work actively to strengthen good features for the enterprise and to lessen, side-step, and protect it against threatening ones. From the desired future in that mapped environment, strategies and whole lines of practical actions can be drawn to the present and work plans be made to start now.

This is the essence of 'Future Searches', and it produces results quite different from improving current workings by making incremental adjustments in policies, organization, priorities, and ways of working. Contrary to problem-solving approaches, future search highlights success experiences that may prove useful for establishing the desired future. Contrary to limiting discussions to the smallest possible number of partners, namely the currently most powerful or at least the most vocal, and relying on hard-nosed negotiation of differences, future search includes all partners in the task-environment and works to establish common ground: a shared vision of the future to desire, first, and then the best policies and actions to bring it about. Contrary to paying minimal attention to the environment, since it is 'out there' beyond influencing and can only be tolerated, future search from the very beginning involves all partners together in shaping the future they have agreed to aim for. In that it recognizes that the environment is not at all 'out there' but that, for the most part, we are each others' environment. As comic character Pogo put it so memorably, 'we have found the enemy—and he is us'!.

Of greatest significance is that future search taps into the larger, long-range thinking that living and working in turbulent environments requires. Overarching goals and values have to be worked out and agreed system-wide so they can effectively guide change efforts and hold them together in the overall strategy and also serve for monitoring progress. In turbulent conditions, the key values to reduce uncertainty to manageable levels and ensure development include equity among diverse people, justice, and opportunities for all to develop and unfold their capacities. Collapsing the traditional hierarchies, opening system boundaries, and increasing information to share of many kinds are all in line with taking a good look at the future together (see Exhibit 2.1).

IMPLICATIONS FOR POLICY-MAKING

Active Engagement in the Environment

...evacuation from the Dunkirk beaches prevented the capture of the core of the regular army, including many of the generals... (it was) imperative that Britain build a large land army in a hurry...no measures tried in the first few months seemed to be effective.

...a group of psychiatrists at the Tavistock Clinic saw that the right questions were asked in Parliament in order to secure the means to try new measures. As a result they were asked to join the Directorate of Army Psychiatry, and did so as a group.

—Eric Trist and Hugh Murray

Step by step, respectfully and thoughtfully, it is possible to explore new ground and to identify important areas in which people can learn to behave differently—developmentally—and to design interventions to help them do so. Training is one kind of intervention that may help, but it is *not* the only one, nor one to be adopted mechanically. In proceeding toward development in this active manner, broad cultural generalizations serve an *alerting* function by pointing out accepted relationships of unusual sensitivity and deserving of special care. But they need not rule out exploration of any line of action.

Many interventions in the course of our work in Indonesia in the 1980s were of this circumspect step-by-step kind and were effective though contrary to long traditions and, many times, disadvantageous to individuals and even to dominant groups. The Government's policy to decentralise decision-making served as clear reference for exploring fresh ways in the light of local conditions, even when they ran counter to common experience and advice.

For training in particular, for instance, the selection of participants and their subsequent placements and allocated responsibilities changed from a mostly personal to a functional basis. Traditionally, supervisors recommended staff for training programs from within a narrow set of occupational grades and academic attainment, and otherwise by personal choice; higher officers then approved or disapproved these selections and sometimes substituted other candidates. In this project the provincial organization agreed to base the selection process instead on functional criteria which the consultants helped it derive from the prospective tasks. Assessments were then based on actual evidence that the candidates possessed the potentialities, personal interest, and commitment which these functions called for, and organizational commitment as well to make these staff members available with sufficient frequency and reliability to undergo the new training and consulting assignments. Initially laid down for programs in this project, these norms for selection spread to other programs also, without special effort. Furthermore, to make their local 'resource system' as strong as possible, provincial health offices agreed to look for candidates for advanced training also in kindred provincial organizations, both public and private, even though this too constitutes a departure from established practice and involve inter-ministerial arrangements, including payments and other complexities.

Among the innovations included in this project, a few deprived officials of some customary income-generating activities. If they were trainers themselves, they lost income when it became standard practice to devote much more time than available budgets provided to assessment of needs, program design, session preparation, and, later, impact evaluation and follow-up. Other officers lost income when the use of guest lecturers in programs was greatly reduced. Case sessions were substituted for lectures, which also made it possible for younger officers to lead sessions. Whereas lecturers had to be at least as senior in rank as participants, this was not necessary for 'leaders' and 'facilitators' in discussion sessions of cases or other prepared materials; change of title helped this change along.

Finally, an important shift was achieved by the project in the relationship between the national and provincial offices of the health system. In Indonesia, as elsewhere, this relationship is subject to complex considerations, including overriding political ones, and any change in the relationship involves subtle but significant shifts by each level in its perception of the other. Classically, the Center issued what it labeled 'guidelines' to establish program contents and schedules, staffing patterns and, often, detailed curricular and training materials to be used throughout the country; provincial offices regarded such 'guidelines' as instructions to be followed. As this project progressed and proved useful, first one, then more provincial offices began to propose to the Center new programs they wished to try out which, if successful, they wanted to institute. The provincial offices also suggested specific modifications in the programs and schedules sent by the Center. When the Center was asked whether such provincial initiatives were acceptable, the national head confirmed that central guidelines were indeed simply intended to describe *minimal* conditions and programs, and that the Ministry expected provinces that had participated in this project and gained fresh insights through it to 'go on from there and do better.'

This set of examples, all from one project, of interventions that deliberately and actively engaged the existing culture and developed some new norms can serve two purposes here. It can reconfirm that there indeed are concrete useful ways of thinking about and working with cultural dimensions in making training policy. It can also set the stage for what the rest of the book offers, namely, steps policy-makers and change managers can take to improve training so that it can meet not just this or that immediate need, e.g., to adopt a new technology or to run a new procedure, but can contribute to more basic development, which necessarily includes developing the culture itself.

Areas of Freedom: Three Dimensions

Sensitivity to the general culture and respect for it does not run counter to development but rather hand in hand with it. To familiarize oneself with the culture in general and to be alert to likely areas of particular sensitivities and difficulties is therefore useful. But a general acquaintance does not suffice and may stultify if used to discourage exploration of what might be possible within a particular context. Every culture is a multilayered fabric, and elasticities and possibilities for modification and substitution differ from layer to layer.

Important guidance comes then from the cultural features in particular environments. As attention shifts from general to particular features, a complex composite of several cultures comes into play. Some cultures differ along ethnic–geographic lines and so also between different parts of the country. In rapidly growing cities, some of these differences become submerged while others persist, and the new generation is often less attached to them than its parents. Professional cultures, such as those of physicians, or public servants or, as in the earlier set of examples, the two in conjunction, often take precedence over ethnic differences. They also sometimes overrule limitations to what women or young graduates generally may or may not do. In health systems, a lead given by doctors counts for more than that same lead given by others.

So, it is useful to particularize culture to the actual locale in which change is desired, i.e., the cultural mix and dynamics important *there*. A line of action possible in one factory or provincial office may not be possible in another, or at least not possible until its 'culture' changes. And even within the same unit, one department or work group may offer a better start than another.

Recent performances and tendencies, current reputation, leadership, staffing, and other resources can provide information for the cultural mapping required for developing a particular system and to mark promising places for starting: areas of freedom to develop work agendas, methods, and often people to initiate the effort. Initial steps, if kept small, can quickly confirm, modify, and detail the map and route(s) for developing new norms and incorporating them into the culture. Whether the new norms will replace the old, or only modify them, or coexist with them, usually becomes clear only later. More often this occurs last, and the culture diversifies and grows in the process.

After detailing and carrying out the initial action, the essence of the third phase is to sustain it with interventions that work, to build on and around them, and to so permeate the system and its culture so that true developments become institutionalized. As shown in the set of examples from Indonesia, several agendas and diverse methods are useful for this purpose at various times and places. It is overall movement and sufficient involvement that matter.

> The project in Indonesia, scheduled initially for three provinces, expanded to eight; one year's commitment led to a second, then to three more. Successful training in one province at a time led to national advanced programs for selected trainers, and membership for some of them in a national inter-provincial consultancy service. By the time the project ended, interventions and programming had expanded and were continuing simultaneously at four levels in the national system. Furthermore, additional work spun off from the health sector to local planning and local government in the Ministry for Internal Affairs.

Two points are important to remember when sorting cultural contexts into phases, levels of generality, and other categories. First, while such segmenting is of practical use in mapping, mobilizing, focusing, sequencing, and managing the required efforts and in monitoring their effectiveness, it is merely a serviceable tool and does not reduce the complex reality of any cultural context. Multilayered and intricately interwoven reality runs on, unaffected by such mapping. Matching surveillance and action with the patterns that may be important to a particular development must be, and remains, the overall aim. Even institutionalizing development, the third 'phase', does not 'follow' an earlier phase. On the contrary, it begins as soon as multiple constituencies of potential participants (whether individuals, groups, or organizations) likely to be affected by the development form expectations about its implications. Their awareness raised to anticipation, they study the intervenors' first appearances and actions for clues as to how they will proceed, how far they can be trusted, and what all is likely to result.

The second and related point is that cultural contexts at all levels of generality remain important right through, opening fresh opportunities one moment, closing old ones at another. In the late 1980s, world interest, publicized and focused by United Nations agencies, favored program initiatives for child survival. Then, programs—*any* programs—concerned with the upgrading of women's position in society received pervasive support (except in some sharply identified countries which are widely ostracized). By his known interest in computers and high technology, Prime Minister Rajiv Gandhi in the late 1980s opened wide opportunities in India for improving work planning, supervision, and management through improved local management information systems. But it is also important to remember that in this same generally favorable climate, some local contexts favored such developments while in others they languished or energies were directed elsewhere.

RANGES OF INFLUENCE

How far and how actively policy-makers interact with the cultural contexts often determines whether an initiative will be still-born or confined to a quite particular situation or, on the contrary, will spread far and permeate the wider culture. Elliot Jaques' mid-century work with the Glacier Metal Company in London focused on the culture of the factory, the title he gave his seminal book.[5] The culture outside the factory gates and the personnel as go-between received just enough attention to safeguard that boundary. When Glacier established a branch factory in the very different setting of West Scotland, the boundaries drawn along these lines came to contain the culture of the *firm* as a whole.

Pilot schemes and intensive area and demonstration projects have been a favorite modality for introducing changes in developing countries. How much of the wider culture their design incorporates, even in embryo, is a better predictor of their effectiveness than their initial scale. Most have belied early promises of wider application because they have failed to incorporate and engage the bureaucratic, political, and, often, economic dimensions of the wider culture. In training itself, progress with quite specific changes, whose benefits are self-evident, often depends for success on changes in reward structures, relationships between people, and other aspects of the culture

---

[5] Elliot Jaques, *The Changing Culture of a Factory* (London: Routledge, 1951). For a fuller, recent discussion of culture, see Edgar H. Schein, *Organizational Culture and Leadership* (San Francisco: Jossey-Bass. Inc., 1987).

of the wider HRD system of which it is a part and of the organization-in-its-environment as a whole.

The introduction of case teaching into management programs, for example, runs into characteristic difficulties. At the personal level are problems with the faculty. Usually from academia and holding professorial titles, they are more accustomed to imparting knowledge to students than in joining them in the exploration of data from the field which all have received and have studied prior to the session. Moreover, case research and writing call for extended periods in the field, a less familiar setting, and for acting as listener, observer, learner, not as teacher. Back in the institution, allocations of time, funds, responsibilities, and often physical layouts as well, have to be changed for case teaching. Furthermore, the different culture of case sessions—participatory, active, creative, exploratory, with the leader shaping and guiding but not imposing views—puts pressure on other faculty members and sessions that operate along traditional lines. Administrators, too, feel the pressures to behave collegially and to flatten organizational structures. Grading performance in case programs requires more complex criteria and processes than standard examinations. Beyond the institutions, in the larger training system and often subject to country-wide standard regulations, the writing of teaching cases usually receives no recognition in the upgrading and promotion of faculty.

To provide a reasonable basis for success, a wide range of considerations has to go into helping an institution introduce case methods of instruction. At the very least, the institution has to commit time and resources to the attempt to modify the cultures accordingly, within and without, so that they support the development, or at least tolerate it, and certainly not negate it.

This understanding of development and of the cultural contexts of training policy, especially the need and manifold opportunities for engaging cultural contexts deliberately and actively, provides a proper setting for the rest of this book. In moving on to training strategies, next, assume that this more basic cultural work has already been well started and is substantially on the way. Strategic thinking subsequently guides contacts between the organization and the developers of programs of intervention. While in actuality there will be many overlaps, in practice (and also in this book) it is nevertheless important to insist on this basic progression, which differs notably from simply choosing particular training programs, methods, and materials, as if it were off the shelf. To keep on doing this is tempting for decision-makers at the top, simple, and it also keeps control in their hands. Development is basic and pervasive, so also more troublesome. But it is quite feasible given the inclination.

Change strategies, programs of training to help implement them, and training systems to provide the training—all have to model the developments they urge participants to learn and to undertake. Composing, supporting, and monitoring the training effort and the infrastructure for it that policy-makers and change managers need to deal with and create will be discussed in Part 2. The chapters leading up to that part will assume that the decision-makers have indeed promoted cultural developments so that they guide and support participants and their organizations and communities to the kinds of futures they desire.

Reading 2.1

What is a Future Search Conference?

MARVIN R. WEISBORD*

Future search is my term for a unique conference framework for planning among diverse interests. The structure enables us to make social, technical and economic breakthroughs that *cannot* happen within top-down meeting, training or management paradigms. It is uniquely-applicable to ambiguous 'problems without boundaries.' Nothing else I know comes close for thorny dilemmas like the environment, labor-management relations, runaway technology, global business, AIDS, homelessness, better schools, affordable housing, more-livable communities.

Meeting Design Equal to Our Aspirations

The conference is designed to a set of proven principles matched to the desired outcomes. I have worked in every time frame from three hours to three years, on a vast array of economic, technical and social problems. I can't think of a better way to fill 16 hours than searching for common ground.

A future search conference brings together 30 to 72 people for 2½ days. Their purpose is a consensus on a future plan for a community, organization, or issue. All agree to take responsibility for its implementation. They engage in five small group tasks, each requiring two to four hours. The first task establishes their common stakes in the future of the planet, assuring a much better dialogue than is customary. They pool their perceptions of current trends into a more complete picture than any one person had before. They draw implications that require no 'right' answers. There is no pressure to change yourself or anyone else.

*Copyright 1999, Future Search Network, www.fsn@futuresearch.net.

Changing Our Assumptions About What's Doable

Later mixed groups devise ideal future scenarios for their search topic. Action planning takes place *only* when the conference reaches consensus on an ideal future. This feature alone transforms the action potential. It assures each person that the plans they will implement align with a future they all want. Under these conditions, we often discover capabilities we did not know we had. We take actions we did not know were possible.

Staging a future search means changing our assumptions about large group conferences. In these meetings I have learned that most of us can bridge lines of culture, class, gender, ethnicity, power, status and hierarchy *if* we work as peers on tasks of mutual concern. We can do this despite prejudices, stereotypes and 'isms' that lie deep in each of us. We can do this despite the 'shadows,' individual and collective, that complicate our lives. We can do this despite initial skepticism and the gloomy predictions of what will or won't happen. Freed from pressure to reconcile conflicts or solve intractable problems, we often discover common ground none of us knew existed. Instead of trying to change other people, we change the conditions under which we interact. THAT at least is doable!

TYPICAL FUTURE SEARCH AGENDA

Purpose: Future of X—5 to 20 years out

Task 1: The Past: Society, Self, Search Entity ('X')
Task 2: The Present: Trends Affecting X
Task 3: The Present: 'Prouds' and 'Sorries' re Us and X
Task 4: Ideal Future Scenarios for X
Task 5: Consensus Scenario and Action Planning

Most big meetings involve speeches, expert advice, panel or small group discussions, training, and/or top-down 'roll outs'—of missions, visions, strategies, technologies, and new structures. They assume lacks *in the people* that only the conference planners can remedy. Despite countless meetings based on this assumption, most institutions I know are coming apart at the seams. Our methods do not equal our aspirations. We know WHAT we want (empowerment, cooperation, service, mutual respect, productivity, quality, shared responsibility, etc.). We do not know HOW to infuse these qualities into our institutions.

Tough Issues Involve Value Choices

Suppose we were to start by assuming that the tough issues of our time require value choices more than expertise? That taking responsibility matters most when there are many 'right' answers? That we already have the skills we need? That what we lack is opportunity, access to each other, and permission to search instead of 'solve?' Future search conferences are designed to these latter assumptions. They build on skills, knowledge, and experience that people *already* have—without more training, exhorting or expert advice. They work simply by *removing structural barriers* between us that keep us from knowing, taking responsibility, and acting. They enable us to use the brains we were born with.

In my enthusiasm, I do not mean to imply that this work is easy, or that one 2½ day meeting can make up for years of inertia or conflict. Searching is not easy. The hardest part is planning how to get the right people in the room. That sometimes takes longer than the conference itself. But the meeting is simple, astonishingly so to me, who has spent the last 30 years chasing rainbows with some fancy methods and concepts that are, sad to say, not up to the task. Search methods are *so* simple as to be easily dismissed. Yet they are profound enough to create enormous anxiety in us about control, conflict, and failure. In these conferences, *everybody* works as peers on the same tasks. The outcomes cannot be predicted, except that they are likely to be renewing and productive.

Why Stop Short of Success?

No wonder sponsors often balk at the very components essential for success. The broad stakeholder base, for example—inviting people who don't usually meet. Or exploring the global context—the past, present, and future of our world and ourselves before confronting the planning issue. Or working as peers in self-managing small groups, including strangers who have never met and people who have a history of conflict or failure. Or spreading out the 16 hours of working time (excluding breaks and meals) over three days. Or holding off action planning until we have a consensus on the future. Sponsors often assume *their* stakeholders are different. They won't show up, stay, or spend time talking about the past. They can't afford three days, and would never agree anyway. Folks new to search may compromise key components, reducing both the anxiety and the chance for anything new. Be aware that when we hold to these minimum conditions we usually make breakthroughs. Ask any leader who has sponsored a conference.

My Advice is Just Do It

The core conditions for success are derived from 30 years of experience and hundreds of search conferences in many cultures. The theory, practice, history, and uses are well-documented in *Discovering Common Ground* (Berrett-Koehler, 1992). The book integrates diverse cases into a set of principles that make the results repeatable by skilled people who share the core values. There are several ways to explore future search conferences. One is to talk to people who have run or attended them. Another is to read the book. A fourth is to attend a Search Net workshop. My advice is to pick your task, recruit a planning group, find a facilitator, and just do it.

3

MAKING THE ORGANIZATION INTO A LEARNING SYSTEM

From Organizational Learning to a Learning Organization
Culture and Processes in Learning Organizations
Highlighting Organizational Goals and Values
Values Common to Learning Organizations
Distinctive Mechanisms for Value Clarification and Organization-wide Commitment

The Environment as Partner in Learning: The Learning System
Reaching for a Learning System in One Go
Including the Training (Resources) System in the Learning System

Exhibits
3.1 Two Models of Assessing Environmental Uncertainties and Characteristic Linkages
3.2 Values of Effective Learning Organizations at Three Phases of Changing
3.3 Common Means and Mechanisms for Fostering Key Values

Boxes
3.1 Organization-wide Learning and Learning Organizations: Six Contrasts
3.2 Characteristics of Learning Organizations
3.3 Building Learning Organizations: Four Company Examples
3.4 Social Structures as Defence against Anxiety
3.5 20th Century Images of Organization
3.6 Instruments for Assessing Structures and Processes of Learning Organizations
3.7 Systems Thinking in Some Prominent Competitive Enterprises
3.8 Systems Characteristics of Organization in the Environment
3.9 Changes in Roles and Functions

Readings
3.1 The Company of the Future
3.2 Institution-building: The British Army in World War II
3.3 Image for Decentralizing Indonesia's Health Services

Not that profit and product are no longer important, but without continuing learning they will no longer be possible.

—H. Owens

Organization-wide learning, widespread and as a clear concept, dates only from the 1970s, and that learning had to be continuous only from the 1980s. Continuous learning that also embraces the environment—the organization-in-its-environment—is the top agenda from the 1990s.

Simply charted, this progressive widening would look like this:

Learning is
for INDIVIDUALS
for the TEAM
for the whole ORGANIZATION
for the ORGANIZATION-IN-ITS-ENVIRONMENT: THE SYSTEM
Learning is continuous and lifelong: so the
LEARNING ORGANIZATION
is the LEARNING SYSTEM

The lower half of the chart concerns policy-makers and change managers most particularly. Only in the smallest enterprises—a small city block, a family store or workshop, or a professional group practice—can change, and training for it, be with people face-to-face. In most organizations, routine orientations for entrants, updated rules and standards and, perhaps, an annual meeting and seasonal party is all that people share organization-wide—till some event precipitates an organization-wide learning effort, and then probably another to back up the first. A disaster threatens or happens, an acquisition, expansion or diversification calls for a major reorganization, a shift to new premises, a new regulation or a currency devaluation in a major market are classic provocations, or a radically new technology or method comes in sight that promises escape from age-old, high-cost headaches; the electronic office and TQM are examples.

Having organization-wide learning in view, then, is already a long way from viewing training as something for individuals, or for neighbors on a block, a class, or a team at work or play. The next step however, and each step after, does not follow at all smoothly. Each calls for reconceiving the change effort and so also the training for it. The very next step makes occasional into permanent effort, and this can usually not be done with merely stretching what is already there but often calls for programming, resources, and integration of a different order, and reorganization. The next step again then broadens the perspective beyond the organization to include people outside, and not just as clients, suppliers, or more or less distant regulators or other officials as before and one-by-one, but as essential partners and together.

FROM ORGANIZATIONAL LEARNING TO A LEARNING ORGANIZATION

> Organisational learning occurs when members... act as learning agents for the organisation, responding to changes in the internal and external environments of the organisation by detecting and correcting errors in organisational theory-in-use, and embedding the results of their enquiry in private images and shared maps of organisation.
>
> —Chris Argyris and D. Schon

Turbulence, newly and reluctantly recognized as the now normal state of the environment and fed by instantaneous global information and tremors of all kinds, causes the shift to a continuously learning organization. It is a basic shift, to a different disposition for the organization as a whole. It orients and prepares the organization differently, different even from the recent past when its people expected and then also buckled down to making a learning effort from time-to-time and here and there in the organization, and even when lately that exigency occurred ever more frequently. So the shift is not just for more economy of effort and smoothing out interruptions of normal living and working.

Urgent as it is, understanding this move, from spasmodic organization-wide learning to a continuously learning organization is essential, and can be achieved by collaborative effort. Exhibits and extracts from major works may serve best for an overview and also for connecting readers with the works themselves for fuller exposition of views of special interest to them.

Box 3.1 contrasts organizational learning with a continuously learning organization on the six dimensions highlighted in organizational studies since the 1970s. What Chris Argyris calls 'double-loop learning' sets the stage for the rest: not only is something learned that improves task performance (= single-loop learning), but the organization too takes note and modifies its policies, structure, ways of

Box 3.1

ORGANIZATION-WIDE LEARNING AND LEARNING ORGANIZATIONS:
SIX CONTRASTS

Organization-wide learning	*The Learning organization*	
1. Single-loop learning	Double-loop learning	(Argyris, 1977)
2. Incremental	Transformational	(Argyris and Schon, 1978)
3. Lower-level	Higher-level	(Fiol and Lyles, 1985)
4. Adaptive	Generative	(Senge, 1990)
5. Tactical	Strategic	(Dodgson, 1991)
6. Occasional	Continuous	

SOURCES: C. Argyris, "Double Loop Learning in Organizations", *Harvard Business Review*, September–October (1977), pp 115–25.

C. Argyris, and D. Schon, *Organisational Learning* (London: Addison-Wesley, 1978).

C.M. Fiol and M.A. Lyles, "Organizational Learning", *Academy of Management Review*, Vol. 10, No. 4 (1985), pp 803–13.

Peter Senge, *The Fifth Discipline: The Art and Practice of Organisational Learning* (New York: Doubleday, 1990).

M. Dodgson, *The Management of Technological Learning* (Berlin: DeGruyter, 1991).

operating, and whatever else is necessary to support that change and to promote further changes. In both cases, learning only registers when it shows in improved performance.

The key difference lies in the scope of that performance: in single-loop learning, even if it be organization-wide, the organizational framework remains unchanged; in double-loop learning, the organization uses the learning for changing its framework as well. Indeed, when that becomes its culture, it expects and is continuously prepared for using innovative inputs for improving performance directly and also improving itself. Basic to this shift is what Harold Bridger, a founder member of the Tavistock Institute in London, calls the 'double-task': learning for improved performance plus learning *how* the improvement is effected, for use next time and also to guide adjusting the framework so it can support further learning.

In a series of exhibits, Madhukar Shukla contrasts learning organizations with traditional organizations along familiar dimensions. We reproduce them in Box 3.2 and also, in Box 3.3, his summary descriptions of organizations around the world that illustrate what learning organizations can be like.

Box 3.2

CHARACTERISTICS OF LEARNING ORGANIZATIONS

Industrial Paradigm	*Learning Paradigm*

The Concept of Business Organisation

• Organisation is a system of control	• Organisation is a system for creating knowledge
• Organisation is a portfolio of product markets	• Organisation is a constellation of competencies and capabilities

The Concept of Strategy

• Target focused	• Vision based
• Focus on competition	• Focus on collaboration
• Market dominance	• Market creation
• Shareholder returns	• Customer satisfaction

The Nature of Controls

• Individual focused	• Team focused
• Regulate behaviour	• Enable initiative
• Power of position	• Power of knowledge
• Use information to control	• Use information to empower
• Control through rules and procedures	• Control through vision, culture, and technology

SOURCE: Madhukar Shukla, *Competing through Knowledge: Building a Learning Organization* (New Delhi: Response Books, 1997), pp 296, 298, 300.

Culture and Processes in Learning Organizations

In learning organizations, innovation, implementation, and stabilization are the three phases that match the well-known Lewinian model of unfreezing, moving, and refreezing for learning in groups. Each phase has characteristics of its own.

1. Innovation assumes organizational openness to change; even better, eagerness to change. Exposure to new ideas and practices, reflection, and experimentation are essential to it along with ongoing processes for examining and testing the innovations' fit with the organization's economy, priorities, and direction.

2. Implementation assumes an accepting climate, a readiness to introduce into normal operations new ideas and practices of tested promise. Processes for recording and accumulating

Box 3.3

BUILDING LEARNING ORGANIZATIONS:
FOUR COMPANY EXAMPLES

Oticon

Oticon, a Danish hearing-aid company, responded to competitive challenges by changing into a 'spaghetti organisation'—an organisation without a centre. It razed walls, eliminated secretaries, erased job descriptions and specialities, and did away with formalised rules and procedures. The employees now formed project-directed completely autonomous groups; they decided their functions and targets and physically arranged themselves as they saw fit to get them done.

UBEST

UBEST, a Calcutta-based telecom software company, is unique in many respects. It is a hierarchiless, flat organisation, in which no one has a designation. Its members work in overlapping project teams. The organisation follows the flexitime system and its members have the freedom to decide on their own workload, timing and pace of work, and work-related expenditures. There is no system of approvals, and written communication is discouraged.

Federal Express

In 1988, Federal Express organised its 1,000 clerical workers into superteams of five to ten people. These teams were trained and given the authority to make improvements in their work. Without any formal supervision, in just one year, these teams were able to bring down costs due to incorrect billing and lost packages by 13 per cent.

Intel

Chip-maker Intel is organised into several dozen small 'councils', which not only manage the research and product development activities, but are also responsible for the traditional support functions (e.g., purchase policy, operating procedures, employee compensation). The performance of the teams is judged against the targets set by them. According to its CEO, Andy Grove, the aim 'is to remove authority from an artificial place at the top and to place it where the most knowledgeable people are'.

SOURCE: Madhukar Shukla, *Competing through Knowledge: Building a Learning Organization* (New Delhi: Response Books, 1997), pp 292, 293, 302.

experiences are important in this phase, as are ready mechanisms for organization-wide review and, if warranted, securing top-level support for continued practice and the resources and changes in structure and processes this will require.

3. Adapting and integrating change(s) into the normal ongoing life of the organization is the third phase. Continued use of the innovation(s) along with systematic monitoring and fine-tuning requires organizational change and leads to this internalization/institutionalization.

The very first phase, of shifting the organization to a new culture of openness to learning and changing, usually presents the greatest hurdles and often gets delayed till it cannot be put off any longer. And very understandably so. Traditions of hierarchical decision-making and long-established relationships and practices which have given the organization an aura of steadiness, and people up and down in it a sense of security that comes with knowing where they stood (even if short of their wishes), are now all in doubt, shaken or to be forsworn altogether; and all this upset is threatened in order to get ready for a wholly unknown future. Box 3.4 quotes studies of the deep resistances with which people commonly confront organizational restructuring; often, the very prospect of it holds terrors beyond clear formulation, enquiry, and reassurance.

Box 3.4

SOCIAL STRUCTURES AS DEFENCE AGAINST ANXIETY

...deep conflicts of individual members are projected into these structures and cultures. Any change in the organisation tends to disturb these projections which are important to the identity of the individual. This is one reason why change is resisted even when its apparent benefits are great.

...interventions have to pay attention to changes in structure and role as well as in psycho-social climate.... The threat of the genuinely novel is too often so great that the novelty is denied. Proper briefings about the new are not held, required training is not given, not enough time is allowed for unlearning the old and mourning its loss, or working through the anxieties surrounding the consequences of the new. The penalties for not doing so are severe.

SOURCE: Eric Trist and Hugh Murray, *The Social Engagement of Social Science: A Tavistock Anthology* (University of Pennsylvania Press, 1990), Vol. 1, p. 376. Every effort has been made to trace the copyright holder(s). In the absence of a reply, permission has been assumed.

Merely dismantling traditional structures and ways is not enough to maintain reasonable calm while things all around shift and change, even when those traditions have become controversial and changing them is still a mere possibility. A void or unknown to follow the threatened dismantling would touch off high restlessness and anxieties, and activate tendencies to rigidity and freezing at the very juncture when trusting relationships and flexibility in action are decisive for shifting the organization.

Highlighting Organizational Goals and Values

Essential for avoiding fearful anxiety about the turbulence ahead is a shift away from defensive over-activity to deliberately positioning the enterprise in that future. Creating a distinctive vision for it and accompanying it with explicit goals and the values to express it provide the new points of reference for making the transition. Happily, this is also what continuing good functioning in complex and turbulent conditions also requires.

Composing and articulating a vision for the organization that its people can really see themselves in and work toward is an ardous, usually drawn-out process. At the admittedly gigantic General Electric, it touched off a spate of 200 one-week programs off-site for mid- and higher management, each one of which the CEO opened and spent additional time for. Such high investment in a meticulous process, that must itself evolve to best serve its basic purpose, is justified by the prospect that it will in fact not merely prepare for the new disposition and culture but in fact begin to enact them best as experience from day one. The involvement and commitment of individuals and units will be much deeper and lasting than in similar-sounding goals and values worked out by a board or task group and enunciated as company policy.

In fact, the more open, free-flowing, and wider the participation in this initial process, the better the goals and values will serve as touchstones for choices, actions, and tracing progress. Wider-ranging information and ideas belong there, of course, including the kinds of far-out ideas brainstorming encourages, and also quite personal feelings, thought associations, and images—anything in short and however presented that gives clues to what things *mean* to people and groups, or might mean if instituted.

Anxieties about the impending changes are then certain to come out in the open—the hitherto held back personal as well as those already shared, such as fears of skills getting shelved or of organizational downsizing; some anxieties will be relieved in the hearing and others with better information or good-enough resolution. If the process is open enough, it leads also to sharing of mental associations, dreams, long-held assumptions, and images about organized activity and life in general by which people habitually act, often without even knowing it. In the sharing itself, and then the churning of it, people get to know and trust each other better—itself an important gain toward greater openness. And the contributions get modified, aligned, and sorted, some in and some out, till good-enough goals and values get distilled which people and units organization-wide can live and work and be known by. 'Own' is the current term for the high and pervasive commitment that makes for a learning organization.

Depending on people and situation, to 'own' associates quickly with streams of images and onward behavior: responsibility, importance, and desirable to some; burden, nuisance, and to be avoided to others. If the images with which people habitually summarize a situation they 'see' and what they make of it get closer, it makes all the difference to what they then do about it. Exhibit 3.1 shows the two very different lines of action taken by executives who 'see' the need for organizational change as quite minor and only temporary, and by executives who 'see' the need as great and permanent. The actions each takes or avoids follow in logical sequence; the fateful difference is in their starting points: their very different assessments of what they were facing.

Exhibit 3.1
TWO MODELS OF ASSESSING ENVIRONMENTAL UNCERTAINTIES AND
CHARACTERISTIC LINKAGES

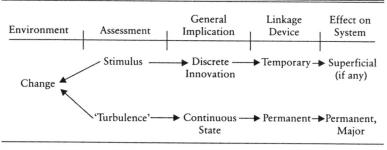

SOURCE: Rolf P. Lynton, "Linking an Innovative Subsystem into the System", *Administrative Science Quarterly* (1969), Vol. 14, p. 296.

A previous reading (Reading 1.1) traced the changing imagery over recent decades about organizations and prevailing conditions, and the stage each set for HRD practice. Box 3.5 sets out the prominent images Garth finds side-by-side, all in the twentieth century. Reading 3.3 displays and discusses the tree-image we ourselves used in our work in Indonesia and the roles this then gave to the key actors in decentralizing the health services there. We include these as further evidence for valuing images and broadly organizing metaphors, unfamiliar as that may be, for their direct practical use.

Box 3.5

20TH CENTURY IMAGES OF ORGANIZATION

Organization as:

MACHINE:	bureaucratic; scientific management
ORGANISM:	open systems; contingency management
BRAINS:	information-processing; self-management
CULTURE:	context creation and context management
POLITICAL SYSTEM:	pluralis. system; interest(s) management
PSYCHIC PRISON:	repression(s) sensitive; managing unconscious forces
FLUX AND TRANSFORMATION:	loops, not lines; flux management
DOMINATION:	parasitic system; exploitative management

SOURCE: Summarized from Garth Morgan, *Images of Organization* (Thousand Oaks, CA: Sage Publications, 1986).

Making British Airways 'the world's favourite airline' served for an encompassing goal of this high order; also Hewlett Packard's determination to get only into product lines that added significantly new features to computers then on the market. 'Favorite' put the general run of customers first, as 'most luxurious' or 'most advanced or fastest' or 'most profitable' would not have done. BA was clear too that sustaining its image of the world's favourite airline meant developing congruent policies and practices *internally*: becoming and also continuing to be the most favourite with passengers was possible only if BA was also the world's favourite airline to work for. HW continued to concentrate investments and efforts on technical advances even when other companies were profiting from quick markets.

Experience confirms that clear organization-wide goals and values continue to serve well the essential steadying function in times of change: limit expectations, order the major choices that remain, and guide the organization to work congruently inside and in the environment.

Values Common to Learning Organizations

Ordering values into greater and lesser categories is hazardous because many are interconnected in complex ways, identify an extreme of a continuum to move towards, and also differ in historical and local contexts and in formulation. The following lists are merely illustrative:

First order values are overarching: e.g., open, honest engagement between parts of the organization (as also between persons); avoidance of harm, to society as well as within the organization; personal respect for all, across diversities including dissenters (along with supporters; evenhanded justice irrespective of position; encouragement to fulfil individual aspirations such as career advancement; safety nets for casualties of the organization's and life's exigencies; acceptance of differences of view; commitment to agreements openly arrived at.

Second order values are means to achieve and maintain values: e.g., surfacing of differences; managing conflicts openly; proceeding on best information; going out to collect it; decision-making closest to the scene of action; going for help.

Exhibit 3.2 sets out dominant values of effective learning organizations at successive phases of changing.

The summary of a 1995 study is useful here for interconnecting the values again. For Popper and Lipshitz, continuous learning is itself the apex (showing appreciation for and willingness to invest resources in learning activities). This value, in turn, requires values of experimentation (showing appreciation for and willingness to incur losses to obtain valid information), transparency (willingness to expose one's operations to inspection), and egalitarianism (judging the actions and opinions of organization members on their merit and not according to the members' rank, prestige, or any other personal attribute). The last value in this hierarchy is accountability (taking personal responsibility for implementing lessons learned), without which learning from experience would not be translated into action.

Exhibit 3.2
VALUES OF EFFECTIVE LEARNING ORGANIZATIONS AT
THREE PHASES OF CHANGING

Innovation	• openness, welcoming new ideas • searching and experimenting • mutuality, accepting of others' views
Implementing	• rigor, thorough work • respect for tradition, blend new with old • support for both innovators and hesitants
Integrating to Last	• perseverance across teething problems • rigorous recording and reviewing actual experiences with innovation; creative adaptation in use

Distinctive Mechanisms for Value Clarification and Organization-wide Commitment

However they are summarized, it is shared values like those listed that ensure that the mechanisms the organization develops and operates for establishing, maintaining, and integrating its values do really produce the needed learnings and do not degenerate into mere ritual: obeisance to stated aspirations.

In Exhibit 3.3 we show means and mechanisms that learning organizations commonly used to make key values pervasive, and Box 3.6 then mentions some instruments for assessing the structures and processes of learning organizations.

THE ENVIRONMENT AS PARTNER IN LEARNING: THE LEARNING SYSTEM

…building into organizations a new response-capability is required more than ever by the changing society.…

—Eric Trist and Hugh Murray

'Use systems thinking' is the fifth dimension in the book with which Peter Senge established learning organizations as a universal concept,[1] the fifth and the most important. The others are: develop

---

[1] Peter Senge, *The Fifth Discipline: The Art and Practice of Organisational Learning* (New York: Doubleday, 1990).

Exhibit 3.3
COMMON MEANS AND MECHANISMS FOR FOSTERING KEY VALUES

Openness, experimentation, mutuality, and teamwork:
- meetings for sharing new information and for brainstorming innovative approaches to issues
- exposure to outside experts and practitioners in relevant settings elsewhere
- reward experimentation itself, successful or not, and certainly useable innovations large and small
- publicise and regularly update lists of issues that call for innovation
- have representative standing committees to review proposed changes and provide resources for trials
- periodic meetings with policy-makers on innovations and issues to resolve

Flexibility of structures and processes:
- contingency planning, with attention to alternatives
- build in relevant traditions and also opportunities to mourn their loss
- maintain good records of experiences as well as experiments: organizational memory
- organize task groups to prepare alternative action plans for common review and recommendation/decision
- set up 'temporary systems' for specific purposes: task groups, project teams, linkage mechanisms

Building organizational as well as individual competencies:
- develop and maintain data pool of competencies already somewhere in the organization and reward using it
- identify eager learners and encourage understudying internal experts, e.g., by regular pairing and supervised practice
- record, review, and share innovations on trial
- use outside training opportunities, both for specific organizational purposes and for individual interests

personal mastery, use mental models, build shared visions, and understand the power of team learning. By 1990, when the book was published, most organizations were already in such complex, unpredictable, turbulent environments that they dared not limit systems thinking to the organization, off by itself, but had to include its environment. All stakeholders in the particular enterprise, outside as well as within organizational boundaries, were essential partners in the learning system for the enterprise: the organization-in-its-environment as one.

The rub for policy-makers comes with this partnering, to keep giving it high importance and on center-stage. More than enlarging

Box 3.6

INSTRUMENTS FOR ASSESSING STRUCTURES AND PROCESSES OF
LEARNING ORGANIZATIONS

Instrument	*Dimensions*	*Authors*	*Date*
1. Organizational Learning Diagnostics (OLD)	Organizational Learning Mechanisms at Three Phases for Change	Pareek	1998
2. Organizational Learning Inventory (OLI)	Organizational Learning	DiBella	1997
3. Learning Advantage	Learning Orientation and Facilitating Factors	Cavaluzzo	1996
4. Organization Learning Climate Questionnaire	OL Climate	Ramnarayan	Undated
5. OL Questionnaire (1)	Senge's Five Aspects Suggested by Senge	Deshpande and Pendse	Undated
6. OL Questionnaire (2)	Garvin's Four Aspects	Deshpande and Pendse	Undated
7. FLO Foundation	Faster Learning Organizations	Guns	1996
8. Learning Organizations Processes (LOP) Survey	Eight Processes of Learning Organizations	Pareek	1998

the learning arena is involved; the very basis for the relationships
with the world outside has to be basically recast, away from spasmodic, one-way calls by one party or another for a particular service
(banking, maintenance, water, effluent disposal) or for financial
support for a community program or a new wing for the hospital, or
contacts with clients or customers or contractors, a pretty minimal
engagement, in short, with one party or another at a time and limited as far as possible to one's own agenda. The new pattern starts
when all parties in the enterprise get together to fashion goals and
values for it into the future, sharing out the parts to be contributed
by each, and committing to each other to live and work as agreed.
The direction is the same for making a learning organization of any
size, only now the core values—of openness, trust, sharing, and flexible readiness to change—have to be developed with people and

agencies outside the organization as well, whom policy-makers know less well and do not have around so continuously and, above all, who have lives, agendas, and resources of their own. This means yet more views to take into account, yet more time preparing and meeting, taking real possibilities of having to modify plans, perhaps even having to abandon plans or doing them all over, having to consider the plans of others and having to fit in with those.

No wonder disbelief, anxieties, and hesitation is often the first reaction to so taxing a prospect, and, next, prime policy time goes into devising stratagems to make do with some lesser version—such as persuading outside parties to buy into goals and values and change strategies already set; or only dealing with outside parties one-by-one and with some perhaps not at all; insist on having one's way or else; buy support; drive a hard bargain; threaten to leave unless...; look around for more licence or more tax advantage elsewhere; or just to give up and retire. For a time, the lesser may even suffice, at least to still qualms in the environment and avoid open challenge; large, powerful organizations often achieve acquiescence that way. But advantage gained that way is short-lived at best and may spell disaster. For certain, it will deprive the organization of the learning and readier changing with the times that only collaborating on a mutual basis can ensure. Everything short of that only postpones what has to be done, for which habits of thinking and acting have to be developed.

Improbable, even fanciful, as this recasting may strike policy-makers new to it, examples of such partnering—task-focused in composition, roles and, processes, and clearheaded for the longer term—are quite numerous and widespread. Box 3.7 shows some from perhaps the least promising sector: highly competitive businesses.

Solid outcomes of systems thinking take many forms—in-house career counselling and retraining for possible work elsewhere; recruiting priorities for including inner city school leavers, handicapped or ethnic minorities; participation in providing community-wide safety nets for all manner of exigencies; joint school-work programs; collaborative work on land use and environmental planning, legislation and enforcement. In seeing this partnering as it works, expertise and other resourcefulness for getting something done evidently cut across positions in the community and also organizational hierarchies. Competitors in one matter become partners in

Box 3.7

SYSTEMS THINKING IN SOME PROMINENT
COMPETITIVE ENTERPRISES

THE DISORGANISED ORGANISATIONS

Dell Computers
Dell Computers, the fifth largest PC company in the US, owns no plants, but leases two small factories to assemble computers from outsourced parts. Unlike other companies, Dell sells its PCs, which are built to customer specifications, directly to the customers through mail-order. In addition, Dell offers to its customers more than 650 softwares, a full range of modems and other PC accessories. But it neither makes nor stocks these products. It simply orders them from other companies who deliver directly to the customer.

Reebok India
Reebok India, like Reebok's worldwide operations, is designed as a network organisation. It has outsourced shoe manufacturing to Phoenix, Aero and Lakhani, retailing to Phoenix, logistics to Nexus Logistics, and warehousing to Bakshi Associates. Its stores will be designed by Aakar, and advertising will be managed by Hindustan Thomson Associates. Even selection has been outsourced to Prospects.

COLLABORATING TO COMPETE

- CMC Ltd and HCL-HP are fierce competitors in the systems integration market. However, they collaborated extensively with each other (in terms of information sharing and training skills) when they were putting the stock exchanges on-line. The reason for this was that CMC had already developed the software for the stock exchanges but was finding it difficult to sell it on the costly Tandem machines; HCL-HP, on the other hand, had cheaper computers, but was finding the development and import of software costly. Hence, the alliance was beneficial to both.
- BPL and Videocon are both contenders for dominance in the consumer electronics market. However, when the colour tubes facility of Uptron was put up for sale, both companies joined hands (along with Toshiba) to take it over and run it.
- Philips India and Videocon are competitors in the market. However, the semiconductor unit of Philips India supplies components to Videocon for its Bazooka model.
- Godrej Foods sells tomato puree; so does Hindustan Lever Ltd (HLL), under the Kissan brand. Both brands of puree, however, are produced at the Godrej factory in Bhopal—using the tomato paste supplied by HLL. HLL, incidentally, supplies paste also to its competitor, Nestle, for making tomato ketchup, which competes with its own Kissan Ketchup.

Box 3.7 contd...

'HOLOGRAPHIC' ORGANISATIONS

Amtrex Appliances Ltd
In April 1993, Amtrex started to mould itself into what its CEO described as 'a horizontal-circular structure'. Most of its activities were reorganised around a number of teams: '100% OK Teams', 'Customer Care Teams', 'Teams for Accelerated Innovation', and so on. To ensure customer focus, the company re-engineered itself into a process-based organisation, and redefined each function as a part of the service chain. The company also invested heavily in information technology to network the various parts of its processes, so that relevant information was available all the time to anyone, anywhere in the organisation.

Eastman Chemical Co.
In January 1993, Eastman Chemical Co., a division of Eastman Kodak, changed itself into a circular 'Pizza Chart' organisation. Each function, geographic region, or 'core competence' is represented by a pepperoni on the pizza. The white space around the pepperoni is where the actual collaborative work takes place. Hierarchy has been abolished, and functions are not supposed to have separate goals. People work in self-directed work teams; all managers are members of at least one such team.

SOURCE: Madhukar Shukla, *Competing through Knowledge: Building a Learning Organization* (New Delhi: Response Books, 1997), pp 292–93, 299, 301–2.

another. Joint exploration and collaboration is the dominant mode, not negotiating, bargaining or maneuvering in secret to better the other party. Prevalent too is sharing information and expecting and proposing improvements on ideas and plans, with differences of views stated openly and conflicts voiced early and for best resolution, maybe by experimenting and testing to see what works best.

Before long, systems thinking and these ways of working become as habitual as the more limited ways were before. In Box 3.8, Shukla summarizes this emerging learning paradigm of organizations-in-the-environment in contrast to the earlier 'industrial paradigm', and the new organizing principles.

Box 3.9 reproduces the changes in roles and functions in moving from 'relatively closed ...to [a] relatively open system' that Harold Bridger has derived from his lifetime of international consulting.

Box 3.8

SYSTEMS CHARACTERISTICS OF ORGANIZATION-IN-THE-ENVIRONMENT

Industrial Paradigm	*Learning Paradigm*
• Clear boundaries	• Permeable boundaries
• Pre-designed	• Evolving design
• Minimise skills	• Maximise skills
• Segmented tasks	• Integrated processes
• Functional, hierarchical groupings	• Open, multi-functional network

THE NEW ORGANISING PRINCIPLES

In spite of the differences in terminologies, there is considerable similarity among the blueprints suggested for the new paradigm organisations. The following are some of the basic principles:

- Organise work around integrated processes, not around segmented tasks.
- Create flatter structures, with parallel instead of sequential teams.
- Make teams (not individuals) accountable for the total task; empower teams to take all relevant decisions pertaining to their work.
- Make organisational boundaries permeable in order to bring teams in contact with customers, suppliers, and each other.
- Evaluate the performance of the teams on the basis of customer feedback. Use peer rating to evaluate individual performances.
- Invest in and reward acquisition of new skills by the individual.

SOURCE: Madhukar Shukla, *Competing through Knowledge: Building a Learning Organization* (New Delhi: Response Books, 1997), pp 300, 304.

Reaching for a Learning System in One Go

[In China] people born in the year of the rat must take care all their lives not to fall into traps....

—Tiziano Terzani

For deciding how best to proceed, the simple chart at the start of this chapter now turns out to be grossly misleading. It suggests that the focus of training can expand step-by-step—individual learning first, then teams, then on to covering the whole organization—and in lengthening time—from occasional programming to an ultimate state of continuous learning and changing by the organization-in-its-environment; like rungs up a ladder of greater and greater accomplishment, building on experience on the way up. We know this not to be so. Gains do come with expanding the focus—greater openness

Box 3.9

CHANGES IN ROLES AND FUNCTIONS

Change from (relatively closed system)	*Change toward* (relatively open system)
Control and coordination retained in the superior managerial role	Control and coordination retained in superior role for policy, but shared with relevant staff for operational goals
Prescriptive tasks for subordinates with some delegated authority	Decision making and discretion devolved to relevant staff when responsible for the action involved (i.e., executive and consultative mode)
Managing mostly within the confines of the system	Managing at the boundary (i.e., reconciling external and internal resources and forces)
Allocation of jobs to persons and 'knowing one's place'	More interdependence in working groups, but more anxiety about one's identity and independence
Managing to eliminate conflict	Managing the conflict by exploring its nature together
Accountability and responsibility located together	Accountability and responsibility may be separate
Single accountability	Multiple accountability
Hierarchical assessment and appraisal (often uncommunicated)	Self-review and assessment plus mutual appraisal of performance and potential
Career and personal development dependent on authority	Mobility of careers and boundary crossing for development, greater responsibility for own development
Power rests with those occupying certain roles and having high status in hierarchy	Power rests with those having control over uncertainty
Finite data and resources utilized toward building a plan	Nonfinite data and resources leading toward a planning process, maintaining a choice of direction in deciding among options
Periodic review and tendency to extrapolate (projection forward)	Control and planning requiring continuous review, prospection as well as projection forward
Risk related to an information gap	Risk related to information overload
Long term/short term based on operational plans (periodic)	Long term/short term based on continuous adaptive planning process

Box 3.9 contd...

Concentrating on 'getting on with the job' and 'trouble-shooting' activities	'Suspending business' at relevant times to explore work systems and ways of working
Difficulty with 'equality' and 'freedom'	Difficulty with 'fraternity'

SOURCE: Harold Bridger, "Courses and Working Conferences as Transitional Institutions" in Eric Trist and Hugh Murray, *The Social Engagement of Social Science: A Tavistock Anthology* (University of Pennsylvania Press, 1990), Vol. 1, p. 244. Every effort has been made to trace the copyright holder(s). In the absence of a reply permission has been assumed.

with more people and also between units in the organization, leading to habits and more or less durable mechanisms of collaboration in learning and changing—and these are themselves good preparation for the next step or steps. The trouble is that each stopping place also produces new boundaries that exclude others—people and units—and that spells trouble; immediately, since they are in positions to damage the organization's performance and image, and also later, when subsequent enlargement does include them and they then resist buying into programs, processes, and relationships already set. The mixed feelings, of old and new, create many problems—of backtracking, testing good faith, reworking 'perfectly well-functioning arrangements just for the sake of reworking them'. In short, habits of thinking and acting that promise well and even function well in one position, create obstacles on the way to another. And nowhere do these short-term gains make more difficulties than in the kind and quality of relationships between partners-to-be of all kinds.

The widening of focus over these decades has been disjointed and not at all the smooth progression the original chart suggested. Redrawn, with thickest lines between 'steps' where the disjunction is most severe, the chart reappears like this:

Learning is
  for INDIVIDUALS
      for the TEAM
        for the whole ORGANIZATION
    for the ORGANIZATION-IN-ITS-ENVIRONMENT: THE SYSTEM
Learning is continuous and lifelong, so:
                    the LEARNING ORGANIZATION
        the LEARNING SYSTEM

It is on the way to partnering as the defining condition that the transition from one position to another is most taxing since it calls for foregoing established status relationships and replacing them by task-oriented collaboration among just any people and agencies that bring the required expertise, standing, and connections. To do it once, and all together, is trauma enough; to do it with some in the organization now and others later, and later again in the effort to complete the learning system so that it also includes the outside stakeholders who are even freer to express their resentments, would be no policy-makers' choice if they could possibly help it.

Taking decisions in a field rent with such severe disjunctions is quite different from getting into it step-by-step. It means deciding in one go where to position the organization in it and setting that as the direction and condition for planning and resources right at the start. Fast or slow, across misjudgments and errors, over and around obstacles—the position to take must be quite clear and public, in word and deed, for the reversal of past practice to convince prospective partners. Anything less would diffuse the energies much needed for the change and keep lingering doubts and regrets alive.

What new position to choose for the organization then deserves the most careful study and courageous consideration; courageous because calculations of risk had better be resolved in favor of a larger option. High turbulence in the environment may be way off, at least for a decade; or the shift to truly partnering relationships may really be out of the question till the founder leader or a father retires, even dies; or inviting a rival organization till *its* head changes. When the goal is clear enough, many tactical possibilities open up on the way to it and are worth pursuing because they promise to cost less in the end than aiming too low. Also, policy-makers can make themselves more courageous and obtain clarity by setting one or more parts of the system the task of trying out the inclusions and new modes and mechanisms for more far-reaching collaboration on behalf of the whole, as R&D and pilot units do for other innovations in enterprises of many kinds.

The decisive consideration is the position the organization can best reach ten or fifteen years into the future and what best relations with its environment it is likely to be in then, hopefully shaped in part by the organization's own active participation in making it so. Practical work on establishing this vision and deciding on actions to bring it about is the stuff of Future Searches and of other methods for helping stakeholders position joint enterprises in the future they desire and see what creating it will take.[2]

Including the Training (Resources) System in the Learning System

The training system which is to help in this change effort is also best included as a partner, to ensure that the training of key participants is well aligned with the task and to have its expertise available in visualizing, designing, and putting on-the-ground the processes and structures for the transformation and for living and working effectively in the new position. The training system in view here comprises all resources that can be mobilized for this place, time, and purpose; the professional system for developing training and people and institutions in that field is the focus in Chapter 9 in the companion volume.

Including training as a partner is important too for keeping training fully informed and focused firmly on achieving the intended change. Like other professional groups, trainers left to themselves tend to diffuse that immediate task and sideline work on it so they can pursue others they generate themselves and commonly at conceptual and methodological clarifications or other more general goals. Both have their place and, to ensure high quality resources in the future, it is important that organizations invest also in developing the training profession. But in order to inform and contribute the most to change efforts, making training a full partner in the learning system and not just a resource to it is the best.

Reading 3.1

The Company of the Future

ARIE DE GEUS*

In a world that is shrinking politically, the world of individual businesses is paradoxically growing. In the global village, the temptation is great to move out of one's regional or national niche into a wider and therefore more

---

[2] Reading 2.1 gives an overview of Future Search. More details and methodologies are in the companion volume for trainers (Chapter 6).

* From Arie de Geus, *The Living Company: Habits for Survival in a Turbulent Business Environment* (Boston: Harvard Business School Press), pp. 119–202.

unfamiliar environment. Even those companies that resist the temptation run the risk that the outside world will invade their home turf.

Over time, as a result, fewer and fewer companies will live and work in an environment over which they have a lot of control. More and more companies will be growing potatoes in the Andes, as it were, rather than in a glass house. With their habitat shrinking, economic companies might become an endangered species—pushed back into isolated, small niches and legally protected national parks.

In short, in the global village, the economic companies risk being the economic losers. The shrinking world will need more and more living companies.

What, then, does a healthy company of the future look like? How do we recognize when we are on the right track toward a healthy living company? And if a company does not look very healthy, what could the concerned management do to restore it?

A healthy living company will have members, both humans and other institutions, who subscribe to a set of common values and who believe that the goals of the company allow them and help them to achieve their own individual goals. Both the company and its constituent members have basic driving forces: they want to survive, and once the conditions for survival exist, they want to reach and expand their potential. The underlying contract between the company and its members (both individuals and other institutions) is that the members will be helped to reach their potential. It is understood that this, at the same time, is in the company's self-interest. The self-interest of the company stems from its understanding that the members' potential helps create the corporate potential.

The nature of this underlying contract creates trust, which results in levels of productivity that cannot be emulated by discipline and hierarchical control. Trust also allows space and tolerance both inside the hierarchy and toward the outside world. These are basic conditions for the high levels of institutional learning that will, on occasion, be very necessary.

The company has a will; thus, it makes choices. As a result of making choices, it may diverge from the conditions or the values in its environment. Continued disharmony with its world will lead to a crisis and may be mortal.

To avoid a crisis and to perceive a diverging environment, the company must be open to the outside world. Openness to the outside world means that there is tolerance for entry of new individuals and ideas. However, members know 'who is us' and 'who is not us.'

The membership of the community is variable, not only through the individuals who enter and leave over time, but also by enlargement or reduction of the whole over time.

Sometimes, members are forced out or converted into supplier or contractor status (which is a money relationship)—as when their value system is not harmonious with the company's value system. This shift is healthy for the institution, because harmonized value systems are a basic requirement for corporate cohesion. Sometimes, reduction in membership takes place, because an inner group of members redefines 'who is us' and enlarges the definition of 'who is not us.' This may not be healthy, because of the shock to the trust levels of the remaining members.

The human members of a healthy company are mobile, both in the different jobs they perform during their careers and in the places where they perform those jobs. They network, they meet, and they communicate across the whole organization. There is mutual trust that people will act fairly, and the leaders are as honest as one can expect from human beings. People know their trade. Power is distributed; there are checks and balances in the power system, and the present leaders understand that they are but one generation out of many still to come.

Besides members, the company will have physical (capital) assets, which the company uses for one or several economic activities to earn a living. Once survival is assured, the economic activity is used as the basis from which the community develops its potential.

While it is engaged in a particular activity at a particular place, the work community is surrounded by suppliers (of materials, of capital, of human labor and intelligence), by customers, by the regional or national community, and by other stakeholders who are all part of its world and with whom it must maintain a state of harmony.

If survival is at stake, the community will scuttle assets and try to change the content or nature of its economic activity before it scuttles people.

Everything the company does is rooted in two main hypotheses:

1. The company is a living being.
2. The decisions for action made by this living being result from a learning process.

Not just the economic aspects of a living company, but the psychological, sociological, and anthropological aspects complement, rather than fight, each other. The relevance of these aspects is explicit in the definition of a living company as 'financially conservative with a staff that identifies with the company and a management that is tolerant and sensitive to the world in which they live.' Both descriptions make clear that the priorities of the management of a living company cannot be exclusively expressed in economic terms.

If corporate health falters, the priority should be on mobilizing the maximum human potential, on restoring or maintaining trust and civic behavior, and on increasing professionalism and good citizenship.

Everything starts there. If companies can meet those conditions, I believe that average corporate life expectancy will begin to rise, to meet its potential span; and all of humanity will benefit as a result.

This is not to say that companies should live forever. In the corporate species, however, the gap between average and maximum life expectancy is still so wide that it may be concluded that too many companies suffer an untimely death. A reduction of the corporate mortality rate would seem to be advantageous for all parties: members, suppliers and contractors, the community, and shareholders.

Reading 3.2

Institution-Building: The British Army in World War II

ERIC TRIST AND HUGH MURRAY*

The group who entered the Directorate of Army Psychiatry took a novel approach to the human resource problems facing the army. Rather than remain in base hospitals they went out into the field to find out from commanding officers what they saw as their most pressing problems. They would listen to their troubled military clients as an analyst would to a patient, believing that the 'real' problems would surface as trust became established, and that constructive ideas about dealing with them would emerge. The concept thence arose of 'command' psychiatry, in which a psychiatrist with a roving commission was attached to each of the five Army Commanders in Home Forces.

A relationship of critical importance was formed between the Clinic's Ronald Hargreaves, as command psychiatrist, and Sir Ronald Adam, the Army Commander in Northern Command. When Adam became Adjutant General, the second highest post in the army, he was able to implement policies that Hargreaves and he had adumbrated. New military institutions had to be created to carry them out. The institution-building process entailed:

- Earning the right to be consulted on emergent problems for which there was no solution in traditional military procedures, e.g., the problem of officer selection.
- Making preliminary studies to identify a path of solution—the investigation of morale in Officer Cadet Training Units.
- Designing a pilot model in collaboration with military personnel which embodied the required remedial measures—the Experimental War Office Selection Board.

* From Eric Trist and Hugh Murray, *The Social Engagement of Social Science: A Tavistock Anthology* (University of Pennsylvania Press, 1990), Vol. 1, pp 3–4. Every effort has been made to trace the copyright holder(s). In the absence of a reply, permission has been assumed.

- Handing over the developed model to military control with the psychiatric and psychological staff falling back into advisory roles or where possible removing themselves entirely—the War Office Selection Boards (WOSBs) and Civil Resettlement Units (CRUs) for repatriated prisoners of war.
- Disseminating the developed model, securing broad acceptance for it and training large numbers of soldiers to occupy the required roles, e.g., CRUs.

To meet these large-scale tasks the range of disciplines was extended from psychiatry and clinical psychology to social psychology, sociology and anthropology. The members of these various disciplines were held together by participation in common operational tasks in an action frame of reference. To varying extents they began to learn each others' skills. The group became, to use a term that arose after the war in a project concerned with alternative forms of organization in the mining industry, a 'composite' work group.

Undertaking practical tasks that sought to resolve operational crises generated insights that led towards new theory. This process was familiar to those members of the group who were practicing psychiatrists, but it was new to those coming from other disciplines. This led to a generalized concept of professionalism.

The innovations introduced during the war years consisted of a series of 'inventions':

- Command psychiatry as a reconnaissance activity leading to the identification of critical problems.
- Social psychiatry as a policy science permitting preventive intervention in large scale problems.
- The co-creation with the military of new institutions to implement these policies.
- The therapeutic community as a new mode of treatment.
- Cultural psychiatry for the analysis of the enemy mentality.

By the end of the war a considerable number of psychiatrists and social scientists had become involved in this comprehensive set of innovative applications of concepts of social psychiatry. They saw in these approaches a significance which did not seem to be limited by the condition of war, and were determined to explore their relevance for the civilian society. Obviously, individual programs could not be transferred without considerable modification; entirely new lines of development would have to be worked out. Nevertheless, a new action-oriented philosophy of relating psychiatry and the social sciences to society had become a reality in practice. This event signified the social engagement of social science.

Reading 3.3

Image for Decentralizing Indonesia's Health Services

ROLF P. LYNTON*

Images for Long-shot Strategies

Innovative institutions aim to make a difference beyond themselves. *What* difference precisely and how, and how much it mattered in the light of history many forces will influence, as also the deliberate moves that took it there. A governing idea encompassing it all though is essential for sound working from the very start. And that idea must break through the pull of words from the past, just as a satellite needs to escape earth's gravity to orbit.

In the systems development work for five years in the 1980s with Indonesia's Ministry of Health and its services in the provinces, the image for making that difference was a tree. Purpose determined that the tree be large and strong, for it was to help the Ministry counter the prevailing powerful tendencies to concentrate policy- and decision-making at the center and help provincial governments take on more and more of that for themselves. Since the same centralizing tendencies beset the whole government at that time, countering them would be extra tough, but decentralization had also been declared an overall policy. Hence, how health got on with it and learned in the process could also serve as a pilot for others. And the policy was backed solidly by facts on the ground: the tens of islands—counting only the larger ones—that made up Indonesia, stretching over 3,000 miles, were simply too different for the same service structures, processes, and priorities to serve all well or more or less equally well—ever. So, with national unity sufficiently affirmed, decentralization was the new direction.

My charge was to help develop the manpower for this in the provinces so that they could take over these functions, at the Ministry so that they could let them go, and with both so that they could rework their relationship to support this shift of responsibilities and control. Other consultants worked on policy and organizational issues, and on strengthening the statistical and monitoring components for the shift.

The image started simple, of course, as all really telling images do: just three parts—roots, branches, and treetop, with the trunk to connect them.

The roots were the inputs. Starting with the policy to decentralize, and time and funds allocated locally, inputs also included the foreign consultants and some material aid. Imaging inputs as roots was not to keep their cost out

* From Rolf P. Lynton, *Social Science in Actual Practice: Themes on My Blue Guitar*, (New Delhi: Sage Publications, 1998), pp 229–33

of sight; on the contrary, I make a point of drawing clients' attention to costs. Roots convey two much more important notions. One is that the growth of the tree largely depends on them, for height, strength, and also speed of growing. The other, an important reminder in all third-party assistance, is that inputs become important in the *taking*, not in the giving: they matter to the growth above ground only as and when the tree draws on them.

The *crown* of the tree and its highest fruit, nearest to the sun, were 'changes in norms and structures' in the Ministry and in the provinces and new capacities to sustain them, that is, the changes that would last and be most pervasive systemically. From the ground these crowning fruit would be least visible, even though they would be the most strategic outcomes of the project.

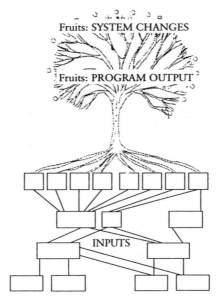

Decentralizing Indonesia's Health Services

Visible fruit on branches at mid-level were program outputs along the way, such as management training, training materials, and local faculty. These fruits, growing in plenty from quite early on and immediately nourishing, were also welcome confirmation that the tree was growing well. But, like the apple within Adam and Eve's reach in Eden, it also tempted to end efforts right there. Nothing was better than this visible fruit for convincing decision-makers, in Indonesia no less than in foreign agencies, to praise the project and see it as successfully over. Keeping attention focused on the systemic developments the project aimed at became more difficult past the fruit ready for picking, especially when settling for them would avoid the struggling undoubtedly involved in working out the transformations of center–province relationships and structures at the top. The tree image showed very simply what was close to hand and what distant, what was visible and what underground (but no less essential), and how all had to work together.

Most importantly, the tree underscored the organic nature of the task—essentially of *all* innovative tasks. Conceptually, its component parts—inputs, program outputs, systemic change—and also how they fit together could be fixed. But then they had to make their way in the real world, with speed of growth, shape, eventual size, and strength all subject to all manner of changing conditions. The accompanying figure shows the tree as it ended up.

The intricate root system shows 16 kinds of inputs (a box for each) and has grown from the two levels envisaged in the prospectus to four and greater depths. Most deeply and securely rooted were the original technical inputs for health services staffs: task analysis, case research and writing, impact evaluation, and occasional later additions. Training and consulting skills were the next level up, and advanced programs above that. 'Consultant interns' were the fourth and newest input, and the most complex, sensitive and spread out in any case, needing the steadiest support at the end.

Above ground, the tree branched out into eight major kinds of program, project, and consultancy outputs. They included inter-sectoral and inter-provincial training and consulting. The crown, to top it all off, identified six areas in which the national and provincial systems, and their work together operated with 'improved norms and structures', e.g., personnel selections based on job criteria, national staff sent as participants in provincial programs, national networking of training and consulting resources, and their recognition as a professional association.

Part II

TRAINING POLICY AND RESOURCES

4

POLICY FORMULATION IN PRACTICE: A CASE

The Setting: A Brief Introduction

Draft Policy in Print: A Sample
  Goals and Culture: The 'Guiding Principles'
  State-wide Coordination, Control, and Technical Support
  Upgrading Quality of Training
  The Training System
  Implementation of Policy and Time Lines

Process Review: Some Questions and Reflections

Exhibits
4.1 Proposed Training System

Readings
4.1 Formulation of Population Policy

The proof of the pudding is in the eating. During 1992–1994, Udai Pareek was consultant to the state government of Rajasthan for developing a state-wide training system for Rajasthan's public health and family planning services (which in India are joint). By summer 1997, the major building blocks for this system had been constructed and positioned, a new apex training institute approved and funded, and the premier candidate in the state appointed director for it—a physician with long experience in institution-building and the state government, and with the highest reputation. The apex institute initiated the process of developing a training policy and the draft policy was documented in an official report. This report we then used in the second seminar for policy-makers that December, on the way to writing this volume, with the institute's director, Dr. Rameshwar Sharma, taking active part. The quotes in this chapter are from that Report.

We run them here alongside the general discussion of issues in policy development, to see how that flow and the resolutions of those issues can emerge in practice, in an actual contemporary setting. The quotes will show what a policy can look like, as a whole and its constituent parts. Following that we review what, looking back, were the key aspects of the process by which the state government created this policy, such as, how the groups were composed that considered various parts of it, the initial support that galvanized the system for this venture, the waxing and waning of that support as it progressed, strategic issues resolved (or unresolved) along the way, and so on; where we assess implementation stands as we write; and with what prospects. As is the wont of such reports, the official report from which we quote confines itself to the outcomes only— the policies as formulated and accepted—and these are indeed the signposts to guide and refer to in the future. Yet, the process 'how' is essential too, for assessing what is really on the ground and reliably on the way to implementing as intended. No policy exists that will not be derailed by administrators who lack the spirit for it. It is attention to process that gives policy formulation life and so also enables others to visualize policy development in their own settings.

Euphoria and relief when a good-looking policy has been put on paper, after much work and anxiety, are probably premature; to stay with the culinary image, there is many a slip between cup and lip. Better to hold them a while, at least till the policy has started to work and worked for a while, seeped into the system, and quietened residual doubts. In Rajasthan, within six months, the routine rotation of key supporters of the new policy and the appointment of newcomers created conditions for putting the policies on hold and dismissing the director, till some months and many upsets, delays, and disturbances later, the state could put the development back on track again.

How much of real life's complexities to take into account and incorporate in actual policy formation—the practicalities—and how much or few expectations of steadiness and reliability to invest in the venture in these fast-moving, turbulent times remain questions to resolve at the outset, and probably conservatively too: where policies are needed to support and sustain significantly different working, as they undoubtedly are for training in most places, doubling the initial estimates of cost—of time and trouble as well as funds—is probably wise. Nothing could illustrate better, than this example from Rajasthan, the importance of the cautionary footnote to all cases:

that it is good for and offered for discussion only, and not to illustrate an especially good or a notably bad way of management, administration or, here, of policy formation. Discussion will reveal the important dimensions to take into account and how they fit together, and indeed have to fit; also the particular circumstances of each set of people, place, and purpose.

In line with this, we will build some discussion right into the text here. Clearly indicated by italicized text, Rolf Lynton will raise questions and seek further elucidation where Udai Pareek's description of the process at some stage is short on detail (that he knows from being there but readers do not) or seems to give too little or too much weight to a possibly significant dimension—perhaps by his very closeness and direct involvement.

THE SETTING: A BRIEF INTRODUCTION

It may be useful to give a very brief background about the setting for action.

Rajasthan, situated at the northwest border of India, is the second largest state of the country with a land area measuring 342.239 sq. km. The state has a population of over 50 million people scattered in 33,000 villages and more than 200 urban agglomerations in its thirty-one districts. This rhomboid shaped state is traversed by the Aravali hill ranges in the southeast while the northwest is an arid land area known as the Thar desert. The thin distribution of population and difficult access to a large number of habitations are a challenge to health planners. Rajasthan was formed in 1950 by integrating several princely states, some of them famous for history and heritage. However, their feudal systems made for backwardness. Even today, Rajasthan is very low on several development indices. It ranks 11 (out of 15 states) on the Human Development Index (HDI), 14 on the Infrastructural Development Index (IDI), and 11 on the Economic Development Index (EDI). The health situation is also bad. Out of 100,000, 823 women die during child bearing or delivery. Out of 1.6 million children born every year, 0.15 million die within one year, i.e., nearly one in ten. Communicable diseases and perinatal and maternal causes account for half the deaths in the state.

The *Report of Training Policy* summarized the current state of training for the state's health services and the need for a new policy as follows:

> The health training institutions have been developed piecemeal over the last forty years with very little horizontal or vertical linkages with other training and service institutions within and outside the state. The issues in the management of these institutions need urgent attention in order to make them efficient and effective, such that the 'service sub-system' perceives them as dependable and credible organisations for seeking help in solving the problem of performance deficit. The management of the training sub-system will be reorganised with strong vertical and horizontal linkages with training institutions and service organisations within and outside the state.
>
> The existing training institutions are finding it difficult to cope with the new demands and expectations due to the changing focus in the Family Welfare (FW) programme implementation with the introduction of Reproductive and Child Health (RCH) approach and launching of new programmes such as National AIDS Control Programme and renewal of focus on National Tuberculosis Control and Malaria Control Programme. The training system will, therefore, be reorganised and strengthened such that it can play an effective role in the current context and keep pace with the fast changing demands of expanding the health care delivery system.

DRAFT POLICY IN PRINT: A SAMPLE

Goals and Culture: The 'Guiding Principles'

- *Decentralization* of planning, monitoring, evaluation and decision-making.
- *Autonomy* to all training institutions for implementation of training.
- *Accountability* in terms of training effectiveness and efficient utilization of resources.
- *Synergy* with the client system.
- *Linking* the training function with HRD, especially the career system.
- *Openness* to continuous feedback, new ideas and developments.

Decentralization and Autonomy

- The training institutions will be given a lot of flexibility to design and develop their work calendars for each year, in consultation with respective Training Advisory Committees, to provide room for training research, evaluation of training and its impact, and consultancy. The State Institute of Health and Family Welfare (SIHFW) will prepare a consolidated State Training Plan and share it with the State Training Advisory Committee.
- All the training institutions will be made autonomous institutions, registered under the Societies Act in their respective districts as subordinate institutions of SIHFW. Necessary amendments in the constitution of SIHFW will be made for this purpose.
- The training institutions will be allowed to generate their own resources through organizing paid programs, consulting, etc. The programs carried out for the state government should also be treated as cost programs nationally. The objective is to make the training institutions self-reliant and encourage them to use the additional resources in enhancing the quality of their training programs.

Accountability

- Training centers, like other units in the training subsystem, will also be cost centers.
- Training capacity and facilities will be evaluated periodically to strike a balance between demand and supply. To begin with, a facility survey will be carried out to find out differences in physical infrastructure and facilities among all the training institutions in the state. The deficit will be removed on priority to enable the training institutions to function at their optimal efficiency.

Synergy with the Client System

WITH OPERATIONS AND SERVICES

- The existing training curriculum will be reviewed and modified, if required, to ensure that only competency-based, high impact training programs are organized. Training Needs Assessment (TNA) studies will be conducted periodically to design high impact training programs. A system of concurrent and impact evaluation will be introduced to ascertain the effectiveness of the training programs. Trainers' performance will be measured on the basis of training impact and not on the number of training programs conducted.

- The opportunity of 'on-the-job' skill advancement is enormous, and has hitherto remained untapped. A lot of emphasis will be placed on job training. The performance of supervisors will also be evaluated on utilization of 'on-the-job' training opportunities. The potential of 'on-the-job training' has not been tapped, particularly in enhancing competencies, developing trust, developing teams, and bringing about much desired attitudinal changes amongst health functionaries. SIHFW/Health and Family Welfare Training Centers (HFWTCs) will provide all assistance to health institutions to make the best use of 'on-the-job training' opportunities.
- The training programs for all categories of health functionaries will be integrated. A comprehensive training program design will be prepared, striking a balance between clinical, managerial and communication skills which are need-based and expressed by the functionaries themselves.
- Special skills development programs will be offered to enable health functionaries and medical officers to pursue their interests and career perspectives on a regular basis. Successful completion of such a program will be considered an additional qualification for the purpose of placement.
- For proper management, a reporting system from District Training Centers (DTCs) to SIHFW will be developed. The system will also be designed for lateral reporting from DTCs to Chief Medical and Health Officers (CMHOs), HFWTCs to Zonal Joint Directors, and SIHFW to the state.
- The role of trainers will be not be limited to classroom training. Their participation in solving performance deficit problems faced by the service subsystem will also be actively encouraged.
- The faculty of training institutions will act as consultants to the health system/clients to help understand and solve the problems faced, and/or suggest/test alternative strategies.

WITH THE WIDER ENVIRONMENT
- Each district will prepare a comprehensive training plan as part of the district plan for health and family welfare in consultation with the District Training Advisory Committee. The plan will

not only reflect training activities but include research and consultancy assignments. The training calendar and nomination roster will be circulated to all concerned well in time.

- A State Training Advisory Committee will be constituted. The Committee will be responsible for direction, monitoring and coordination of all the training activities in the state. On similar terms and with similar objectives, zonal and district training advisory committees will also be constituted.

- Vertical and horizontal linkages will be developed amongst DTCs, HFWTCs, and SIHFW, and other training and service organizations in the government and non-government sectors within and outside the state for dissemination and sharing of experiences and for providing a wide range of opportunities for organizing competency-based learning programs.

- SIHFW and HFWTC and the state health services will favorably consider the potential of organizing exchange visits between and within districts for health professionals and trainers to share success stories. Such visits may be used as a reward for better performers and a motivational strategy for border-line performers.

Linking Training with Human Resources Development

- A perspective Human Resource Plan will be developed for the state to project human resource needs as precisely as possible. The need for NGOs and the private sector will also be considered while estimating the need for human resources.

- The human resource development function cannot be discharged effectively unless comprehensive data on recruitment, movement, training status, and performance appraisal of all the functionaries is readily available to all the training institutions. A Human Resource Management wing will be created at district, zonal, and state levels, and it will maintain the data on computer and provide the information regularly to training institutions and training coordinators. The information will be used for human resource planning and for nominations for training programs and placement.

- To create trainees' interest in enhancing their skills and competencies, an environment will be created wherein good performance is rewarded and poor performance is punished. This type of work culture will promote and/or create interest in in-service trainings. The implementation measures will include:

i. Linking successful completion of training with confirmation, promotion and placement.

ii. Institutionalizing a system of rewards for competence and performance in terms of better placement, out-of-turn promotion, study tours and foreign training.

iii. Providing challenging assignments to good performers.

iv. Poor performers being denied the above benefits.

- This will involve developing a suitable appraisal system.

Openness to Continuous Feedback and New Ideas

- Training research, including evaluation of training and its impact, and health service research will be accorded high priority. The training institutions will play an active role in conducting research and evaluation studies. A system of training evaluation will also be developed. Pilot testing of different approaches by the training institutions will be provided high priority. Some such approaches are the problem-solving approach, area-specific approach, distance learning, and involvement of NGOs and the private sector in effective and efficient competency-based training.

- A forum will be provided in the form of a state-level biannual conference to share the experience of research, operations research, TNA, and impact studies. The best studies will be awarded recognition in the conference.

- Important research experiences will be disseminated to all training institutions, program managers and others who may be interested in them.

- The contribution of training institutions in conducting relevant research is negligible, though the scope and potential are enormous. The training institutions will play a more active role in conducting research—operations research, TNA, evaluation of training, and impact evaluation studies—to understand and solve the performance problems faced by the health care delivery system. Facilities and inputs will be provided to health training institutions through SIHFW to promote research and operations research studies.

- The participation of the faculty of training institutions in research studies will be one of the indicators considered in reviewing their performance.

- Realizing that a large number of health functionaries need to be trained each year, which is far more than the existing capacity of the training institutions in the state, SIHFW will explore the possibility of offering distance learning programs.

State-wide Coordination, Control, and Technical Support

Coordination as support assumed high importance, alongwith making the many training institutions more autonomous.

- All the training institutions in the state will be brought under the administrative, financial and technical control of SIHFW.
- SIHFW will be further strengthened in terms of its physical facilities and staff, so as to enable it to play the role of lead institution in the area of training in the state. SIHFW will coordinate all the training, health service research and consulting functions of the state through providing technical support to DTCs and regional HFWTCs.
- As far as possible, training programs will be organized only in designated training and service institutions in government and non-government sectors.
- Uniform rates of TA/DA, per diem, or honorarium will be adopted in training programs irrespective of the funding agency. SIHFW will prepare the norms. Likewise, uniform norms of payment to resource persons/guest speakers will also be adopted in the state. A flexible mechanism of flow of funds will be established so as to facilitate payment of TA/DA and honorarium by the training institutions.
- The multiplicity of training programs and program-specific trainings will be replaced with a well designed integrated in-service program for all cadres. Only in very special situations may a program-specific training be organized, for which prior approval from the appropriate training committee must be taken.

Upgrading Quality of Training

Staffing

- A special training cadre will be created with clear prospects for promotion and career advancement. Provision for coming in and going back to the service system after serving for a minimum period, specified under rules, will be made.

- Only highly competent people will be placed in the training institutions by open selection and through special selection rules.
- The trainers will work for a period of at least five years in the training system.
- The trainers selected/recruited will be given special pay and other incentives and facilities, higher than those for equivalent positions in the service system, as provided in the special selection rules.
- One of the responsibilities of SIHFW will be organizing special programs on competency enhancement for trainers.
- The trainers in the training institutions are the most valuable resource. The competence and self-esteem of the trainers will lend credibility to the training institutions. Realizing this, high priority will be assigned to developing competencies of trainers. To recruit and retain good trainers in the training institutions, a separate training cadre will be created with a well defined process for recruitment, placement, rotation and promotion. The trainers will be provided the best possible opportunities for enhancing their competencies through regular training and study tours within the country and abroad.
- The trainers will be provided adequate opportunities to achieve academic excellence through trainings, study tours and sabbaticals in and outside the country. The trainers will be eligible to get one year sabbatical after ten years of confirmed government service, and three years in the training system.
- The trainers will be encouraged to pursue research and undertake consultancy assignments. SIHFW will develop detailed norms for consultancy, including the number of days per year.
- The experience of working as a trainer will be considered an additional qualification for the purpose of promotion and placement in the service department.

Training Materials

- Very little attention was paid in the past to developing locally relevant training material. Currently, the material prepared by the Government of India (GoI) and international agencies is being used. In addition to using such material, appropriate and relevant material will be developed by the training institutes in the state at all levels, preferably using locally available resources and material.

- The training institutions will be provided facilities and inputs to develop new material, or adapt existing material, which is need-based and trainee-specific and duly pre-tested. SIHFW will provide necessary technical support and guidance to all other training institutions in the state for this purpose. SIHFW will also review the training material periodically.
- In order to develop, encourage and evaluate a wide range of training material, including multimedia, a special cell will be created in SIHFW.

System Support
- All the training institutions in each of the districts will be integrated into the District Training Center and it will be physically located at one place. The person incharge of the DTC will be of a rank equivalent to that of Deputy Chief Medical and Health Officer (Dy. CMHO). He/she will also be designated as District Training Coordinator. The number of HFWTCs will be increased to six (one in each zone). The rank of Incharge, HFWTC, will be equivalent to that of Joint Director. He will coordinate all training related functions in the zone. Each HFWTC/DTC will develop a Field Practice Demonstration Area (FPDA) at one of the Primary Health Centers (PHCs) to organize community-based trainings.
- All the DTCs will report to the regional HFWTCs. The regional HFWTC will be responsible for providing administrative, financial, and technical support to the DTCs in its jurisdiction.
- The training capacities of DTCs will be suitably augmented by reorganizing and strengthening the physical facilities to be able to bear the type of training load envisaged in RCH and other programs.
- Training institutes will issue certificates of completion to the participants after ensuring that all the requirements of competencies have been fulfilled.

The Training System

For implementing these policies the training system will have four levels with the linkages as shown in Exhibit 4.1.

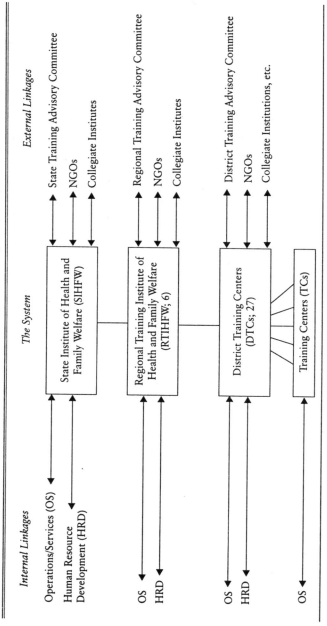

Exhibit 4.1
PROPOSED TRAINING SYSTEM
(for State Health and Family Welfare, Rajasthan, 1997)

Implementation of Policy and Time Lines

- The detailed plan of action for implementation of the training policy will be prepared within six months of approval by the state government.
- The responsibility of follow up of the implementation of the training policy will be that of the State Training Advisory Committee.
- Within one year of implementation of the policy, an expert group will be constituted by the government to find out the status of implementation and suggest corrective actions, if any.
- After a period of three to five years, a policy review will be undertaken by constituting an expert group to study the impact of the implementation of the policy and to suggest policy changes, if required.

PROCESS REVIEW: SOME QUESTIONS AND REFLECTIONS

The following process dialogue between the authors is meant to help the readers reflect on the critical issues of training policy formulation, and more importantly, of its implementation. The dialogue was conducted at long distance, the authors being in two different continents.

LYNTON: *From the wide variety of questions that occur to me as I scan this policy document, I will try to select just six to highlight some strategic dimensions that policy-makers elsewhere may want to watch as they proceed in their own settings.*

First, what made this time—1996–1997—especially opportune for launching this policy effort? After all, by all health and family welfare indices—and indeed all social indices, from family income, literacy, and the position of women, for instance—Rajasthan had been distressingly low for as long as records exist. Moreover it has to cope with extra difficult location, desert terrain, and climate as well as awkwardly distributed habitation and services.

PAREEK: The senior health administrators and selected bureaucrats had realized the importance of health manpower in delivery of health services through the government health system. The late prime minister Rajiv Gandhi, because of his wider exposure to the western world, was convinced that in-service training as a component of

HRD in the government system was essential to making the system efficient, effective and responsive. Some of the health administrators and bureaucrats had undergone such training, both within the country and abroad. According to Dr. Rameshwar Sharma, various international and bilateral donor agencies were also looking into issues in health care delivery and were working out interventions to improve the situation. One such agency which joined the system was the UNFPA. This UN agency was primarily working for promoting family welfare programs in the state and was interested in supporting the development of training infrastructure and training capabilities in the state at different levels. This was also the time a new World Bank project was under preparation. The World Bank consultants were also focusing on these major issues in the proposed project, strengthening infrastructure so as to developing training capabilities to improve service delivery, and promoting demand generalization through Information, Education, Communication (IEC) and involvement of NGOs (1993–1994). As training was given focused attention in the project proposal, and the UNFPA consultants' report on training system was available, the state health system decided to act upon various components of training including developing the training policy.

LYNTON: *About the composition of the policy-drafting body (bodies?). If it was a specially designated one, for this task, how was it composed, e.g., of health secretariat officials only, or other state officials as well? Any NGO or collegiate institution representatives? Any spokesmen for service users—all stakeholders, in short (as in a Future Search)?*

Was there direct involvement of the regional, district, and local levels of the system?

If the task was given to a regular body, how was it composed, and what provision did it then make to give voice to other constituents and regions, district, and local levels in the system?

Did the people in fact then also come? Any regular patterns of attendance and of active participation? I am thinking here, of course, of the difficulty more local and less exhalted participants have in coming in the first place (time off work, transportation, other costs) and also in speaking in the unfamiliar presence of older and high status people.

PAREEK: A group was formed consisting of state-level officials (secretaries, directors, and the state institutes), district heads of health, regional training centers, NGOs like IDS and IIHMR, experts, retired directors of health, local representatives of international organizations (UNFPA, UNICEF, World Bank, Danida), and a few other bureaucrats. They met in a workshop and generated ideas. Then the draft was prepared. Again the group met to discuss and approve the draft. The task of drafting was assigned to the state institute which requested a consultant to prepare the draft, who first discussed it with a small expert group, and then within the institute.

LYNTON: *What time frame was envisaged for drafting the policy—originally, subsequently? Was there a budget, e.g., for travelling?*

PAREEK: The original time framework was one year and a budget of about $4000 was kept for travelling, etc. The person appointed for the task travelled to a few districts for discussion. The time was later revised, because the draft discussed and approved by the larger body had to be approved by the government. The draft lay with the minister for five months.

LYNTON: *Meetings—how many and how frequent were they? What took place? E.g., discussion of drafts? Whose drafts?*

On my mind here is how much commitment any agreement arrived at in the meetings was carried forward with support. Did these drafts get looked at like the many others that officials receive from elsewhere/'outside', e.g., from Delhi, which they pretty routinely note and pass on (significant phrase?) but do not put energy into, and also know how to by-pass when something else suits better. Or are these in fact drafts that they worked out themselves and so were more likely to stand by when it came to action?

This commitment question—and what was done to help ensure commitment—looms extra large in view of the hiatus the whole policy effort ran into when key supporters were transferred out of the state.

PAREEK: Only two meetings of the larger body were held—the first workshop to generate ideas and the second to consider the draft prepared by the consultant but presented as the state institute draft. Smaller groups met about five times to discuss, review, and modify the various aspects. The smaller group consisted of state institute persons, Udai Pareek, an UNFPA representative, one director of health services, and an expert.

LYNTON: *Contents and coverage. Did the work begin with an overall map or make its way ad hoc? If with a map/overview, what was it? And did that get discussed and modified—and ownership thereby strengthened?*

In our chapter here, following the Report itself, we ordered the extracts conceptually. In what order did they actually get (a) started, and (b) settled?

In particular, how and at what stage(s) did 'the Principles' get formulated—early on and complete? Or identified in the course of drafting policy components about this or that, i.e., as something underlying all? How complete does the set look now?

PAREEK: The work began with an overall map, growing out of a previous report on a health training system prepared by me as UNFPA consultant. I proposed guiding principles which were discussed in the first workshop. Some new dimensions were added. The draft was discussed in smaller groups—at that time the need for a clear mission statement was felt and then the statement was drafted, discussed, and redrafted. The various aspects seem to be complete as of now.

LYNTON: *How do you understand now, looking back, the opposition, hiatus, delay, and then resumption that the effort ran into when key supporters of it left? A coalition of opponents that top-level support had kept quiet till then? Awe at the great amount of work that implementing this drastic new order undoubtedly foreshadowed? The competency requirements alone must have disquietened many officials and other staff, is it not so?*

About Dr. S and his dismissal then, I think of the scapegoating that routinely occurs in situations of radical change, so regularly in fact that the most sophisticated institutions send consultants and other kinds of resource people in pairs to work on this kind of task, in the expectation that one will attract the anger, etc., that is bound to come, and can then leave, taking that with him or her, and his colleague stays behind as the reassuring, supportive partner.

Did other(s) see themselves as good candidates for the directorship from the beginning?

Were the two of you seen from the beginning as a pair to fear? To indulge no longer than necessary?

PAREEK: Looking back, several factors contributed to the delay and hiatus as you put it. The change of the secretary was the most important one. Secretaries are becoming more powerful in the system, thereby disempowering the technical and professional directors. Secretaries are general administrators, from the Indian Administrative Service, with no accountability for the function(s) assigned to them, because they hardly stay in a particular role for about two years. So their commitment primarily is to their administrative career. Being highly intelligent and powerful, some do bring about significant and strategic changes, which may be reversed after that person leaves. Now there is subtle rivalry amongst the incumbents, the next person showing his/her upmanship. There is hardly any organizational learning and building on the previous work done. In this case, the next secretary tried to undo what the previous secretary had done—discontinuation of many training programs, cancellation of the World Bank supported campus building of the state institute, stopping faculty recruitment. The new secretary questioned the rationale of many initiatives and took unilateral decisions. One of them was to put the training policy proposal in cold storage.

Since the state institute is an autonomous body, with a governing board chaired by the health minister, the director of the institute 'used' this formal arrangement, directly sending papers to the chairman (the minister), including the training policy draft. This almost questioned the authority of the secretary in relation to training. The training policy document further emphasising autonomy and the strategic role of the state institute, was seen as a threat.

The minister kept the training policy paper with him for five months, and only near the elections (he was voted out of power), sent the paper to the Department of Health (as suggested by the director of the institute) for examination. The directors saw this proposal as a threat to their power (the proposal to shift training responsibility from the directorate to the institute). So, while earlier the directors had endorsed and supported the ideas when participating in the discussion of the draft, they saw the danger when they examined it for implementation. This led to its coldstoring; to letting it die in long isolation.

In a way, Dr. S. became a scapegoat. There was awe at his known academic/professional standing, a strong team, or a 'cheque' if you like, generating new and revolutionary ideas. His removal eased the way to bring back the status quo and traditional power. I resigned my membership of the governing board, the executive committees and other bodies.

No initiative was taken by the new director of SIHFW on training policy as he is a general administrator. Directorship is now being filled by the search committee/selection process. According to Dr. S., 'there was no fear, but the Director was thought to be a person with clout and influence, having direct relationships with the then secretary and the minister. Some health directorate people were also considered for the post of director SIHFW, but were not approved by the search committee'.

Concluding reflection by Pareek: With the previous secretary coming back, with greater power, the document has now been given by the secretary to a small HRD team of the directorate to work out action steps to implement the training policy. Although a small group is still enthusiastic about and is pushing the implementation process, with the weakening of the SIHFW and the entire training system the level of enthusiasm (and, therefore, commitment) in the directorate is low. The secretary also is too busy with other more urgent and important aspects. Unless the training system is seen and treated as central for improving the larger work system, and unless it is manned by, and strengthened with, additional competent persons, the training policy may continue to be fed on nutrition-free sweet words and promises. However, hope is still alive!

Reading 4.1

Formulation of Population Policy

STEPHEN L. ISAACS, CAIRNS AND NANCY I. HECKEL*

What is Population Policy?

It is useful to distinguish between 'explicit' and 'implicit' policies. An explicit policy is a statement or document by a national government announcing its intention or plan to affect at least the country's population growth and perhaps its distribution and/or composition as well. Implicit population

* Abridged with permission from the authors' *Population Policy: A Manual for Policymakers and Planners* (New York: Columbia University, Faculty of Medicine, Center for Population and Family Health).

policies have taken a variety of forms, including documents by governmental ministries and commissions, legislation, sections of development plans, policy declaration of a ruling party, statements by the nation's president or other high level officials.

Because fertility and family planning often are given great attention, population policy is sometimes confused with the fertility policy of family planning policy. However, population policy is generally considered broader than this and includes considerations of migration and mortality as well as fertility.

In contrast, implicit policies are those laws, regulations, and other directives which, although not necessarily issued for the purpose of affecting population growth, distribution, or composition, have the effect of doing so. By aggregating the impact of those policies which influence population growth, distribution, and composition directly and indirectly, one could theoretically arrive at a conclusion about a country's 'implicit' population policy. In this way, one examines what a country 'does', not merely what it 'says'.

There are three reasons why this is extremely difficult in practice. First, policies are, with few exceptions, not generally coordinated to reach a common goal. Second, most social and economic development policies (e.g., education, health, income, housing) are thought to influence fertility indirectly. Measurement of all these policies for their effect on population dynamics could be very complex and cumbersome. Third, the net impact of policies often is not known, at least for many years.

Elements Common to Population Policies

Although they may differ from one another with respect to particular provisions, population policies contain a number of related elements. These can be summarized in the following manner:

- *Rationale.* Policies usually begin with a justification for, or the reasons behind, the issuance of a population policy. This often takes the form of a demographic analysis and the problems presented by current and projected population growth.
- *Objectives and Goals.* Many policies follow the rationale by a statement of objectives and goals. These may be general—phrased in terms of overall development or health goals—or may be written as more narrow, specific goals.
- *Targets.* In some cases, policies set specific demographic targets, such as reaching a certain level of fertility or mortality by a specified year.
- *Policy and Program Measures.* Many policies contain or recommend measures which the country plans to take. These commonly include:
  1. providing fertility regulation services and information;

2. furnishing population, family life, and/or sex education and information;
3. improving the status of women;
4. improving health and nutritional status;
5. providing incentives and disincentives;
6. improving research and evaluation;
7. carrying out specific legal reforms; and
8. implementing policies to affect internal and/or international migration.

• *Implementation and Institutional Arrangements.* Many countries try to assure effective implementation of population policy by assigning specific responsibility for coordinating or monitoring or by establishing a specific entity charged with this.

Numerous policy options are available in these areas, as the range of examples below demonstrates.

Implementation and Institutional Arrangements

Issuance of an explicit population policy does not guarantee that family planning programs will be implemented, that other measures proposed in the policy will be carried out, or that sufficient budgets will be allocated. Thus, some countries have given attention to mechanisms for implementing their population policy. They have established national population councils and have specified the roles of various institutions involved in carrying out the policy.

There is considerable diversity world-wide, but at least three distinct types of national population policy units can be identified:

• Small technical units placed at a high level of government to assure that demographic considerations are included in development planning.
• Interministerial councils whose function is to develop, monitor, and in some cases coordinate population policies.
• Family planning coordinating councils, which have a role in coordinating, allocating funds to, and even implementing the government family planning program.

Even where no coordinating mechanism exists, the concept of collaboration and shared responsibility has been emphasized. For example,

'It is essential that all Ministries and Departments of the Government of India as well as the States should take up as an integral part of their normal programme and budgets the motivation of citizens to adopt responsible reproductive behaviour both in their own as well as the national interest'.[1]

A number of policies emphasize the importance of the private sector in the implementation of population policy. For example,

'Of fundamental import to the success of...the population policy...is involvement of non-governmental agencies in the programme. The programme at the moment is far too dependent upon the Government and the official machinery. This has obvious limitations and the position needs to be remedied. Opportunities have to be created for people's representatives, voluntary groups and individuals to involve themselves directly in the programme'.[2]

A population policy can assign specific responsibility for monitoring and implementation. For example, the Jamaica population policy gives the National Planning Agency the task of assuring that the goals of the population policy are included in the nation's development plans and of monitoring the work of other agencies involved in implementing the policy. The National Family Planning Board is assigned responsibility for coordinating the delivery of services and the provision of family life and family planning education. An interagency coordinating committee is given responsibility for overseeing policy implementation.

The Process of Population Policy Making

Population policies, like policies in other fields, are the product of a political process and often represent a compromise between competing ideas. However, unlike many fields, population issues remain delicate, often are controversial, and frequently have very little political 'payoff' for policymakers. Thus, the enactment of population policies will not always be without difficulty.

Policymakers should, therefore, consider the process of issuing a population policy. Some of the questions which can be asked are:

- How can a constituency best be developed in support of a population policy?
- What are the strongest arguments in favor of a population policy? To whom should they be addressed?
- What form should a population policy take (e.g., should it be a law passed by parliament? A declaration of the Prime Minister? A ministerial resolution?).

[1] National Population Policy statement by Dr. Karan Singh, Minister of Health and Family Planning, New Delhi, April 16, 1976.

[2] Planning Commission, *Revised Draft Sixth Five Year Plan, 1978–83* (New Delhi: Government of India, 1978).

- What methods can be used to educate or to minimize any opposition?
- What is the most advantageous timing?

The Jamaican experience would seem to indicate that the following ingredients are essentials for the successful development of a national population policy.

1. A broad-based consensus on the urgent problem and a need for the policy.
2. Local political support. Efforts should be made to accommodate powerful groups such as religious organizations or other nationalist groups.
3. Highly motivated and influential local leadership, who will commit themselves to the cause.

Once these ingredients have been obtained the policy development process can begin.

The first stage is to assemble and organize the available body of theoretical and empirical information on the country's population trends in the context of social and economic development. Involvement of a broad cross-section of experts, public servants, politicians and others in workshops and task forces should be encouraged. But the work of these bodies should be well prepared, coordinated and directed to clear goals if any success is to be achieved.

A mutually complementary network of institutions that can provide data, conduct research, train experts and provide services is needed. In order to guarantee a relatively smooth functioning of this network, a strong coordinating body is required. It is advisable that this population policy coordinating unit be attached to the government's planning ministry which is multidisciplinary in nature, operates above all sectors and can establish links with the planning units in sectoral ministries as well as the various levels of local government.

With regard to the implementation of the policy, widespread involvement of numerous yet appropriate institutions within and outside the government is advisable.

Finally, wide dissemination of knowledge and news about relevant data, activities, research, and policies through a variety of channels such as the educational system, public and private organizations, and communications media, will prove effective in developing and implementing a national population policy.[3]

---

[3] Population Policy Task Force, *A Statement of National Population Policy* (Jamaica: Ministry of Health, 1982).

Although there is, by now, a considerable body of literature on population policy, definitive studies on process remain elusive. Perhaps this is because political conditions are so varied that the experience in one country will not necessarily apply in others. Nonetheless, in the process of policy formation, as with the content of population policy, there are lessons to be learned from the experience of others.

By giving attention to both the process and the content of population policy, policymakers can improve the chances of both issuance and successful implementation of population policies.

5

BUILDING A TRAINING SYSTEM

Above all, a concept should be robust: robust enough to survive mistranslation into various languages, to survive distortion by political pressures and interservice rivalries, to survive drowning in floods of emotion engendered by… crises and catastrophes.

—Freeman Dyson

By using so broad, generic and, in this context, unfamiliar a word as 'system' to designate the partner responsible for identifying and organizing training resources and for providing the actual training and associated consultation that an organization and its participants need, we have already alerted readers to complexities ahead. Now, starting the practical study of it, 'system' also offers three important pointers: a system has many components; these components are interrelated and cohere; and a system has boundaries, a position in an environment, and connections and transactions with this environment that matter greatly. Clearly, these pointers to the nature of a training system raise concerns far beyond the usual ones of sending some staff to a training course somewhere, 'leaving' training issues to 'the training people to get on with, since that is their business', or expecting a newcomer to 'pick up' a particular set of competencies by simply being 'put with' an old-timer and others at the same superficial level.

To visualize training as itself a system is a useful first step—as long as it is not also the last! Exhibit 5.1 shows the basic model. The 'import', 'conversion', and 'export' subsystems in it represent the more commonly used 'inputs', 'thoughputs', and 'outputs'. Planners, boards, and project directors are quite familiar with these concepts, as also with 'boundaries', 'environment', 'linkages' and 'feedback loops', and many have become quite adept at converting lists of items for program planning or evaluation into system diagrams. It is the onward steps that are often wanting. Once the diagram is drawn, energies flag. As if they were an end in themselves, this labelling and diagramming is more often used to wall off the business-like consideration of practical issues rather than to open it up. And so the language of systems, which should help all trainers find their way more easily in a

Exhibit 5.1
SIMPLE MODEL OF TRAINING SYSTEM

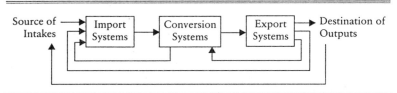

SOURCE: Adapted from E.J. Miller and A.K. Rice, *Systems of Organization* (London: Tavistock, 1967), p. 160.

complex world, is often used instead to strengthen their protective shield against the world's realities.

These realities *are* complex, true, but not intractably or endlessly so. Task requirements make a good start, with their human, organizational, technological, time and territorial specifications and the feasibilities to match with available resources. These clarifications, as they get made, will reveal too what contact to build between the organization and the training system—what kind and for what, how frequent and regular, at what level(s), at what stages of the change strategy as a whole. In this way are fashioned the blocks with which to build the training system for a particular purpose.

The environment of this system under construction can also be identified: only those parts of the otherwise limitless world that are importantly connected with this particular purpose warrant attention and building linkages with. Even with environments becoming more complex and dispersed and systems larger, they can still be bounded and managed if developed step-by-practical-step.

For the partners, training system included, to share together the vision, goals, and values of the enterprise, as a whole and into the future, is of course an essential condition, as we saw earlier: congruence among parts becomes more essential for cohesion with every enlargement, and further dispersal and diversification. Rapidly increasing the volume of training while also rapidly building training capacity is a common dilemma in fast-changing economies and cities that only strong policy guidance can manage well; supporting broad career-oriented training and so also enabling valued staff to move elsewhere is another; urging well-working institutions to expand and diversify to keep pace with pressing demands or rather to spin-off additional, smaller centers is a third. Only systems thinking, and that too into the future, can do justice to such complexities.

In a major review in 1983 of its 'existing internal training system', the State Bank of India developed papers on major issues in 'a futuristic time frame'. That system then included three staff colleges, thirty-eight training centers, and a regular 'relationship nexus' within the organization that included a deputy managing director and chief general manager. The frame took into account the Bank's expansion rates, especially of rural branches, 'emerging' positions and roles, technological changes, and other considerations.

The report based on these papers and their discussions stressed training as a 'planned organizational intervention' and proposed means for making the identification of organization development and training tasks into a 'continuous process'. The 'important areas of concern' the Bank identified ranged from the need for better 'synchronization of organizational growth with the development of the individual employee... through career development' [to] 'modifications of the structure' of the system in the light of these considerations.

TASKS OF THE TRAINING SYSTEM

For the time, thought and funds they put in, the partners expect the training system to make a coherent contribution to the change goals they have set together for the enterprise. What does the training system then have to do to convert these inputs into the desired outputs? Our focus now is on the 'conversion systems' at the center of the simple model in Exhibit 5.1.

The tasks can be grouped and classified in many ways. We identify eight.

Building and Maintaining Support of the Partners

Obviously essential for a training system's very existence and continuation, achieving good enough support is beset with pitfalls. Goal clarity, careful checking of implications, and then tight monitoring are essential to ensure that what looks like support is really supportive.

Particularly important is giving this extra care early, when the training system is newly constituted or restructured and is understandably eager for any and all signs of approval. Satisfaction with an early program by direct users of it, for instance, and promises of continuing support 'if *this* is what you do and we can expect', is easily heard as if these were customers in a shop finding what they want or clients of standard services. Making the same simple connection is hazardous in the extreme when the task is to train for new goals and for changing established practices, maybe in major ways. Early programming, and eager welcome and promises of continuing support, may actually be for standard kinds of training, that is, be important to the hungry users but marginal at best to the core change strategies; and continuing that line of work and even enlarging it to satisfy consumer demand would risk undermining the goal and blunting or deflecting the training effort. Wittingly or unwittingly, it would make training yet another defence against anxieties touched off by impending change.[1] Training, also good training, may then get confined to areas of minor impact and the resources for it may remain small and uncertain. For an initial trial period, such limitations may serve both system and organization well by keeping risks low. These risks include unexpectedly heavy demands on organizations following effective training. But if sidelining continues beyond the initial trial, the system risks dismissal or irrelevance. The more far-reaching the development(s) to which training is to contribute, the more important the system's efforts on ensuring support.

Support, and support of different kinds, has to come in any case from many partners in addition to those that feel most directly profited by training. The first strategic objective for building support is to involve all partners and parts of the organization that are prospective users of the outputs in setting up and providing the training i.e., those who will be affected by it as well as the direct users of it. Even an initial list of these, which can be extrapolated from the training needs, strategies for meeting them and the training design goes far beyond the policy-makers and funders. After policy-makers have given training the green light, others have to be effectively involved in selecting participants, providing space and organizing opportunities, and in perhaps arranging equipment for practicing the new skill. At every stage, staff groups have the power to facilitate, delay or even effectively negate essential steps in the implementation, whatever the decision at the top. Modifying existing norms of training, of effective living and working and of changing the organization involve yet other units. The training strategy may call for new criteria for the selection and subsequent placement of participants at higher levels and in more collaborative arrangements; support from leaders *there* is therefore important. Such changes are usually easier and more pleasantly achieved if knowledge about them has already engendered goodwill in the organization; a general atmosphere of goodwill generates support all around. Then, for thinking through the complexities, for resolving doubts at the inevitable times of perplexity, for coping with stresses which change efforts invariably encounter, and for sharing and learning from ongoing experiences, people in the training itself often look for intellectual and emotional support from professional colleagues.

[1.] See Chapter 2 for the earlier discussion of anxieties and defences often connected with major changes.

Theories of institution building group the supports to be built and maintained into five sets, according to their purpose. The first set comprises supports to *enable* the training system to exist and to work, involving funding to give it system-wide support. *Functional* support covers all operational help: selection and placement of participants, space, equipment, materials, and services for training activities. *Normative* support covers support to set new levels and ways of living and working and so change the culture in the organization and the larger system that includes the environment. *Diffuse* support comes with ensuring widespread understanding and goodwill for training and the transformation it is for. And *collegiate* support assures trainers, program directors, and system administrators that they work in the best ways the profession knows and that their experience also contributes to developing the profession and their standing in it—their own and their system's.

As with goal setting and sharing, many heartaches and excruciatingly time-consuming difficulties later on can be avoided by projecting the pattern of support far into the future and then including all partners in the vision right from the beginning even if only a few take active part then and early programming is heavily influenced by immediate tactical considerations. Presentation of the pattern as a whole and the ways it develops the system makes the training mission concrete, communicates it to its partners, and also establishes its own distinctive style of working and public image.

For each kind of support, specific units and contacts can be identified and used in the course of organizing meetings, distributing documents, announcing programs, etc. Establishing ways to keep this information up-to-date and serviceable deserves early attention; otherwise these tasks tend to become quickly unmanageable.

Building continued mutuality into all relationships is particularly important for maintaining support; all partners need to gain and also feel that they are gaining, otherwise support wilts. System supporters for enabling and normative purposes are at greater risk of neglect than those involved in the more frequent and often discrete functional and collegial linkages. Maintaining top-level support exemplifies the difficulty. Whereas functional linkages are needed and used frequently, and many transactions are directly associated with payments or other benefits to these supporters, top-level support is an obvious and powerful need only at the time of annual budget appropriation or some emergency. But policy-makers take it amiss if such highly active occasions are the only, or almost only, contacts they have with their active partners. It is important that the system find additional and more mutually satisfying ways to keep in touch. The least step is to provide policy-makers with information on a regular basis that shows the training system effectively busy on priority developments. When major system developments are proposed and examined, policy-makers can again be heavily involved in thorough reviews.

The head of a banking institute in India made this record of a thorough review by top-level policy-makers initiated by the training system.

> In 1983, on the eve of the establishment of the second apex-level institution for training and development of the State Bank Group (India), a document was presented to the Top Management Group and a two-day seminar organized at the new Staff College with the following objectives:
>
> 1. To have a review of the Bank's Training System in its retrospect and prospect.
> 2. To have an in-depth and meaningful in-house debate on the critical areas of the Bank's Training System.
> 3. To discuss areas of expectations, concern and action.
> 4. To crystallize thinking on the Bank's Training System so that it remains continuously attuned to the needs of the User System.
> 5. To have a productive exchange of ideas for providing direction to the future course of the Bank's Training System as an enabling mechanism for sustaining growth and promoting organizational excellence.
>
> As a result of an in-depth debate that was highly participative in nature a number of action points have emerged on which we are working at present.

Building organizational support at working levels is also very important, especially wherever trained people are trying to work more effectively and need their colleagues' collaboration to make improvements. Working support goes far beyond fostering an atmosphere of general goodwill at the work place. It is very concrete, and often quite pedestrian and routine. Occasionally it requires additional programs in conjunction with formal training.

> In 1983–1984, the Bank of Baroda (India) decided to relocate training programs in industrial relations for zonal managers from training centers to the zones themselves, to build more of the programs around issues specific to the zone and to involve zonal executives in the programs given to the managers. A member of the core faculty writes:

The decision to do this programme on location was based on the feedback from managers that their effectiveness in managing IR at the branch level depended on the quality of support from zonal authorities. It was, therefore, decided to conduct this programme right at the zone so that it could address the specific needs of the zone and also involve zonal executives directly.

We have conducted ten such programmes. Very important [feedback shows] that before such a programme is launched, we diagnose IR problems of the zone with the help of personnel and trade unions. The programme is designed in the context of this diagnosis. On the last day of the programme [there] is a four-hour interface session where the entire zonal team, including personnel specialists, participate and answer the queries of branch managers. Here, during this session, managers raise a variety of issues and quote instances of inadequate support. Later on such issues are thrashed out and, where policy matters are involved, they are referred to higher authorities.

Building Training Competencies and Capacity

Increasingly competent planning, running and follow-up of training programs, and more of them, is direct evidence of success with this task. It is a particular responsibility of policy-makers to ensure enough steady attention to the less visible system aspects on which that success rests—recruiting enough trainers, for instance, and building them into coherent staffs and into appropriate institutions that last. Enough staff too for activities that grow out of training, e.g., organizational consulting and action research, for networking professional resources outside to draw on for specialized or temporary additions to the continuing staff, and, often neglected, for staff time and opportunities for further professional development and for proper breaks between programs. Building permanent training departments, centers, and institutions generally will be in focus again for more detailed discussion in the next chapter.

Administrative efficiency and building overall training capacity to meet the scale and pattern envisaged at various stages of the change strategy deserve particular attention. Efficient, reliable administration is part of the modelling the training system has to offer. It increases credibility, for itself and for training generally, as it performs well the functions and changes it trains others in. Deliberate steps may be required to offset and counter the disdain that trainers, like members of most other professions, have for administrative staff and tasks.

More subtle still is attention to the culture and tone of the whole training effort so that it lives and portrays, as it were, the goals and values the system aims at by living them ahead of the time for all. For trainers and staff it is a circular process, feeding on itself: a well-functioning organization of training and implementation of programs, and the sense of successful pioneering build staff competence in their system, which then probably raises competence and effectiveness further.

Developing Training Materials

This task supports competency building and also reflects it. The most useful materials are developed from within the work settings which training is to address; e.g., the materials development for industrial relations trainings in the Bank of Baroda cited earlier. The production of a steady flow of fresh training materials is characteristic of strong training systems, as also making new materials widely available and drawing on already existing materials from anywhere in the professional network. Practical developments along any of these lines come with taking active, deliberate steps, most by the training system itself; policy-makers can ensure that they get taken. Ten percent of staff time should probably be allocated to materials development.

Building the Internal Structures, Processes, and Policies

Routinizing activities, forecasting and providing for new requirements, and underpinning operations with a firm and adaptable framework of structures, processes, and policies is another task; one that often gets postponed to that day (which never arrives) when pressures for current activities lessen. The result of postponing is the great waste of time which occurs as people try to cope somehow—ad hoc and again and again—with nelgected aspects of the system's operation that could be routinized.

Leaving staff uncertain about how or even whether 'things work' quickly leads to disparaging comparisons, true or untrue, with how things are so much better managed in the operating enterprise and lowers morale. System heads and management teams have to persist with allocating 5 percent of their time to firming up this essential framework, probably devoting more time early in developing or drastically renewing the training system.

Strategic Planning

Logically, this task should come first and the others then be extrapolated from the plans. Attempts to go with this logic usually begin and also end with an impressive series of interlocking figures to show the new order of training to go with high aspirations.

> An example in our experience was the decision of Indonesia's Ministry of Health to increase nursing positions in the public health services by 220,000 in fifteen years. The working papers then divided the recruitment of this massive increase among existing and already planned training centers, and used those figures in turn to arrive at the additional trainers all this would require and shared out *their* recruitment and training. And these figures, of course, led up to budget requests to match.

Step-by-step, each following tightly and incontrovertibly from the last, simple chains of calculations like that can jolt policy-makers and the wider public into recognizing the new orders of magnitude that high goals imply—but at the risk that the figures end just there. And adding the essential context that would give them further use would reduce their compelling simplicity: an impasse.

Strategic planning to be useful must go beyond the simply mechanical—and therefore piecemeal—and, while getting under way early, has to keep going. For one thing, the new order of magnitude (or other transformative change) that major goals involves means entering new ground, much of it unforseeably new. So strategic planning must be open to experience and often also to experimenting, to see what works and what does not, and how much, how quickly, and at what cost. Which means that it cannot just come at the beginning but, once ballpark magnitudes are in mind, keeps running right along with implementation and is informed by it all along. Also, it must cover all components and *all* relevant parts of the environment.

It is useful to go down the list of all components, inside the system and in its relevant environment, and map what effort of the projected scale and nature would be needed in each. Right then, constraints on one or two components may rule out the initial goal, e.g., the rate at which new trainers can, in fact, be found and developed, and the capacity of the operating organization itself to actually place, absorb, allocate, supervise, and manage new staff. Funding usually receives the most attention, but people and managerial constraints can be far more stubborn. Subjecting all components to systematic review in the light of projected training needs can identify those which are in fact *strategic*. Plans can then be made to concentrate efforts and other resources particularly on these. And even then some component(s) usually remain intractable and realistic limits to goals.

Mapping and initial planning for components individually and in subsets is followed by an important step to fit the pieces together into an integrated system under the projected conditions. This produces a composite map of a situation (B), which can be compared to the current situation (A). Strategic planning is complete only when a path has been worked out by which the system will move from A to B and when the decisions, resources, and other external and internal supports required for this movement are in hand.

Networking Training Resources

Another task of the training system is to make the best use of all resources available anywhere, including those outside the immediate system. Crossing its own boundaries in order to secure additional trainers, materials, and other resources which it cannot provide from within, or provide as well or as economically, leads to the identification, development, and management of external networks of training resources.

This task, focused as it is outside the system, is least familiar. It runs counter to strong personal and traditional inclinations to reserve resources for internal use only, as if for oneself or for one's family, and to regard their use by others as a weakness, as giving resources 'away', and even creating unwanted competition. In this perspective, calling on outside resources is a regrettable necessity and to be terminated just as soon as internal resources can be built up.

The perspective for building strong systems is quite different. It values keeping the organization lean, clear priorities in allocating effort and resources, and developing its own particular strengths and being well-known for those in the profession.

The strongest systems have the flexibilities and economies of drawing on special strengths elsewhere. They also highly value stimulation and assurances that come from working with competent colleagues in sister systems; in fact, colleagues in the network in turn count on them.

The second important part of this task is networking within the system itself—one's own. It is unhappily characteristic of training systems, and especially those in developing countries, that trainers and other resources are either too centralized to be in effective contact with provinces, regions, and local situations where training is needed, or so dispersed and isolated that individual efforts yield little result and are always in danger of petering out, one by one. Clustering and networking address these needs.

Since August 1983, the Indonesian Ministry of Health has operated a strategy of building training capacity at the provincial level through a series of steps:

1. Select three provinces for the first phase, then three more provinces (out of 27).
2. Compose any initial provincial 'training team' that includes promising and available 'trainers' from related ministries and service and educational agencies, private as well as public, i.e., begin the external network.
3. Make a series of technical inputs to this provincial team and develop action projects for putting the new techniques to use. Selected central staff join as active participants, i.e., develop the internal network.

Within six months of starting, the core training team of six in one large province developed a network of fifteen additional trainers. Networking was also supported by special funds for provincial team meetings and for joint field activities and materials development. A periodic newsletter from the central training unit—in the Ministry itself—added to regular communication between all team and network members across the country. By early 1984 direct contact among provinces and inter-provincial programs had also begun.

Box 5.1 sets out a plausible in-house division of the training function among managers at several levels and various HRD specialists. For networking with outside resources, a variety of special arrangements are possible. One useful distinction is to keep training for strategically key functions in-house and to sub-contract specialized training outside.

Sharply focused and tightly managed in-house training resources, up-to-date information about pools of trainers and materials available for various kinds and levels of training in the network, and

Box 5.1

IN-HOUSE DIVISION OF THE TRAINING FUNCTION

Top Management provide role model behaviour for others and identify key competencies for strategic goals and plans.

Line Management analyze each employee's role and list detailed functions and competencies required; identify training needs of employees in terms of relevant functions and communicate these to HRD department; encourage employees, provide opportunities to take responsibility and initiative and to learn on the job; provide counselling; help employees to develop problem-solving skills; sponsor associates for training; obtain feedback from associates about their learning during training; discuss opportunities for trying out what they have learned; provide such opportunities and institute group discussions, etc. to help associates learn to work as a team.

Personnel provide required facilities for training and facilitate employees going to training.

IR develop training plans for workers, organize training of workers, and develop plans for multi-skilled training of workers.

HRD play the key role in designing systems to identify training needs; collecting information about training needs from the managers; keeping updated on trends in training; collecting information about available training programmes; disseminating information about training opportunities to line managers; analyzing training needs and planning in-house training; and managing training institution/unit (functions and facilities).

Source: Udai Pareek, "Partnership in Human Resource Function" in *Indian Journal of Industrial Relations* (1997), Vol. 32, No. 3, pp 345–53.

smoothly working mechanisms for securing them are major outcomes of good networking and also support its further strengthening.

Managing Boundaries

Effective training often sparks onward actions of the most promising kind, since they are welcome to the organization and command realistic support from the very start. Managers come to count on further supportive activities by the training system, such as counselling or coaching of key staff, organizational consulting, and/or training beyond that planned and provided for originally. Such spin-offs are a good indicator of effective training and will bring training more organizational support.

The development of training capacity in the initial Indonesian province sparked eight action projects in the first six months, of which three became major multi-phase strategies. One of these called for an additional three weeks of senior consultation time. The other two required consultation time and, additionally, funds for provincial officials to participate in a series of local learning opportunities. Together, these two action projects cost half as much again as the initial year's training in the province as originally planned.

Spin-off action projects and other consequences of effective training present dangers for which good boundary management is required. Successful systems, especially in understandably success-hungry developing countries, are at high risk of being overwhelmed and washed away by the overloads organizations urge on them in the wake of successes. Weak systems have the opposite tendency, likewise destructive: they risk insulation and atrophy for lack of contacts across their boundaries.

To cope with the risks of success, two lines of action have yielded promising results. One is to seek fresh clarification, periodically and together with all fellow partners in the organization and in the larger environment, of the system's primary task, to sort fresh demands into agreed priorities and sequences, and then to attempt only as much and as many as will not endanger fine performance of the primary task. Agreement with the work system at large along these lines is very important; otherwise pressures on the training system will continue and this or that organization will feel deprived each time the training system rejects an attractive project. The next line of action is to ensure that these clarifications and decisions are translated into mutually acceptable plans matched with additional resources, and are then made public.

Monitoring and Controlling Performance

Each task to be performed by a training system has a purpose, and its performance can be assessed in terms of both outcomes and the processes by which they were attained. Regular monitoring yields the data the system needs to improve its immediate functioning, structure, and, looking forward, further development. This system function, important to carry out routinely for all tasks, also addresses the often intricate interrelationships between particular tasks and the performance of the system as a whole. The basic training system model presented earlier in Exhibit 5.1 is elaborated in Exhibit 5.2 to

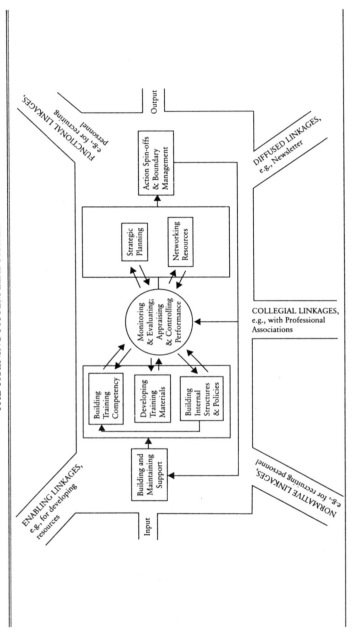

Exhibit 5.2
THE TRAINING SYSTEM ELABORATED

show all eight tasks and link them conceptually with the five constituencies the system has for its basic needs and purposes.

THE DYNAMICS OF SYSTEM DEVELOPMENT

There is no one way to develop a training system. It is too dependent on time and local circumstances, and on the needs and resources of the enterprise and its organization—all of which vary widely. The rigorous formulations commonly found in systems literature, comprising tidy and complete steps in one direction, may hide this main point, and, by their apparent clarity and finality, confuse newcomers and discourage them. A six-point list of this type is given in Box 5.2—useful as far as it goes, but that is not very far. To the overriding generalizations that there is no one way to begin and that several starts may have to be explored before one works, three other operational steps are worth adding along with the appreciation that they are not a neat sequence or ever ended: the focus shifts to a new activity, the orchestration becomes fuller.

Box 5.2

STEPS TO DEVELOP A TRAINING SYSTEM

The process of training systems analysis essentially involves a series of carefully sequenced activities as follows:

1. Formulate a clear and unequivocal definition and specification of the system under consideration to include the need for the system and the delimitation of its boundaries.
2. Develop lucid and functional descriptions of the components of the system and the ways in which they interact.
3. Determine and define the system objectives in terms of optimal system operating performance and output.
4. Identify and specify the criteria to be used for evaluating the congruence of system objectives, performance, and output.
5. Identify and select alternative groupings of system components for evaluation in terms of practicability, desirability, and cost benefits, and determine the trade-offs involved.
6. Test selected alternatives to collect data upon which decision makers may base their choice of the configuration of system components for implementation.

SOURCE: Summarized from W.R. Tracey, *Evaluating Training and Development Systems* (New York: Amocam, 1974). Every effort has been made to trace the copyright holder(s). In the absence of a reply, permission has been assumed.

Steps and Activities

The first practical step is to work on training systems development alongside contributing, through training, to alleviating some severe pressures that organizations are actually experiencing, e.g., a severe shortage of nurses in the health services, violence in the neighborhood, patently inadequate supervision of costly materials or technologies, or a major shift in technology. Second, no matter what the specific need and the contribution training can make to meet it, several systemic tasks will certainly surface and demand attention quite quickly as training begins. Support building, trainer competence, resource networking, materials development, and presently, of course, monitoring performance and control, all predictably appear early. Only just behind (or remaining hidden just below the surface) will be the other tasks of reviewing and renewing organizational structures and processes and of ensuring that the new work is part and parcel of deliberate strategies and plans. This emergence of systematic tasks can be counted on no matter what the starting point, because the tasks are closely connected.

The third (possibly discouraging) practical generalization is that none of the eight tasks is ever finished and laid to rest. A cyclical pattern seems inherent: one or two tasks move to center-stage, are reworked to a new level of performance, then give way to the next upcoming one. Later, each comes full circle again (and again) for renewed attention, maybe in a fresh sequence and at different levels of system performance. This spiral pattern is true for each task and also for developing the system as a whole. Nothing seems to be gained by hurrying to the next task before the current one has been sufficiently accomplished; only then is attention to the next fruitful.

We hypothesize that the upward spiral of system development can continue until it exhausts the readiness of an environment to accept and support it. The immediate and most powerful environment of training is, of course, the home organization(s), but broader supports and hindrances to further development may also set early limits, such as the traditions and tolerance of a country's civil service. Until these limits are reached, performance levels for each task of a training system and the constituencies with which it is linked can continue to widen and strengthen both parties. System malfunctioning and disintegration may likewise be cyclical, and may only be reversed when they become too awful to tolerate.

The initial six months of work in 1983 on trainer and training system development in the health services of a large Indonesian province showed such a cyclical pattern upward. Exhibit 5.3 shows the sequence in which tasks received primary attention and also the time spans for which they held. The figure is only illustrative; we expect system development elsewhere and at other times to show variations in sequence and time spans. But these will indeed be variations on the basic theme of system development proceeding in cyclical, spiral patterns.

The judgement of when enough progress with a task has been made to enable system developers to go on to the next is happily easier to make in practice than to define in abstract terms. When the levels of performance in adjoining tasks repeatedly hinder further progress with the task in focus, attention should be shifted to those others—one or more. Even after attention has moved on, the momentum may well continue to carry the earlier task forward as information comes in about how well the work is progressing and hindrances to development are removed. So, for instance, there is no such thing as total acceptance and support from the start; 'enough' is well short of that. Initially, especially when an organization's past experiences with training have not been encouraging, proposals for developing the training system may be merely tolerated, and extra resources for it, if any, may come through minimal reallocations. Even small amounts of national or international funds can make a crucial contribution in this first phase. But as developments get underway and some early training yields practical results and promise beyond expectations, tolerance changes to lively interest and on toward more active involvement. Later, additional resources (actually already available locally) are 'found', commitment to the developments is publicized, and an active search by the organization for yet more resources produces notable results. In the Indonesian province, this progression took six months. Progress with any one task contributes to and reinforces progress with all the others.

As the training system continues to shift attention to different tasks in turn, round and round, with conscious, deliberate intent informed by orderly monitoring of progress and problems, the map of tasks and their interconnections becomes familiar to many and using it becomes habitual. Thus, when all levels of the system are routinely receiving general attention and the system is so organized that it can keep all under regular surveillance and servicing, specific

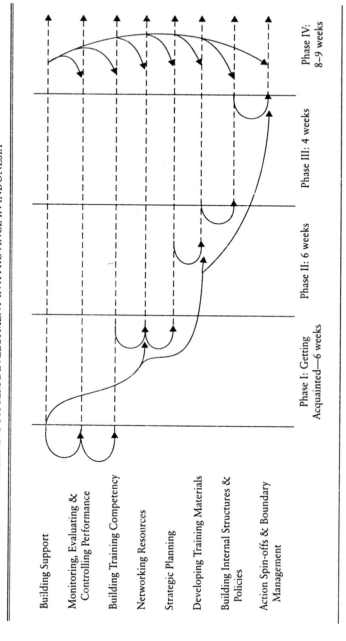

Exhibit 5.3

TRAINING SYSTEM DEVELOPMENT IN A PROVINCE IN INDONESIA

concerns will move in and out of focus at different levels and at different times. When both overall surveillance and shifts in focal attention between components and between levels become routine, this shows that system development has been truly 'learned' and has become an integral part in its operations. This holds true not only for the training system itself, but also for the organizations which it serves and, to a lesser degree, for all constituencies in the large system.

Four Phases

As shown in Exhibit 5.3, developing the training system and its eight tasks in the Indonesian province in the initial six months moved through four phases. These can be characterized as follows:

PHASE 1: *Getting approved, funded, and more widely acquainted*— enough to proceed. Monitoring, evaluating, and controlling performance begins right here. Work with trainers on competence development (for one district administrators' program) was the legitimating activity at this stage.

PHASE 2: *Competencies development* became the primary area of attention: having proved its usefulness. The initial training could be built on. A special technical input program attracted additional trainers. The provincial network of trainers and of their institutions began here.

PHASE 3: Continuing success created criteria and motivation for *reviewing and firming up the training strategy and budget* for the next year. New choices were made. Many outdated programs were revised and rescheduled. Implications for allocating staff time, funds, and facilities were worked out. Implications for longer-term plans for program and resources development then came into focus. These raised issues in improving system structure and processes and in strengthening formal system linkages to operational and service units in the organization.

PHASE 4: The technical inputs had, from the beginning in Phase 2, included practical exercises in participants' work situations, and several exercises had quickly proved of practical value to the organization and so also contributed to growing system-wide recognition and support. Within two months, three of these action projects had been developed into major province-wide strategies for addressing major problems of the organization (a severe current and prospective shortage of hospital nurses; the unacceptably low standards of services management at the district level; and inadequate coordination between the two major provincial offices). The organization was then eager to invest its manpower and substantial amounts of other resources in working on these important problems and to involve in this, in preplanned stages, units at various levels of the provincial services. Since work on these problems had national priority also, the provincial government secured additional resources for two of the three projects from the national level and responded to the great interest there in the possibilities of spreading the learnings and changes to other provinces.

Some Cautions

Rapid success with training systems development is fertile ground for seeds of destruction also. What in good time would be very attractive onward developments can overstrain the planning and management capacities of a barely begun training system, leading to its collapse if undertaken too early. Regular reviews of system boundaries and careful boundary management offer the best immediate protection. Behind it, the enlarging of resources, improving system structure, and firming program strategy can then receive attention. Top-level support from the organizations and the whole system is essential for deliberate, orderly responses to demands for program expansion and diversification, so that they can be held to match but not exceed the capacity as it grows.

By using the catch-all word 'system' to designate the partner responsible for training and associated consultation, we now have a setting for making three points. One is that the functions we have listed are composites, enveloping manifold variety and application in many possible situations. Second, to be used well and economically, the components required for any particular development effort need to be fitted together, that is, dovetailed into a single training system. And third, while the training system may include one or more components that actually specialize in training and consulting (e.g., have fulltime staff and constitute the training department in the organization or a training center outside), it is the other components that actually carry out more continuous and overall more important training functions. If specialized training components in the training system are not to spin-off into self-serving irrelevance, they need particularly strong ties to the operating system. Only in that operating system will it grow vigorous roots in purposeful action.

NATIONAL, REGIONAL, AND GLOBAL SYSTEMS

When all resource components needed for an actual training effort are clearly in view and can be quantified and synchronized for the particular purpose(s), only then can the training system for it be put together as a whole. Successive drafts can then test and refine it to fit particular pertinent detail. This is true for systems of all sizes, but there are also important practical differences between systems of different sizes. As size goes up, complexities increase of course, e.g., greater diversity, more stakeholder constituencies to include in more elaborate structures and processes; but in addition to these there are also some additional dimensions to deal with and, even with resources of a different order to call on, in principle, also fewer options. This is particularly the case for country-wide systems and even larger heavily political units, such as regions.

Individual organizations and enterprises of all kinds can shop around and outbid each other for people with scarce skills and expertise, such as trainers, computer programers, medical administrators, and engineers. They also expect the national system to ensure sufficient capacity in these fields overall, if not right now because the technology, say, is quite new, then very soon. So training systems to ensure sufficient overall capacities are primarily in view at the national (and higher) level. In expanding populations and economies, there is at the same time little scope for shifting resources from one program or institution to another. Immediately, practical questions are of these kinds and order: will the nation-wide system, perhaps augmented for a while with regional and international resources, yield training (of *all* required kinds) on a sufficient scale, and/or will that output be sufficiently well-paced and coordinated to meet the requirements of the planned projects, expansions, and technical and administrative improvements? Can it sustain this level of effort? Are the estimates sufficiently sound for coping with the imminent retirement of the 'independence generation' of experienced administrators (which is predictable) and concomitantly for accommodating turbulent (i.e., unpredictable) changes in the environment? These are the types of questions that system development is meant to address at higher levels in developing countries. That complex scene characteristically includes pressures to develop training capacities in several major sectors at once; to compete for the very same handful of trainers that private enterprises try to attract with better salaries and conditions; to develop training capacities in widely-scattered provinces while simultaneously strengthening nationally acceptable standards of training; to multiply training opportunities even at the cost of purpose and quality; to shift experienced trainers away from training into training administration (or more distant tasks still) and from outlying places—but close to the action—to headquarter positions, and to train the workforce for foreseeable changes in service needs while also multiplying and improving the quality of the same workforce for current services.

Augmenting in-country capacities with regional and international resources brings other complications, as also does letting national experts join the international traffic. When, and for how long and on what conditions do foreign resource people actually contribute to building strategic in-country capacity and not run the high risk of stifling the emergence of indigenous resources to build up the required system? Issues of minimum concentrations of expertise for take-off and sustaining good training in a field, of assessing the growing strengths of emerging systems, and the skillful management of transitions to independent functioning come to the fore here.[2] Foreign programs simply marketed must be especially suspect for undercutting indigenous efforts and emerging professionals, and for holding back local support for building indigenous systems.

National systems are also quite properly meant to ensure that the population at large has *underlying* basic capacities, e.g., in literacy and mathematics, and that historically neglected groups are included. An extension of this responsibility is foreseeing impending shifts and shortages in expertise and providing both training for enough newcomers and retraining of workers rendered obsolete, most likely in technology and economics. Tasks in soil, water, coastal, and other ecological management will predictably explode in number, complexity, and controversies in the coming decades, and meanwhile require building up of the resource bases in preparation for meeting them. Focusing training systems on needs emerging in distant futures

---

[2] Reading 5.2 conceptualizes issues of minimum concentration and shows a large country, in this case India, having much easier options than smaller countries.

and building them with the flexibilities to accommodate actual developments as they come into sharper view calls for scanning and collaborative and political competencies of a supreme order.

At the levels at which these concerns have to be included (and then parceled out to subsystems), training system development is not only larger in scale than simply using systems thinking for developing a component, or a system at program level, or a temporary system; it has complexities of an entirely different order. In line with this, a *readiness* to approach the development of a training system as a working proposition, for practical elaboration, improvement, and confirmation over time, is of paramount importance in developing countries. Under such conditions, the proper use of systems concepts and diagrams is as a checklist and general map—to ensure that all essential components are accounted for, can readily attract necessary attention, and are also plausibly interrelated for charting the territory that lies ahead. Practical considerations will also limit further elaboration of conceptual components and their interrelations in terms of the available capacities for collecting and analyzing data and putting these (or about to be available) results to use in influencing and managing the necessary relationships. The territory itself, full of concrete, stubbornly intricate, and often divergent, if not directly conflicting issues, remains yet to be entered and explored. This step can in turn guide the further clarification and development of a training system, and set the direction for next steps.

Overall, then, this system perspective allows the same basic question about training resources to be raised at any level for decision and action. Is training of all kinds and from all sources on a sufficient scale and quality, and is it sufficiently well-placed and coordinated to meet the requirements of planned projects, expansions, and technical, administrative and structural improvements? Temporary systems, as well as permanent units of training, are included in the system; specially arranged and staffed they serve best in many situations. Institutions elsewhere in the country or abroad can also be used and therefore included. Meanwhile, less formal, altogether more extensive, unobtrusive programs also continue in the system, such as understudy, induction, apprenticeship, and effective on-the-line supervision. All these varied and widely dispersed avenues to learning are integrated by an effective system into cohesive training for organizational purposes. The system also links training with public and private agencies that deal with workforce planning and the provision of resources; with organizations which are the immediate 'consumers' of trained personnel; and with professional associations and resources centers, e.g., for quality maintenance and economies of scale in developing materials and for strengthening support in the general culture for good training.

Training goals, properly set by organizations, guide decisions about training strategies (e.g., what training to provide through full-time programs and what parts through part-time and/or on-the-job training and/or at a distance), about the resources needed for training and their allocations, and—a very strategic consideration—what components to include in the training system itself, i.e., where to draw boundaries. Issues internal to the system, such as task sequences, development of the kinds and numbers of trainers and other system resources required for achieving the goals, likewise stem from the same set of estimates and considerations.

Reading 5.1

Developing a Temporary Educational System

JACK GANT, ORON SOUTH, AND JOHN H. HANSEN*

... a temporary educational system is, by definition, a product of, and an influence on, the permanent systems that comprise its constituencies. Those constituencies include the funding or sponsoring agency, the permanent systems to which staff and participants belong, and the site organization where the temporary system will operate. The members of the permanent systems (constituencies) have needs, goals, expectations, skills, and resources which will be combined in the temporary system to produce a program that is unique. The temporary system, then, starts and ends with its focus on the permanent systems.

Each of the constituencies of the system contributes to its development in various ways at various times. They may reinforce mutual interests and, at times, may conflict when priorities or expectations differ. Collaboration is critical to the development process if all the parties are to benefit.

* From Jack Gant, Oron South, and John H. Hansen, with the assistance of Binky Hart and Johme Mills, *Temporary Systems*, 1977, pp 65–74.

The development of a temporary system may be described as a set of five interrelated, progressive stages or phases including planning, building, operating, closing, and following up.... During the planning phase, the dimensions of the temporary system are defined; during the building phase the system's dimensions are adjusted to accommodate the needs, objectives, and resources of new members. The primary focus of the operating stage is teaching and learning in order to achieve the program's objectives. During the closing phase, participants will be involved in activities designed to transfer what they have learned to the permanent systems to which they will return. The follow-up phase occurs in the permanent systems where learnings are now being applied and disseminated. (See Figure 1.)

Throughout the five phases, the system becomes stronger. New members are involved, objectives increase and learning resources are added. Figure 2 suggests that the temporary system evolves upward in a spiral fashion.

The environment of the system is designed to maximize the chances that each member feels safe enough to risk active involvement as the system grows. Each stage relies on previous stages; each stage contributes to subsequent stages.

While each of the phases in the development of the temporary system differs in some ways from the others, some common elements can be identified. Each phase has a purpose and a membership which is engaged in fulfilling that purpose. During each phase, a specific set of tasks must be accomplished so that required outcomes are produced. The following is a description of each phase accompanied by suggestions for performing key tasks.

Planning

The purpose of the planning phase is to define the dimensions of the temporary system. The planning process is critical to all other phases and is conducted by representatives of the sponsoring agency and the administrative and instruction leaders. During this stage they address the questions: What is the system going to accomplish? Who are the participants? What resources are available to the system? When and where will the system operate? What are the primary activities that will be conducted? What information is needed by planners and participants? How will the system function?

These questions lead the planners to specific tasks. The tasks are:

1. Goal Setting

Planners engage in stating the changes that are expected to occur among participants and, ultimately, the changes that should occur in the permanent systems. Planners can assume that participants, relieved from the pressures of the permanent systems, will be prepared to work hard. On the other hand, time and resources are limited in the temporary system. Therefore,

Figure 1
TEMPORARY SYSTEM COMPONENTS

Planning	Building	Operating	Closing	Following-up
Goal Setting	Acquaintanceship	Microdesign	Forward Action Planning	Providing Support
Recruiting and Selecting Participants and Staff	Stating and Redefining Goals	Forming and Using Work Groups	Forward Support Planning	Evaluating
Specifying Norms	Redefining Roles	Conflict Management	Forward Network Planning	
Data Planning	Building the Governance System	Decision Making	Planning for Evaluation	
Choosing Time and Territory	Identifying and Using Resources	Recreation		
Locating and Allocating Resources	Monitoring			
Macrodesign				
Analyzing Constraints				

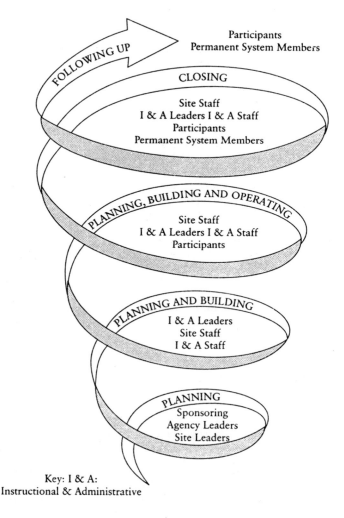

Figure 2
THE SPIRAL NATURE

goals must be clearly stated, measurable, and achievable within the time allotted. Goals are likely to specify anticipated changes in knowledge, skills, attitudes, or interpersonal relationships, and may also involve commitments of participants to tasks they will undertake once they have returned to the permanent systems.

In the process of goal setting, planners of temporary systems should consider both their own expectations and the expectations of constituent groups. Objectives are always set with a focus on the permanent system, i.e., the organization which receives participants upon their return. Agency sponsors, participant representatives, planners, and instructors should all be involved in the goal setting process. Goals should be set for participants to indicate expected outcomes of the program. Goals should also be set for the temporary system itself to spell out how it will function to support the goals of participants. Planners should continue to be aware of long-range goals of the permanent system and should ensure that these goals are known to participants and reflected in the objectives specified for the temporary system.

Goals should be set by interfacing with key people in constituent groups. These representatives may be interviewed, surveyed, or where the constituent group is large and diverse, a Delphi technique may be useful. Planners should be careful to limit objectives to a manageable and achievable number. Though they must take care not to overload the system, they must be certain to provide time, space, and opportunities for staff and participants to modify or add to the objectives.

2. Recruiting and Selecting Participants and Staff

In some temporary systems, participant selection, which is accomplished prior to the planning team, is a task of the sponsoring agency. Planners may have the task of selecting the instructional staff, administrative staff, and participants. For each group, planners establish the selection criteria that are compatible with the system's goals. In order to minimize socialization problems and internal conflicts, participants are likely to be highly specific groups of personnel who can devote themselves to the system's learning tasks.

3. Specifying Norms

Determining the social behaviors that should characterize the temporary system is a task of the planners. Any social system develops norms which define and govern group behavior. In temporary systems, planners have the unique opportunity to establish norms that are specifically intended to encourage learning and creativity. The norms of the temporary system may be different from the norms of the permanent systems and may include:

1. *Egalitarianism.* The hierarchy is minimized and all members may initiate ideas or participate in decisions that affect them.
2. *Authenticity.* Members are expected to be open, frank, and honest and to be free to express feelings.
3. *Innovativeness.* Members are encouraged to be curious, to seek solutions to problems, to raise questions and try new answers.
4. *Effortfulness.* Limited time in the temporary system is likely to encourage people to work hard to achieve the goals. Energies are channeled into the learning tasks.

5. *Risk Taking.* When removed from their permanent systems, participants are likely to be willing to try new behaviors or take on unfamiliar roles and tasks.

6. *Experimentalism.* In solving problems, experimentalism is encouraged by the fact that a temporary system protects members from the usual consequences of failure.

7. *Interdependence.* The standard supports available in the permanent system are not available. Members, therefore, come to rely on each other to achieve the goals set forth by the temporary system.

8. *Open Conflict Management.* Participants of a temporary system are expected to deal with conflicts among themselves openly, rather than to conceal disagreements....

The planners or designers should apply the specified norms to the planning process. In this way, the planners can be assured that they are capable of modeling the norms which they are specifying for the temporary system because they will have applied them and established them in their own planning process. One way in which members can determine whether or not the norms are being observed is to review planning meetings. Such questions as: 'How are we working', as opposed to 'What are we achieving?', is a good question to use as the planning team evaluates its way of work.

4. Data Planning

Planners need a variety of types of information to steer the development of the temporary system. The information is to be used for planning, for monitoring the system during its operation, and for planning follow-up activities once the system is closed.

Evaluators of the temporary system participate in the data planning process. Evaluation is based upon system goals and is likely to require the collection of data before, during, and after the program.

If an outside evaluation team is to be used for evaluating the success of the temporary system, it is essential that the planners negotiate early with the evaluation team. Agreement should be reached on what data are required, the method of collecting the data, and questions to be answered by the data. It is extremely important that the data collection process NOT interfere with the operation of the temporary system....

Another decision on evaluation and data collection concerns feedback to staff and participants. Unless otherwise established by the funding agency, even data collected by outside evaluators should be fed back to staff and participants.... Staff should have veto power over any research data to be collected. Participants should also be informed and their agreement sought.

5. Choosing Time and Territory

The site of the temporary system must provide work space, recreational facilities, housing, and meals. Representatives from the site organization should participate in planning and should be aware of any unusual demands that the temporary system might place on that permanent system.

The site should be far enough away from the permanent system to protect it from permanent system interruptions and distractions; yet, close enough for week-end excitement if the temporary system is to cover more than one week.

The learning facilities should be flexible (and have) a retreat atmosphere....

6. Locating and Allocating Resources

... Goals and resources are closely related. Time, money, and energy are applied to the achievement of each goal and should be distributed to maximize the success of the various program activities. The planners should keep in mind that the time of the personnel (planners, participants, and staff) is the most expensive resource....

7. Macrodesigning

Planners design an overall flow of activities that will occur during the operation of the system.... The macrodesign attends to such living and learning needs of the participants and staff as:

1. The physical environment.
2. The human resources inside and outside the system.
3. Involvement of the participants in a two-way influence in goal setting, contract defining, and problem solving.
4. A reduction of dependency needs on staff and increased participant responsibility and skills.
5. Openness to redesign on the basis of data from the ongoing process.

The living and learning needs require attention in both macro- and microdesigning.

In putting the macrodesign together, decisions are made on time boundaries, major themes, unit or weekly objectives, the unit of planning and delivery, and outside resources. In considering time boundaries, plan the starting and ending time so that all participants and staff can begin and end the temporary system together. Early departures erode the temporary system and diminish the impact of the closing phase of the system.

8. Analyzing Constraints

During the planning process, planners need to be aware of any constraints in the system which might interfere with the attainment of goals. Constraints may be logistic or material; they may relate to people or resources. Careful analysis may remove some of the constraints. Others may be unavoidable and should be shared with participants.

9. Pre-system Communication

Prior to their arrival at the program site, participants should receive information about the temporary system... a statement of the goals of the system and... the commitment they are making when they become members of the temporary system.... Pre-system communication affects the norms of the temporary system and should be carried out in a manner consistent with the desired norms.

Reading 5.2

National Policies and Minimum Concentration

JOHN P. LEWIS*

The concept of critical mass of expertise invites attention. The numbers in a professional or paraprofessional cadre can be said to have reached a critical mass (regardless of whether some of the final training still is being done overseas) when the cadre has developed a distinct self-awareness and a credentialing process; when it is internally networked and has mechanisms for recognizing superior professional status; when the members have recognized specializations; when they are afforded a full professional life and are enlisting recruits at least at a replacement rate; and, when, in particular, members' net migration abroad has not, from the viewpoint of the nation's interest, become dysfunctional.

Such critical mass is much likelier to be attained when numbers are large. A large cadre, having a greater assortment of members, is likelier to have one who, if not an interchangeable part, can be a serviceable replacement for another pivotal member who departs. It has a much larger number of professional interfaces. For a large cadre, an absolute number of out-migrants is a smaller relative loss. Moreover, a large cadre has a better chance of generating and sustaining a sufficient ferment of pioneering, ongoing, professional activity at home to become a magnet, attracting back some fraction of the profession's numbers sojourning abroad before their work lives are over.

The Indian economics profession can be cited as a case in point. In 1975, I participated in a comparative study of the development of economics in India, Pakistan, and Bangladesh. At that time we determined that, of all the Pakistanis with overseas post-graduate degrees, more were employed in the World Bank and IMF jointly than in all Pakistani universities. The Bangladesh profession was being similarly decimated by emigration. In India by

* From John P. Lewis, *India's Political Economy: Governance and Reform* (Delhi: Oxford University Press, 1995), pp 44–45. Reprinted by permission of Oxford University Press, New Delhi.

comparison, brain drain was no problem. In absolute terms, of course, there was more of it. And the quality of some of the emigrants was extraordinarily high. But they were not really *that* much missed. They continued to visit. The production of new first-class Indian economists continued apace, both at home and overseas. The key chairs in government and in the policy analysis and academic communities were occupied by mostly able persons, and people kept coming home from the World Bank and elsewhere to government and institute jobs, lured by the attractiveness of the work and colleagues despite the financial disincentives.

Not all Indian professions and disciplines are so well positioned in these regards, but the condition is not uncommon. It would appear to extend, for example, to much of engineering, the natural sciences, and medicine. And where critical mass prevails, the disadvantages of brain drain may be greatly reduced. It still can be the case that, as the beneficiaries of publicly subsidized education, highly trained emigrants are the bearers of reverse foreign aid to such places as the US. But this would be true also for a small exporting country and small exporting professions. In the critical-mass cases, the opportunity cost of emigration is less. Indeed, it is likely the emigrants' remittances exceed what would have been their social products at home. Higher education is such a labour-intensive industry that it could be to India's continuing comparative advantage to export a considerable variety of trained professionals.

6

MAKING THE LEAD INSTITUTION STRONG: LOCATION, LEADERSHIP, SUPPORT, AND OTHER POLICY ISSUES

Institutional Design

Leadership Selection

Organizational Position and Linkages

Ongoing Policy Support for Training

Four System Trends to Watch—And Quickly Rectify
  System Maps Incomplete: Important Partners Missing
  Imbalances in Linkages and Their Use
  Overloads and Partners in Conflict
  Distorted Development Stemming from Improper Position

Policy-level Monitoring of the Unit's Internal Development
  Stages in Institutional Development: Characteristic Dilemmas
    and Resolution
  Institutional Climate
  Leadership Traits in Promising and Failing Institutions

Support for Steady Development and Also for Innovation

Exhibits
6.1 The Innovative Core: From Appreciation to Key Characteristics
6.2 Internal Components and External Linkages
6.3 Schematic Map of Components and Linkages
6.4 External Linkages of a Field-oriented Center in a Public University
6.5 Stages in Institutional Development
6.6 Typical Leadership Traits in Promising and Failing Institutions

Boxes
6.1 Ethos for Building the Training System
6.2 Four Pillars for Building an Institution

Readings
6.1 Organizational Health in Training Institutions
6.2 Linking the Training System into the Operational System
6.3 Common Issues in Developing and Managing System Linkages
6.4 Building a New Institution: Practical Issues
6.5 Continuous Improvement Network: The Concept

... the interplay of individual choices and collective effort within a social frame...was profoundly different from the popular image of solitary hero-figures...open and pluralistic...not a unitary organization but a loose alliance of many overlapping groups. That structure gave Paul Revere and Joseph Warren a special importance as the linchpins of the revolutionary movement—its communicators, coordinators, and organisers of collective effort.

—David Hackett Fischer

At the core of any training system is an institutional mechanism to orchestrate and integrate the diverse efforts in its various parts, to take primary responsibility for overall performance and to lead. Forms vary. Common ones are a training department or staff college inside the organization itself, as the State Institute of Health and Family Welfare in Rajasthan discussed in Chapter 4; or, outside, a freestanding training center, a network of professionals on long contract, an institute in a university designated for public service, or, as in Boston angrily on its way to rebellion and independence, a 'loose alliance of many overlapping groups'. Any and all, the essence is to provide the 'social frame... for the interplay of individual choices and collective effort'.

'Organisers of collective effort' comes close to what policy-makers have in mind for the unit they need somewhere in their organization to lead the training effort; 'linchpin' and 'revolutionary movement' do nicely for highlighting the innovative mandate as its very core and also the steady persistence with it that major organizational change demands. These two, innovation and persistence with it, specify the key characteristics that a core mechanism has to have and also the care, protection, and support policy-makers must expect to give it into the future.

The decision-chain—this or another—starts with how policy-makers assess the needs of their organization in its setting of time, place, and other particulars, for now and more importantly ahead in prospect. Where to position training in the organization and how to interlink it with the other parts of the organization and the larger system as a whole, selecting its leadership and holding it accountable, and giving the innovative effort enough scope and backing, all flow, with severe logic, from this initial appreciation and policy-makers committing themselves to act in line with it. If time and situation look pretty normal to them, a variation on well-known themes, the decision-chain differs essentially from the decision-chain to follow for organizational transformation.

Exhibit 6.1 diagrams the two decision-chains in sharpest contrast. With equal logic the chains run in quite different, even opposite, directions.

To highlight this contrast and trace it back to how policy-makers *see* the task from the very beginning is extra important, because the decisions taken from one perspective will not do at all well for readying the training unit or the organization to change later to the other; more likely they will be obstacles in the way and have to be undone. Worth recalling too, as a rule of thumb, is that the greater the innovation and transformation to be set in motion, and the more lasting—more like a permanent state than a once or twice only heave of effort—the clearer and more consistently different the policies had better be. Better delay getting the training unit started or the existing unit reworked and repositioned to new purpose till sound policies are really in place.

For the planned transformations we focus on in this book and to reach new states of preparedness and economy of effort in turbulent environments, relying, revolutionary Boston-like, on one or two 'linchpin' persons would be sheer irresponsibility. The core mechanism, its nature, and position warrant the most careful choosing and working out and positioning because of the fateful differences these can make. The decision to put (or keep) a training department in-house at the core of the system, for instance, can then be accompanied with the resolve to monitor its development on system-building dimensions and not on, say, quick improvements in current operating performance (to justify expenditure on training programs). If making a free-standing institution outside the core mechanism looks like the better way to go (as it may well be if major transformation is the aim), the particular institution to settle on must be independently strong enough to withstand opposition from funding and regulating agencies that are really against major change. That this institution has highly creative staff speaking for it would also not be good enough if it turns out to be one of the many free-standing institutions that are so small and weak that key staff are always on the lookout to move elsewhere and turn over fast; only if the new

Exhibit 6.1
THE INNOVATIVE CORE: FROM APPRECIATION TO
KEY CHARACTERISTICS

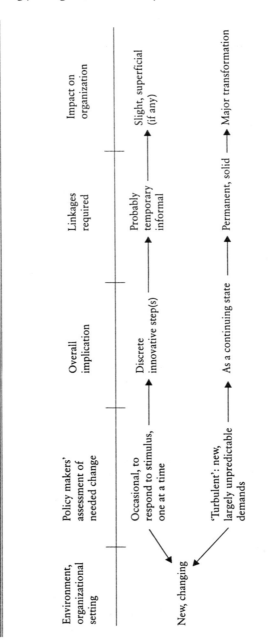

contract is large and long enough to shore up its overall strength should policy-makers go for that institution.

Experience suggests patterns and sequences with regularities across widely different settings that are useful enough, at the very least, for policy-makers to bear in mind when mapping and considering options at various phases of the life of their unit and on the way to reaching sound decisions. Experience also points to dimensions and times when policy-makers would do best to hold back from intervening, that call for understanding and waiting, not action, so that the institution's leadership has the scope and support for working things out and continues to be clear about *its* responsibility for doing so; this keeps lines of accountability clear as well.

INSTITUTIONAL DESIGN

For scanning the many possible options and examining their practical implications, listing the essential components of a lead unit and showing schematically how they connect can make the complexities on the way to fateful choices more manageable.

The basic input-output model in Exhibit 5.1 showed the training system as the 'conversion system' in the middle. Exhibit 6.2 now shows the components of its lead unit (as institution-building theory identifies them): ten in all, one set of five to cover all internal and the other five all external functions. Exhibit 6.3 charts the dynamics of their working.

Exhibit 6.2
INTERNAL COMPONENTS AND EXTERNAL LINKAGES

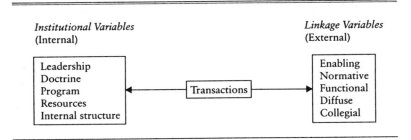

Exhibit 6.3

SCHEMATIC MAP OF COMPONENTS AND LINKAGES

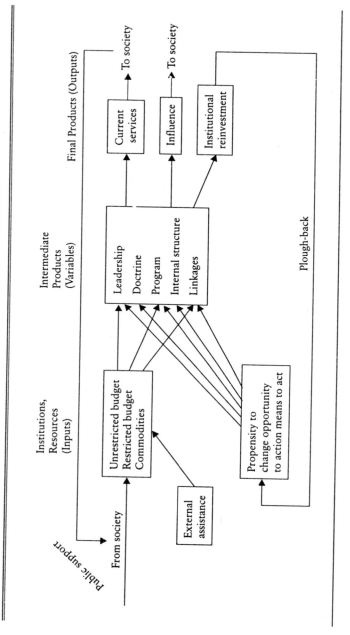

The mission and the in-house culture that policy-makers design the lead unit for, to give life to their vision of what the organization needs in its current and future environment to aim to do and to be like this is what institution-building theory calls '*doctrine*' and is the key reference for developing all other components. For the training unit to be a linchpin of major ongoing change in the organization and its larger system, two other components also call for the most careful attention: its leadership—selecting and supporting it and holding it accountable—and its position and connectedness with the organization and the wider system. For the first—leadership for the core unit—the essence is to choose someone to head it who, among the impressive set of other competencies needed for that role, is most certainly capable of bridging the gap between the innovative training unit and the organization and larger system it is to help change. For the second—the position of the unit and its sure organizational connectedness—the essence is to determine a location and linkages for the unit that protect and support its innovative function. Where high innovation is the aim and/or conditions are turbulent, two components of leadership and linkages are as closely tied together as Siamese twins and present the greatest challenges, together or apart.

LEADERSHIP SELECTION

How wide the gap is, between the current state of the organization and the future that policy-makers want training to help it achieve, makes all the difference to the leadership to select and support for the core training unit. Where the gap is large, that leadership has to be competent and credible in what amounts to two very different cultures and keep innovation going without losing its client. This is the most exposed and conflict-ridden situation and many—perhaps most—people who are attracted to apply by the challenge of it are really unsuitable for handling it. At the opposite end are organizations that have grown up and have survived in fast-changing fields, in information and high technology development for example, and they essentially challenge training to keep them ahead of developments (at the very least to enable them to keep up). Leadership in the one must buck the stream and redirect it, whereas in the fast-flowing stream training leadership must stay afloat, abreast and, if possible, ahead.

Even now, with high technologies occupying the airwaves, the two-cultures situation is more common by far as well as the more demanding, so we will concentrate on it here. Most organizations and their people persist with traditional forms and ways even where their clients, markets, and other externalities have long changed. From time to time, when discrepancies become too blatant and inefficiencies and costs so high that clients, staff, and/or backers protest or stay away, policy-makers have tended to adjust things just enough to carry on. That common progression, of minimal and incremental changes that alleviate pressures, actually complicates the situation further by making ready adjusting into a widespread habit and favoring the people good at that; it sidelines capacities for clear visioning and transformative policies that the situation really requires, starting right now and into the future. This is the difference, on the ground, that Exhibit 6.1 showed conceptually.

Top candidates for heading the training unit then would be competent and credible in *both* cultures and good at bridging them. Administrative and team-building competencies are additional qualifications. Policy-makers expect the head to speak specifically for training in meetings and in other contacts with partners in the organization and in the larger system; to initiate lines of developing training further; to propose and advocate specific policies, strategies, and resource allocations for it; and to pick up on training components and implications for training when the primary focus is elsewhere. More generally too, it is this head in particular that policy-makers can rely on to ensure that the longer-term and wide-ranging developmental aspects of change strategies receive proper attention in all planning and monitoring discussions; when others miss those or give them too little weight, she or he will highlight them.

If the organization prizes getting things done most directly and quickly—clarity and economy, reliable processes, and time-frames for seeing well-defined tasks through so people can get on to the next round of tasks and achievements—the culture of training and the people in it are geared differently, and must remain so if helping continuing organization-wide change is its mission. The training culture prizes exploration, innovation and experimenting; anything, in brief, that may help key people in the organization and the larger system acquire needed new capacities and root them well, and then also join with enough others to give the enterprise new life. Candidates for heading the training unit have to rate high for discussing and sharing purpose, open exploration, reflection and readiness to change, generally inclusive and collaborative working, and ready acceptance of personal differences. These traits are also good for networking with colleagues and sister institutions outside. For representing training with policy-makers, funders, administrators, and other partners in the larger system of stakeholders, the head needs credibility also with *them*.

Few heads come competent and at ease in both cultures; if they come highly recommended, it is usually for work in one or other of them—and, true, they must come from *somewhere*!. Those who have come up in old-style organizations may be the worst equipped for helping organizations change significantly, and especially their own. The experience they bring, and that the selectors also feel kinship with, ties them most strongly to the past: reassuringly familiar but not to new purpose; they may not even be able to visualize anything very different. Used to traditional line-and-staff thinking, for instance, they most readily see training as a service and so a staff function, and are inclined to wait for line managers to come forward with their requests; and then, unless policy-makers step in briskly and insist on the transformative priorities and on training taking the lead, training that simply accords with managers' requests will most surely lead only to multiplying and/or streamlining the same, no longer adequate programs. Or, if they come out of command-type organizations, as many applicants do from service in the old-time armed forces, they put the highest value on good order, efficiency, and clear accounts. If the head comes from within the organization, then the long familiar relationships which looked like such a great asset for selecting him or her may turn into the extra hostility due a turncoat when this supposed friend and colleague makes a move to take training in a new direction and threatens to upset things.

Bringing the head in, instead, from the training and consulting field has other challenges, with relationship-building in the organization and large system right at the top. Maybe here will be the greatest temptation for professionals used to independent practice to seek to impress selectors with the training equivalent of getting the trains to run on time. Worth listening for, too, is the subtler and lasting inclination professionals often bring to insinuate agendas and priorities of their own, out of the feeling that with their expertise they really do know better what needs to get done and how to do it than the organization's long-time policy-makers and managers. With training their full-time task, they would be quite able to find quiet ways to take it off on agendas they prefer, and even stress those more and more as training recedes into the isolation that they themselves led it into by this substitution. What expert outsiders see as important may in fact have much to say for it in substance and future orientation, but it would miss the practical purpose even then if they developed training in ways that distance it from the people who use it. Not far down that road, the intended users will write training off.

Some dilemmas then confront selectors whichever way they turn. Not even quite new organizations that have developed institution-like cultures to cope with state-of-the-art technologies in these fast changing times escape having them. Familiarity may make hearts grow fonder, as the saying goes, but the growing similarity of cultures adds other complexities to managing the training–operations boundary. For finding cover when challenged by policy-makers, each side makes the most of its singularity. Different again and usually less visible in considering a newcomer is his or her capacity for the internal management and onward development of training, for which the head of the unit is also responsible and accountable. Many excellent candidates on all other scores will have problems when it comes to combining training and relationship competencies with these essential internal functions. In addition to establishing each candidate's capacities, it is worth noting indications on his or her inclination or impatience with allocating effort and time to them.

One criterion seems to stand out for selecting the head of train-ing: how the candidate is likely to use the power of that position. Heads who share power readily with their colleagues and support their initiatives are well set to develop training into the many-rooted learning system it needs to be; and this then also models learning ways of being and working in the organization and in the larger system. With that sharing, training and organization development become congruent, and training can help most in the continuing trans-formation.

It is easy to see how the opposite of centralizing and building power up at the head of the training system, even personalizing it there, would undercut training and discourage colleagues from giving their best. Outside partners too will be on guard against manipulation mas-querading as leadership, and so stay distant and less involved. Im-portant in many leadership roles, for training the power equation—

the head's disposition to share it or hold on to it—is pivotal, because it is so central to that task and culture and nothing in sight can make up for a basic defect in it, and also because it feeds on itself in either direction—strengthening colleagues and training in one, discouraging and destroying in the other.

Only rarely is partnering with other institutions the experience candidates bring, but colleagueship—the experience of it and the disposition to it—should stand out in their presentation and in meetings for selection. It is the only mode for sustaining innovation into the future and also for building the innovative function securely into the training system's reputation. On that the leadership of training and the system's policy-makers must be fully aligned; so with newcomer candidates this is the dimension to check most of all. Not easy. Words about power and sharing it are many, and impressions gained in a sit-down meeting or two may not show how this head would be likely to handle actual situations. Contact with earlier colleagues and organizations is then necessary and worth going to the trouble to get. Deep down commitment to partnering is needed in the leadership of the training system as well as open, steady and, whenever necessary, active support from policy-makers.

Power-handling aside, with so many unknowns to head into and a wide variety of partners to live and work with, policy-makers will do well to consider final selection also in the light of the organization's own ongoing capacities to make up for this or that deficiency any of the two or three top candidates may show in actual practice. We keep on referring to leadership—the function and not just the person to head the unit—because most innovative training requires more continuous and also more diverse leading than one person is good at or can carry on by him- or herself. In selecting the head for the unit, policy-makers will therefore also want to take potential colleagues into account to make up competent leadership all round. The aim then becomes finding the combination that fits best. And, even with that, policy-makers will continue to have important balancing responsibilities for making it all work.

For candidates to come forward, the exacting and exhausting responsibilities of leading a training unit also promise wide scope for highly creative and satisfying work. That is what draws very creative people to doing it once they are satisfied that policy-makers mean what they say about wanting training for organizational change and continuing development. In Boxes 6.1 and 6.2, two experienced

Box 6.1

ETHOS FOR BUILDING THE TRAINING SYSTEM

Ethos can be defined as the underlying spirit or character of the beliefs, customs, or practices of an entity or a group. At the base of ethos are core values. The eight important values relevant to institution building are: Openness, Confrontation, Trust, Authenticity, Proaction, Autonomy, Collaboration, and Experimentation. In addition to being an acronym for these values, OCTAPACE is a meaningful term, indicating eight (octa) steps (pace) to create functional ethos.

1. *Openness*: Openness is spontaneous expression of feelings and thoughts and sharing of these without defensiveness. Openness is in both directions, and receiving and giving. Both these may relate to ideas (including suggestions), feedback (including criticism), and feelings.
2. *Confrontation*: Confrontation is facing, and not shying away from, problems. It also means deeper analyses of interpersonal problems. All this will involve taking challenges. The term confrontation is being used with some reservation and means 'putting up a front' as contrasted with 'putting the back' (escaping) to the problem. A better term would be confrontation and exploration (CE).
3. *Trust*: Trust is used not in the moral sense. It is reflected in maintaining confidentiality of information shared by others and not misusing it. It is also reflected in a sense of assurance that others will help when such help is needed and will honour mutual commitments and obligations. Trust is also reflected in accepting what the other person says on face value, and not searching for 'motives' of what has been said.
4. *Authenticity*: Authenticity is the congruence between what one feels, says and does. It is reflected in owning up one's mistakes and in unreserved sharing of feelings.
5. *Proaction*: Proaction means taking the initiative, preplanning and taking preventive action, and calculating payoffs of an alternative course before taking action. The term 'proact' can be contrasted with the term 'react'.
6. *Autonomy*: Autonomy is using and giving freedom to plan and act in one's own sphere. It means respecting and encouraging individual and role autonomy.
7. *Collaboration*: Collaboration is giving help to and asking help from others. It means working together (individuals and groups) to solve problems. It means team spirit.
8. *Experimenting*: Experimenting means using and encouraging innovative approaches to solve problems. Using feedback for improving, taking a fresh look at things, and encouraging creativity.

SOURCE: Summarized from Udai Pareek, *Beyond Management* (New Delhi: Oxford and IBH), Chapter 26.

Box 6.2

FOUR PILLARS FOR BUILDING AN INSTITUTION

I tried to adhere to four principles of institutional development as the pillars on which [the] Institute should rest. *First*, I wanted all of us to be clear about the *mission of the Institute*. While the individuals constituting an institution may have different agenda, priorities and emphases, for any successful Institute there must be an overriding concern shared by practically every member. I thought that the mission statement which we tried to emphasize time and again summed up very well the purpose and objective of the Institute. The statement was, '*our mission is to bridge the gap between micro realities and macro initiatives*'. This gave us a rationale for working at the grassroots level with NGOs, Panchayati Raj Institutions, and different formal and informal groups on the one hand, and reviewing, examining and suggesting approaches for state and national level programmes and policies on the other.

The *second* pillar on which I thought the Institute should rest was the *values* which ought to be imbibed, knowingly, by the majority of the group. These values should not remain abstract. They have to be translated in terms of day to day conduct and behaviour without chanting them as mantras. I believe that our *concern for the vulnerable sections*, and our responsibility to contribute in whatever way we could to ameliorate their lot served as a cementing force for the group. At another plane, our obligation to the society to fulfil our tasks to the best of our abilities was emphasised as an over riding consideration. The concrete manifestation of these values was in creating a work ethos in which each individual was motivated to fulfil his/her responsibility without shirking, without putting blame on others, without delaying and dithering. In the present atmosphere prevailing in the society to preserve and to enhance this sense of responsibility to ones own duties, ones own 'dharma', is a very uncommon feature.

Another way in which the underlying philosophy of the institution got manifested was the *insistence on transparency and efforts for sharing*. Whether it was the Thursday meeting, easily accessible master-file, frequent consultations/meetings etc., the purpose was to share the information and inhibit all those tendencies, which unfortunately are too common in our society, which enable the individual to corner power because he or she monopolizes some information. Beyond sharing information, there was a respect for the judgement of people who participated in various activities. Various types of arrangements which we made in terms of thrust areas, committees and responsibility centers, reflected the participatory approach. The committees' format, in which practically each and every faculty participated in one way or other in the management of various academic activities of the Institute with reasonable authority and autonomy, helped in creating a sense of belonging. This did not mean that [the] leader had to abdicate his responsibility but it did connote a participatory culture.

The fourth pillar of this strategy of institution building was *projecting the right image of the Institute among its various publics*. I believe that there is no

Box 6.2 contd...

need to feel shy if we are doing some good work. Let others, who are supporting us in a variety of ways have a sense that they are 'backing a right horse'.
Many a time false humility disguises real weaknesses.

SOURCE: Vijay Vyas, *IDSJ News* (January 1997).

heads identify aspects they have found important; others appear in
the readings following this chapter. Pareek fosters eight values
which, together, make the institution's 'ethos'. Vyas has learnt to
build 'four pillars': mission, values, sharing among colleagues, and
projecting the right image among the various publics.

To graft new on old so that it transforms the whole organization
and the still larger system of partners; to staff, design, fund, and provide programs to prepare people for work on this transformation
and at the same time also enlarge and build the staff; to lead this
work, so intriguing and demanding that it can absorb all hours, and
also make time for family and personal renewal and rest; to make
well-tested programs routine (to increase participant numbers and
lower costs) and also at the same time develop and instigate new
methods, materials, and structures; to keep collaboration going with
so many and diverse partners and also update the linkages and the
ground they cover as task and future become clearer—there is no
end to the opportunities for exciting work to lead and for stretching
personal and professional capacities in doing so.

Equally unending too, of course, are the conflicting pulls and pu-
shes from all over this busy scene, and the see-saw of elations and
frustrations as a result of keeping efforts coherent and on course
through it all. Most draining of energy and high spirits for heads we
know is the inordinate time and effort that administrative detail and
sorting out disputes take—and meetings (no end to meetings and how
this confirmed their worst fears when they agreed to head training).
Heads of free-standing training centers and other institutions have
fund raising to do as well, which supercedes all when a shortfall
looms.

The worst-case scenario takes over when the same or nearly same
issues come up again and again because, say these heads, there is
never time to work them out properly and *really* settle them, as they
could and should. Being head then not only puts one's own professional work on hold (bad enough but they half expected that), but
the respect and joy they started with for the work and opportunities

as head drain away. Some turn sour, settle for doing least, or count the days till this imposition is over. Senior staff taking turns as the head, as many academic departments require, limits the sentence—same for all. It also confirms this bleak image of being head.

All in all, effective leadership of a training system can be so creative and also so conflictful and relentlessly demanding that the role ranks high for time-limited occupation, say five years. Academic departments limit chairs that way, but that is more for sharing out hated administrative duties (hated for interfering with the research and publishing that really count in that system) and conflicts abound even there, even when there is no mandate or inclination to put the department—never mind the university at large—in closer touch with the world outside and the turbulent conditions that training prepares organizations for. More directly relevant may be the experiences of the armed forces in some countries and of some international organizations and agencies with making leadership of the training system a regular step to high promotion. This gives training and leadership in it high recognition and also limits the time anyone occupies the role, and so sets up the unit head better for pacing her- or himself through the high pressures and low periods in that position, and also for accepting for that set period the often severe shortages of personal and family time and time for professional reading, reflection, and further development.

ORGANIZATIONAL POSITION AND LINKAGES

A very practical issue to ask candidates to address in the selection process is where they would like the training unit to be positioned in the organization and then see what dimensions they take into account. Nearness to the top and/or to where strategic groups work? Indications to let colleagues in on the thinking? Attention to purpose for which contact with this or that part of the organization would be needed? Are outside partners in view, too? Developing relationships for the long haul? Or, for a unit that already exists, how might the candidate approach reviewing its position, recognizing the implications of it, and go about strengthening it? In either case, how would the candidate keep track of the many dimensions of developing and leading the unit and its many linkages? Along with the concrete steps he/she proposes, is there evidence too of leaving room for new things to emerge, of readiness to hold off decisions, and manage with the ambiguities of that?

When announcing the opening and eliciting candidates for heading the unit, policy-makers will, of course, have indicated the position they envisage for it; hopefully, they indicated too that that is open to review and revision along with selecting the leadership. Only on very general lines can the position be envisaged in advance of thorough homework and talking with partners. Having it in-house is one such: having trainers and operational staff in ever ready contact promises to keep training 'practical', but also risks them getting mired in mere repetition or, at most, minor variations instead of setting the organization up for major change. The straight alternative—to locate it distant from current operations for most free innovation—carries the opposite risk that trainers take programs off into realms of their own or fail to build good enough bridges for new learnings to permeate the organization back home. On the basis of mere generalizations of this order, the unit will likely turn out to be 'too close' or 'too far out'. And, if the position is decided with no clarity about its implications and expectations, and the actions aligned with them, the leadership will flounder between the two. Asked which of the nine organizational relationships that they managed they found most difficult, all twenty heads of population centers ranked managing the position in the middle highest and very difficult indeed. Their organization pulled them back, they reported (even those that had innovative policies and strategies on the books), and outside agencies pulled them forward. When governments and international funding agencies tipped the scales in favor of innovating, that silenced the opponents, but without usually reconciling them; driven underground, the opposition became still more difficult to handle and live with than before. Within a year or at most two from starting, all centers had drawn closer to one set of partners or the other and had more difficulties with the receding partner.[1]

Difficulties in managing will of course persist and, after laying out the issues and stakes intrinsic to the choices of role and position, we

---

[1] Rolf P. Lynton, *Institution-building for University Population Programs: A Short Guide for Policy Makers* (Chapel Hill: University of North Carolina Population Center, 1974). See also Rolf P. Lynton and John M. Thomas, 'The Utility of Institution-building Theory for Strategies and Methodologies of Consultation' in Dharni P. Sinha (ed.), *Consultants and Consulting Styles* (New Delhi: Vision Books, 1982). References to this work in this chapter are mostly to the latter.

will turn to the continuing work policy-makers face in supporting the leadership in the position it has chosen. The point here is that organizational position, like leadership, carries such heavy practical and symbolic consequences that it needs the most careful working out on the way to chosing among identifiable options. Some positions suit a situation better than others, just as leadership selected to fit an organization and its situation and vision well will more likely succeed in some position(s) than others. To involve candidates in mapping the options and their implications, and indicating how they would approach making a practical choice holds promise in selecting the leadership; next make working it out and coming up with a solid recommendation the first special task of the chosen leadership.

Position and linkages hang together. Working out what the training unit needs to carry out its innovative mission in its setting—and what partnerships it therefore has to develop and nurture—focuses the options for its position in the organization, and may in fact identify it. Policy-makers then also decide the unit's position in the light of wider organizational considerations, their own and the organization's tolerances for innovating and the uncertainties it brings.

Exhibit 6.4 shows the linkages typical for population centers that universities on four continents were developing in the 1960s and 1970s with agencies and communities outside. Omitted on this map are the collegiate linkages between the twenty centers in the global network and also with other professional colleagues and institutions in their own universities and outside.

'Enabling' linkages provide the institution with legitimate authority to start and to operate and to give it access to the funds and other support it needs. 'Functional' linkages provide for substantive exchanges with the environment. 'Normative' linkages deal with the establishment of standards in the institution and with its attempts to influence norms in the environment. 'Diffuse' linkages are for building widespread understanding and support for the institution. 'Collegial' linkages at the inter-institutional level are for professional exchanges about best practices and benchmarking, for instance researching and sharing information from parallel strategies, and also for working on some developments jointly and with resources in common. All five kinds of linkages have the double purpose of relating the core institution closely with its environment and also of influencing that environment.

Exhibit 6.4
EXTERNAL LINKAGES OF A FIELD-ORIENTED CENTER
IN A PUBLIC UNIVERSITY

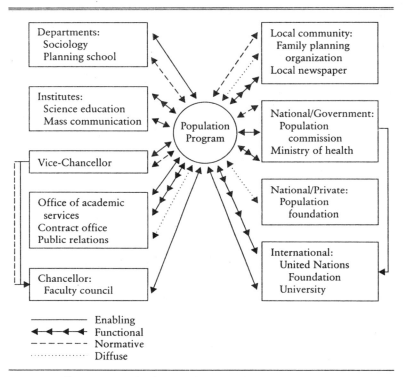

SOURCE: Rolf P. Lynton and John M. Thomas, "The Utility of Institution-building Theory for Strategies and Methodologies of Consultation" in Dharni P. Sinha (ed.), *Consultants and Consulting Styles* (New Delhi: Vision Books, 1982), p. 92.

Exhibit 6.4 also summarizes the outside partners by types, which is appropriate for policy-level attention. (Operating the network requires detailed listing of partners.) Even with some grouping, the linkages one of us took responsibility for as dean of a professional school numbered 148 and each program director had his or her list and network as well (which partly overlapped the others').

Beyond its use for overview and planning, the classification of linkages has practical values for the detailed designing, management, and evaluation of linkages. It facilitates checking existing linkages for appropriateness to purpose and for mutuality; both are required for effectiveness and stability of each linkage. Beyond this, if linkages are mapped and examined jointly, they will reveal unattended or neglected relationships and other aspects of patterns important for institutional policy and planning. Such maps provide valuable data for decisions on institutional leadership, notably governance, internal structure, resource allocation, and operations.

Ongoing Policy Support for Training

With leadership selected and the core unit in position, it is important to let them get on with developing the training system on the agreed lines along with the day-to-day running of it. Any attempt of others to micro-manage how it is working and progressing would interfere and confuse. The function policy-makers now have and into the future is to ensure that developing the unit and the system receives sufficient attention *as a whole* and with eyes far enough into the *future*, even while the head and the team there are also engaged without let-up in ongoing programs and associated activities.

For that onward monitoring and guiding of the *institutional* development of training, scrutiny of immediate 'outputs' from current programs and activities—their scale, immediate 'impact', costs, and the like—is of very limited use and that is true too for anecdotal reports about any as well (however dramatic and encouraging or discouraging). For assessing and ensuring institutional health and growing strength, these are best treated as symptomatic and to be combined with cues to progress on the underlying developmental dimensions. This is proper caution generally too for keeping up with departments and other parts of the enterprise without undercutting the leadership there, but it needs special emphasis for monitoring and guiding training. One reason for extra caution is that outcomes of training that show up early, such as a sharply improved output or fewer disputes or an apparently smooth change-over to new methods or to a new location, may have been achieved at high but hidden costs to collaborative working and morale. A second and very different reason is that policy-makers who would not consider themselves qualified to voice their opinion about, say, an engineering issue, do have personal views about how people are best trained and are inclined to push these. Their views deserve noting, but not acting on by themselves.

Instead of immediate impacts and reactions, policy-level monitoring and guiding calls for attending to *trends*, and those trends are best looked at in sets and as patterns. Trends in participant numbers, costs, and measurable consequences back home, for example; accessions and turnover in training staff; new or revised programs and new populations in programs; updated maps of the core institution's relations with system partners, frequencies of contact, content and outcomes; and where in the system these initiatives came from. Two sets of generally salient trends will be discussed in the next sections and others in the chapter on evaluating training in Volume 2 of this book in combination with data to show the all-round consequences of training in the realities of back home settings and also the use training staff have made of these same data for improving and augmenting programs. In regular, say quarterly, reports, policy-makers can require the core unit to show the important trends and point to notable changes and anticipations, and come prepared to discuss them.

Here we will focus on two sets of measures policy-makers can use to keep training well aligned with the overall purpose, direction, and change strategies intended for it. Many measures for that are indirect, the kind statisticians call unobtrusive. Even with those, conclusions are bound to remain indefinite for understanding and guiding so far flung and costly an effort as training and for its subtly and insidiously far-reaching effects which may even be fateful for individuals and for the organization. In such highly complex situations a rule of thumb helps: the more indefinite the product and the more difficult to measure, shift attention to making sure the processes for getting there are best designed, are transparent, and work well. Policy-makers would do well to pay special attention to the processes the leadership sets in motion and by which it operates and develops training. They can check for inclusion of partners, range of agenda, usage of linkages, and also for the clarity, transparency, and reliability of the unit's ways of working. Sound processes will promote the desired ends even where the ends themselves are so difficult to foresee and specify and indeed have to remain generously open to shifts and changes to cope with turbulent conditions as well.

FOUR SYSTEM TRENDS TO WATCH—AND QUICKLY RECTIFY

Four aspects in the unit's relations with its world outside warrant regular attention: system coverage and updating it; how the linkages are actually used; any overloads and conflicts among partners; and imbalances that can be traced to the unit's position in the system. Requiring the head of training to be sure to report on these in every quarterly or half-year report would signal the special importance these have in policy-makers' eyes.

1. System Maps Incomplete: Important Partners Missing

When listing important partners to include and be represented in decision-making and guiding, some come up readily and others are commonly omitted. Clearly in view and included are: the governing body of policy-makers, funders (additional and potential) and suppliers, major customers and clients, and the surrounding community/ies, local administration, and regulating agency/ies. Others, also strategic for the purpose, tend to be missed or improperly represented. Commonly among these are poor and long-neglected populations (who may actually be the neediest clients), young people (though they will be the key actors in the envisaged future), and among these, the less accessible because they are less organized, distant or geographically dispersed. Often thought of, sure enough, but deliberately omitted are doubters and opponents of the transformation the training system is to foster and sister institutions who could augment the resources available for mounting and sustaining change in any one organization (and also could turn into competitors for funds and limelight). In terms of purposes, linkages essential for enabling training to start and keep on functioning come easy; linkages with normative, diffuse, and collegial partners need reminding and insistence.

Wide inclusiveness, right from the very beginning, of all partners needed then and also of others needed as the unit develops and the environment changes is highly advantageous, even if it has to be followed with patient nurturing of hesitant partners into active participation. It gives change goals and strategies the inclusive image and underlying goodwill that will advance them best, and it also avoids the often much heavier costs of bringing missing partners on board later. Aggrieved at having been left off initially, most then insist on having their say now, even if that means reopening agreements hard-won earlier and in operation.

Even the decision to invite and encourage (or to exclude) particular opponents is worth basing on favorable calculations of risks. Experience gives two clear pointers: one is that it is better to know what the opposition is and what are its source(s) than to guess, and better too to have it out in the open and respected than hidden and belittled; the other is that when opponents get together with advocates to work out something concrete and practical, they find common ground. Steadily positive experiences with this now include partnerships among direct competitors in business (of which examples were mentioned in Box 3.3), organizations opposing further environmental degradation with the offending manufacturers or agro-businesses, and political parties with quite basically conflicting positions on development issues.

2. Imbalances in Linkages and Their Use

Imbalances of two kinds are common and well worth periodic action-oriented attention by policy-makers. Short term over long term is the more obvious. Developing normative linkages, (for raising change to an organization-wide norm, for instance) and diffuse linkages (for spreading goodwill for it widely, locally and through public media) tend to get postponed again and again, and quite understandably so, by immediate preoccupations with pressing everyday activities. While functional linkages work smoothly from constant use and enabling linkages have to function too—at budget times at least (though neglecting them at other times also becomes hazardous)—linkages for less urgent purposes remain undeveloped and often fade from view altogether. Collegiate linkages tend to get neglected for the same and also for another reason: colleagues and sister institutions outside may be or may become competitors or at least show up shortcomings in the unit and its leadership. Better stay away from them. Static on this score will surface for policy-makers at budget and resource contracting times. Ready access to the best training resources wherever they are is their direct concern—*that* defines the training system they are after; but they also want to make sure that the leadership and staff of their own unit continue well respected in their field and so also stay in the best position to network with others. By the reporting they expect and by incisive enquiry, policy-makers help keep all kinds of linkages visible.

In the network of population centers in universities, enabling linkages were few and used very unevenly over time. They were used most at the beginning of the programme, then atrophied within a year; in years 3–4 and 6–7, when crises characteristically occurred in the programs, they were increased in number and strength and used actively, usually under pressure from the university at large.

Normative and diffuse linkages were virtually absent. This portends low legitimization and outside support to protect the institution against attack and to support continued innovation. Yet protection was especially important during the early critical period in the existence of new and highly experimental programs before they were strong enough to deal with their environments on their own terms.

The other characteristic imbalance occurs when one partner in any linkage steadily initiates or benefits from it more than the other or others. Mutuality is basic for linkages to work and continue to work well. Direct, exact or immediate exchanges of benefits are not necessary but care to make linkages benefit all partners must be evident.

By requiring the training unit to include specific information about the development of linkages in all regular reporting, policy-makers will show their concern with it. There will be other signs too of how well this is going, e.g., continued funding from outside sources and invitations from partners to join *them* in an activity, and, indirectly, in reports in the media and in the course of outside contacts policy-makers themselves have about other matters.

3. Overloads and Partners in Conflict

Making a few linkages serve many purposes looks so easy and efficient that it is very tempting. In fact, overloads and conflicts loom round the corner. Requiring updated maps of existing and planned linkages according to their functions helps ensure that the training unit diversifies its linkages enough to avoid these dangers.

In the population centers, reliance on a few linkages in itself increased the tendencies of programs to close themselves off from the rest of the university and from [the] public outside. For instance, the enabling linkages which some programs had with a government agency frequently imperilled the quality of their functional relationships with other units of the university. Similarly, diffuse external support for programs through extensive coverage in public media tended to weaken their legitimization within the university and their ability to mobilize faculty and departmental resources.

To go for multiplicity and also separability of linkages is a good general rule. Multiplicity provides safety, for one—the institution will not have all eggs in one basket. This is extra important where conditions in the organization itself and/or in the communities and administrations nearby are turbulent or will be so and, notably for funding, where national and international shifts can interfere at no notice. Funding and other enabling partners are in fact especially risky partners for additional functions because they can so readily assume control.

4. Distorted Development Stemming from Improper Position

Defects on this score are probably the most far-reaching, the most difficult to recognize and, if tracing them confirms the origin, the most urgent to remedy. Many overlays hide the source, and policymakers themselves may encourage bandaiding difficulties, one after another, rather than going back to square one—institutional design—and setting about revising and renegotiating it.

Faulty positioning at the beginning results most frequently from faulty appreciation—our old friend!—of the order of change the organization really needed to get used to for functioning well in these times and the far-reaching and possibly upsetting implications of it. In most cases we know, courage, not intellectual clarity, fell short. The prospect was simply too complex and demanding to grasp and to begin grappling with all at once. Or, more accurately, for those who did see the needs clearly, to convince their more hesitant colleagues about. Here now is the time for the second cut.

Transformation, that greater order of change, now becomes the compelling referent for repositioning the training unit. And the same principles apply: it must be separate and autonomous enough to innovate and keep innovating and also linked close enough to remain practical and affect operations. The new position may undercut policies and even structures developed meanwhile, and certainly shift priorities and resources. Two rules are the best guide for following through. The sooner all change, the better is the first; outdated perspectives can only complicate things even more everyday. The second rule is to match incisive reworking with clear, transparent processes for doing it. Repositioning can in fact be a stellar opportunity for engaging partners more closely.

The prospects of meeting great urgencies in the field more creatively combined with ready offers of public and foundation funding for this led universities to establish population centers quickly and then also to tolerate the centers' attaching themselves more and more closely with outside partners. Quite quickly several existed wholly on funds from clients for specific items of work. Some programs had become heavily dependent on one or at the most two major clients, notably, the Planning Council or the Ministry of Health in their country. Others, in an attempt to escape this dependency, had multiplied their work contracts, but at the cost of having to sort out competition between them for faculty time and facilities. Either direction limited the program's autonomy and hamstrung it in its relations with the university. Programs which had at least some basic university or development funds from elsewhere were freer to choose the agencies they wanted to relate with outside the university. They commonly chose agencies with missions and styles of working close to their own and in several cases had been able to influence those missions so that the area of congruence was enlarged.

Irrespective of the mode of funding, programs which had developed their main supports for expansion outside the university invariably experienced serious difficulties within their universities. Funds being available, university administrators had allowed this to occur without anticipating the consequent isolation of the program inside the university. Some did expect this but were unable to stand against political pressure. Among these programs were several which, because they looked so productive and enjoyed outside support, attracted foreign funds in large amounts.

Partnerships that strengthen innovation need counter-balancing then with others that reflect traditional structures and familiar ways; the culture to emerge will be an amalgam of new with old. Institutions that assimilate best have three features in common: a strong, explicit, and well-publicised mission and culture (the combination labelled 'doctrine' in the basic schemas), a governing body and leadership that straddle both eras and, third, eager and well functioning relations with a wide range of partners.

We have stayed with discussing partnerships and linkages this long to emphasize their strategic importance for developing training these days and into the foreseeable future; they define it and hold it in position. Also, because this is unfamiliar ground for most policymakers; altogether abstract and distant for many who have come up through internal management and usually only partially and erratically understood even by others experienced in handling external relations one or two at a time and in one direction—sales or services to clients or from suppliers and banks, pacifying regulatory agencies, or the like. The systematic overview of all linkages and their purposes and of the options and pitfalls they commonly present should make the next steps practical and also more assured.

Good enough maps for this—of the terrain ahead and features in it likely to be dominant—is the first thing policy-makers can routinely require the training unit to provide, along with comments grounded in relevant experiences elsewhere, trends and their implications for framing or revising a policy or monitoring its use, practical options, and possible pitfalls. Mapping frames the issue; the local realities then fill the frame.

The very first to consider for review and revision may well be the make-up of the policy-making group itself, to make sure that the major partners needed for training, here and with this mission, are in it; even partners whose active involvement will come only later. Erring on the side of inclusion is a good rule of thumb, even at the risk of ending up with a larger and more elaborate governance structure than turned out to be strictly necessary, looking back. Getting the signals right helps greatly; wrong is difficult to reverse later. If innovation and training are too innovative for clear mapping, the first composition can be time-limited to be taken up for formal review and revision at a specified date.

On developing the needed linkages, policy-makers themselves can work quite actively, and often on their own too, if they are also in good enough contact with the unit leadership to avoid overlaps and confusions. Opportunities for taking an active hand with this will arise in the course of their other work in the organization and with contacts outside. Surely they will be alert to comments from colleagues, friends, competitors, and in the communities around and public media about how they view the changes going on, and pass these on. Action outside is open, mostly unsolicited, and also uncomplicated by in-house boundaries, loyalties, and risks of undercutting the leadership.

POLICY-LEVEL MONITORING OF THE UNIT'S INTERNAL DEVELOPMENT

In the development of the training unit itself, its programs and other services, internal structures and management, and developing its capacities for the future, policy-makers can act only indirectly—through the leadership they have chosen (and can also replace) and through the policies and resource allocations they make. We keep on referring to the leadership function, not the person heading the unit, because most innovative training requires more continuous and also more diverse leading than one person can carry on, and one hopes that in selecting this head for the unit policy-makers made sure that colleagues were there to join him or her for competent leadership all round.

To satisfy themselves that training is developing well—as they must—policy-makers will receive data of many kind, asked for and as a result of the unit's and others' initiative. They commonly show participant numbers in training programs; introduction of new programs; greater diversity of participants and clients; financial grants and requests for collaboration; and staff changes. Other indicators are qualitative, such as comments from participants about their training or clients about their participants' performance following training, and initiatives taken (or not taken) by training staff. When looked at for trends over time and taken together as indicators (symptoms), they can help overall assessment. And policy-makers can get the leadership to present them for that. In the quite proper endeavor to make their assessment deliberate, comprehensive and systematic, it is important too that policy-makers not downplay their own hunches and the summary assessments they have learned from long experience to prize.

Here again mapping can help order the many impressions and key in policy-makers where and when to look for salient data, and so make their monitoring more reliable and interventions surer and timely. We have found three aspects especially useful: an overview of the initial stages to getting an institution on the ground and functioning, with characteristic issues for each and indicators of settling them; indicators of the unit's institutional climate overall; and leadership traits.

Stages in Institutional Development: Characteristic Dilemmas and Resolution

Our own work with new units as they start and with various kinds of institutions at different stages of development shows the major similarities and sequences set out in Exhibit 6.5.

Exhibit 6.5
STAGES IN INSTITUTIONAL DEVELOPMENT

Critical Issue	Characteristic Features	Dilemma	Resolution
1. *Start*	A few individuals full of ideas and zest. Frenzied activity. Attention oriented outward— power points, sister institutions, customers.	When should the institution be born and how large? Planning for every contingency or have a crash program?	Strong continuing leadership.
2. *Identity* a) Seeking identity	Search for main focus or foci. Conflict and uncertainty. Internal competition for attention.	Perfection of one thing or value all comers?	Clearly explicit long-range objectives as a priority system for decision making.
b) Seeking acceptance	Search for relationships with existing systems. Interorganizational jealousies. Attention outward.	Stress likeness and conformity or stress novelty and differences?	Moratorium to establish standards, largely in isolation.
c) Seeking balance	One or two activities have made a quick start, now threaten to dwarf or belittle others. Jealousies within.	Curb fast starters or let them run loose?	Focus on lagging functions to encourage their momentum.
3. *Growth*	Great demands for services, mostly short-term. Temptation to take on too much load. Meeting demands increases demands.	Consolidate and develop slowly or expand in all promising directions?	Moratorium to reexamine objectives and priorities. Publicize long-range plans.
4. *Maturity*	Success revives interorganizational jealousies, even threatens sponsors. Attacks on autonomy and independence.	Forego identity and submit or revolt and break away?	Develop interdependent relationships focused on tasks.

Exhibit 6.5 contd...

5. *Continuing innovation*	Self-satisfaction. Temptation to rest on laurels. Reluctance to work out new ideas.	Fossilize or break up into progressive and conservative, young and old?	Check objectives against changing situation, rejuvenate institution, build in indices of relevance.

Urgencies together with local practicalities and dominant working style determine the actual start, that is, starting with plans and developments worked out in advance more or less. Neither that choice nor any other down the third column is an all-or-nothing choice. Each commands broad and deep enough consideration to combine both; a 'dilemma' that can only be 'resolved' at a deeper level.

Whatever the start, the new institution then develops through predictable stages, each with a defining dilemma at the core. Till that is resolved, development stalls; it may overlap at the next stage and occasionally also regress, but the sequence broadly stands. Only as currently critical issues and the dilemma they pose get resolved, can the unit move on into the next phase. Too many training institutions settle into a middling stage, well short of hopes and even of plans for them, and never get to making the contribution they were meant to make.

At each stage the characteristic features (in Column 2) are the most open evidence for the unit's progress or lagging. When features of the next set show up prominently, that confirms that the unit has incorporated the previous one well enough to move on. Mere novelty does not denote progress—reflecting old features in a new dress. But not for long. The underlying dilemma will show through.

Institutional Climate

The need to assure themselves that the training unit is developing on sound lines and at the same time give its leadership full scope for doing it their way, makes an overall measure highly desirable, one to take only occasionally or to put together from sets of unintrusive samplings. Institutional climate promises well for the overall measure and a set of five indicators reflect it routinely and in varied enough settings for carrying on with confidence or for alerting policy-makers to problems to address.

In the companion volume we deal at some length with institutional climate itself, its nature, and its centrality in the unit leader's particular role and task (Chapter 8).

Ready indicators of a good institutional climate are:

- Wide sharing among colleagues of responsibilities for programs and participants. This makes the essential link to trainers, in turn helping participants grow into more independent and responsible functioning, which is training at its best.
- The unit's efficient functioning over time. In most organizations nowadays, this shows high flexibility and easy communication among the leadership and professional colleagues and also with administrators and support staff. Working in teams and exploring innovative projects with good economy and little disruption require these.
- The unit and staff diversify professional roles and functions to advance the change goals and strategies of the organization. So training is supported with consulting, counselling, coaching, and also with research and experimenting—whatever is needed for the purpose. They call on additional colleagues outside to collaborate.
- The unit has orderly processes for upgrading professional competencies and rewarding staff members for attaining them. This reflects development with a long view and also high individual commitments.
- Plans and programs for the unit are worked out collaboratively and carry strong institution-wide commitment.

Leadership Traits in Promising and Failing Institutions

Exhibit 6.6 sharpens the focus further on common traits shown by the leadership in particular—the head .and his or her immediate team whom policy-makers see in action most and also interact with most directly—and comparing the ways they typically handle and promise well or by others on the way to failing. Contrasting them so sharply helps fix the differences for ready reference, for watching and testing the many units that are actually somewhere in between and trying to assess in which direction they are tending.

Exhibit 6.6
TYPICAL LEADERSHIP TRAITS IN PROMISING
AND FAILING INSTITUTIONS

Leadership:	*Core institution:*		
Dominant trait	*Promising*	*Middling*	*Failing*
Focus on:	Task and relations	Avoid trouble	Protect status quo
Face-to-face:	Open, engaging, flexible	Passive	Partial, formal
Who initiates:	Any and jointly, partners too		Staff tries
Time frame:	Near- and long		Near, immediate, partial and self-confirming
Evaluation:	Holistic, appreciative, of difficulties too, data-based, for discussion	Minimal: general impressions	Sharp, formal, critical, for top-down instruction
Contacts:	System-wide, follows up	Responds to others'	On own agenda
Image:	Creative, collaborates, deserves support	Conservative, waits for guidance	Under others' control, insignificant, 'only trouble'
Funding:	Diversified, avoid dependence	Original, passive	Single-source, highly dependent

SUPPORT FOR STEADY DEVELOPMENT AND ALSO FOR INNOVATION

For training to keep on combining the steady development required to institutionalize it with the innovating and pioneering that is its particular task in the organization and the larger system, it needs uncommonly wise policy-level support. The right mix is one dimension of this—how much of one with how much of the other; how active and insistent to be with any particular intervention is the other.

For keeping the mix right over time, standardizing and routinizing training too early and too much is the greater risk to guard against than excessive and too rapid innovation. Relentless high alert for innovating is sure, before long, to exhaust the unit or its clients or both, and policy-makers will use the first mis-step or faltering to call for more order and economy. When settling into less exertion and simpler and less demanding options seems to takeover, policy-makers will want to shift their weight and challenge the unit to innovate more.

A particularly potent measure for raising innovative zest again, and also for then keeping it well stimulated, is to broaden and diversify the unit's role beyond training. As a first step, expecting it to support change efforts in the organization generally in direct follow-up of training can be made explicit. A broader consulting function emerges quite smoothly from this. Focused initially and most plausibly on helping operating units map training needs and matching them when selecting participants for programs, consulting on broader manpower planning is a natural next and often is eagerly welcomed where technical or organizational changes are in the offing. In ever-widening circles, improving workstations, team and departmental operations and inter-departmental, organization-wide, and wider relations can come into focus.

How much expansion and diversification to encourage informally, and when to redesign the unit and embed it enlarged in proper policies, budgets and perhaps a new position in the organization becomes an issue quickly. The urgency in settling this depends largely on how informal and formal arrangements play traditionally in the organization and in the wider culture. To minimize uncertainty, policy-makers can set and announce dates for reviewing and updating the expanded role, and also confirm the intent to legitimize and back all that will clearly continue. For the unit's internal development, expanding and diversifying its role—on staffing and a variety of tasks and opportunities to grow professionally, the wider exposure it offers of how effective training now is and how it can be improved, on opening wider vistas and contacts altogether—all this is electrifying of course. For maintaining order and economy and avoiding happy developments from becoming chaotic, requiring the unit to incorporate internal changes in policies and structures, to develop clear processes, and to make them transparent and public is the direction to go.

Recorded experiences to date tell very little about how much, how actively and insistently, and how best policy-makers can intervene.

Maps—ours, others' and those policy-makers' draft that incorporate their organization's particular features and priorities—help direct attention meeting to meeting and also for the reporting policy-makers can require the unit to do. When trends are generally positive and also promise well for the long term, as in staffing and developing unit capacity generally, querying detail is more likely to damage than support. When trends are unclear, as they are bound to be in innovative endeavors of all kind, most supportive may be to clarify the criteria for assessing the trends and when next to discuss them again. When dysfunctional trends are confirmed, swift intervention is usually best. A clear specific instance is persistent gaps in the linkage network with strategic partners. When dysfunctional trends persist and forecast further damage, changing the leadership may be best.

Scenes and casts keep on shifting and changing of course, inside and out, so new opportunities open up and others close.

> In our own experience, the departure of the principal who had backed highly innovative training at the SIET Institute in its early years opened a Pandora's box of so much long-repressed resentment that it almost killed innovating. The particular target there was interpersonal relationship training but that stood in for wide-ranging upsets. It survived, but emasculated and sidelined.
>
> Elsewhere, competing in the more open world-wide market has made innovation imperative and urgent. Boards, reconstituted to include HRD and other expert members, aim at changing 'the whole organizational culture' and fall readily for highly publicised training and other quick fixes. Younger policy makers express difficulties even understanding why their elders hesitate so often over innovations that seem so obviously necessary and urgent.
>
> Leadership for training continues [to be] difficult to find and to keep. In fast-developing countries other positions attract good candidates more, so turnover is high. In highly industrialized Western countries able professionals stay away from organizational commitments, and prefer individual practice and consulting from an outside role.

Important as they are, dealing with crises and being readily accessible with counsel and active support at major transition points must not distract policy-makers from their primary task of creating the best setting for training in their organization and its larger system; also re-creating it again and again as needs and conditions change.[2]

---

[2] *The Creation of Settings and Future Societies* (San Francisco: Jossey-Bass, 1972) is the title of Seymour B. Sorenson's seminal book on institution-building.

Foresight and acting in good time and good measure characterize good policy-making, not high-drama crisis management.

By staying clear of day-to-day exigencies, policy-makers are in a better position to help the lead unit develop habits and strengths in combining and balancing and pattern-making where others would only see either/or choices for separate action. Combining and balancing—new with old, immediate with longer- and long-term, off alone with times together with one partner for some purposes and with many or all for others, fast with slow pacing and with halts, expanding programs (staff, funding) with holding tight—and getting used to viewing whole spectrums and making acting on these habitual and the norm will keep the unit focused on its innovative task.

For the organization as a whole and the larger setting and system, policy-makers determine how far and how best to differentiate training as a separate function and also—its constant companion—of keeping training well integrated with the organization and linked with the larger system. How deep, far-reaching, and permanent the change that the organization has set out on is the essential assessment to guide this pair of determinations, as we have seen. Boundaries and linkages are their continuing core responsibility, along with their design and the formulations and policies to cover them, and their maintenance and updating. This differentiation/integration equation defines the scope of training and its limits at any time: the playing field, the game, the players, and the possibilities of all.

Reading 6.1

Organizational Health in Training Institutions

MATTHEW B. MILES*

Organizational health can be seen as a set of fairly durable second-order system properties, which tend to transcend short-run effectiveness.... A steadily ineffective organization would presumably not be healthy; ....But notice that an organization may cope effectively in the short run (as for example by a speed-up or a harsh cost-cutting drive), but at the cost of

---

* From Matthew B. Miles, "Planned Change and Organizational Health: Figure and Ground" in R.O. Carlson et al., *Change Processes in the Public School* (New York: Columbia University Press, 1965), pp 369–81.

longer run variables, such as those noted below. The classic example, of course, is an efficiency drive which cuts short-run costs and results in long-run labor dissatisfaction and high turnover.

To illustrate in more detail what is meant by 'second-order property', here is a list of ten dimensions of organizational health that seem plausible to me.... The first three dimensions are relatively 'tasky', in that they deal with organizational goals, the transmission of messages, and the way in which decisions are made.

1. *Goal focus.* In a healthy organization, the goal (or more usually goals) of the system would be reasonably clear to the system members, and reasonably well accepted by them. This clarity and acceptance, however, should be seen as a necessary but insufficient condition for organizational health. The goals must also be achievable with existing or available resources and be appropriate—more or less congruent with the demands of the environment. The last feature may be most critical.

2. *Communication adequacy.* Since organizations are not simultaneous face-to-face systems like small groups, the movement of information within them becomes crucial. This dimension of organizational health implies that there is relatively distortion-free communication 'vertically', 'horizontally', and across the boundary of the system to and from the surrounding environment. That is, information travels reasonably well—just as the healthy person 'knows himself' with a minimum level of repression, distortion, etc. In the healthy organization, there is good and prompt sensing of internal strains; there are enough data about problems of the system to ensure that a good diagnosis of system difficulties can be made. People have the information they need, and have gotten it without exerting undue efforts, such as moseying up to the superintendent's secretary, reading the local newspaper, or calling excessive numbers of special meetings.

3. *Optimal power equalization.* In a healthy organization, the distribution of influence is relatively equitable. Subordinates (if there is a formal authority chart) can influence upward, and even more important, they perceive that their boss can do likewise with his boss. In such an organization, intergroup struggles for power would not be bitter, though intergroup conflict (as in all human systems known to man) would undoubtedly be present. The basic stance of persons in such an organization, as they look up, sideways and down, is that of collaboration rather than explicit or implicit coercion. The units of the organization (persons in roles, work groups, etc.) would stand in an interdependent relationship to each other, with rather less emphasis on the ability of a 'master' part to control the entire operation. The exertion of influence in a healthy organization would presumably rest on the competence of the influencer *vis-à-vis* the issue at hand, his stake in the outcome, and the amount of knowledge or data he has—rather than on his organizational position, personal charisma, or other factors with little direct relevance to the problem at hand.

... A second group of three dimensions deals essentially with the internal state of the system, and its inhabitants' 'maintenance' needs. These are resource utilization, cohesiveness, and morale.

4. *Resource utilization*. We say of a healthy person, that he is 'working up to his potential'. At the organization level, 'health' would imply that the system's inputs, particularly the personnel, are used effectively. The overall coordination is such that people are neither overloaded nor idling. There is a minimal sense of strain, generally speaking (in the sense that trying to do something with a weak or inappropriate structure puts strain on that structure). In the healthy organization, people may be working very hard indeed, but they feel that they are not working against themselves or against the organization. The fit between people's own dispositions and the role demands of the system is good. Beyond this, people feel reasonably 'self actualized', they not only 'feel good' in their jobs, but they have a genuine sense of learning, growing, and developing as persons in the process of making their organizational contribution.

5. *Cohesiveness*. ...the organization knows 'who it is'. Its members feel attracted to membership in the organization. They want to stay with it, be influenced by it, and exert their own influence in the collaborative style suggested above.

6. *Morale*. The history of this concept in the social-psychological literature is so appalling that I hesitate to introduce it at all...Yet it still seems useful to evoke, at the organization level,...a summated set of individual sentiments, centering around feelings of well-being, satisfaction and pleasure, as opposed to feelings of discomfort, unwished-for strain and dissatisfaction...in a healthy organization it is hard to entertain the idea that the dominant personal response of organization members would be anything else than one of well-being.

Finally, there are four more dimensions of organizational health which deal with growth and changefulness: the notions of innovativeness, autonomy, adaptation *vis-à-vis* the environment, and problem-solving adequacy.

7. *Innovativeness*. A healthy system would tend to invent new procedures, move toward new goals, produce new kinds of products, diversify itself, and become more rather than less differentiated over time. In a sense, such a system could be set to grow, develop and change, rather than remain routinized and standard.

8. *Autonomy*. ...A healthy organization...does not respond passively to demands from the outside, feeling itself the tool of the environment, and it would not respond destructively or rebelliously to perceived demands either. It would tend to have a kind of independence from the environment, in the same sense that the healthy person, while he has transactions with others, does not treat their responses as determinative of his own behavior.

9. *Adaptation*. The notions of autonomy and innovativeness are both connected with the idea that a healthy...organization is in realistic, effective

contact with the surroundings. When environmental demands and organization resources do not match, a problem-solving, restructuring approach evolves in which both the environment and the organization become different in some respect. More adequate, continued coping of the organization, as a result of changes in the local system, the relevant portions of the environment, or more usually both, occurs. And such a system has sufficient stability and stress tolerance to manage the difficulties which occur during the adaptation process....

10. *Problem-solving adequacy.* Finally, any healthy organism—even one as theoretically impervious to fallibility as a computer—always has problems, strains, difficulties, and instances of ineffective coping. The issue is not the presence or absence of problems, therefore, but the manner in which the... organization copes with problems. Argyris has suggested that in an effective system, problems are solved with minimal energy; they stay solved; and the problem solving mechanisms used are not weakened, but maintained or strengthened. An adequate organization, then, has well-developed structures and procedures for sensing the existence of problems, for inventing possible solutions, for deciding on the solutions, for implementing them, and for evaluating their effectiveness. Such an organization would conceive of its own operations (whether directed outward to goal achievement, inward to maintenance, or inward-outward to problems of adaptation) as being controllable. We would see active coping with problems rather than passive withdrawing, compulsive responses, scapegoating, or denial.

The Special Case of Educational Organizations

... educational systems have special properties which condition the propositions of organizational theory in reasonably predictable ways....

1. *Goal ambiguity.* For many different reasons, it has seemed difficult to specify the output of educational organizations very precisely. Some of this is realistic: change in human beings is going on, with presumably cumulative effects over a long period of time. But part of this output measurement difficulty also seems to be a form of organizational defense or protection against criticism from the surrounding environment....

This ambiguity and pseudo consensus around output measurement encourages the institutionalization and ossification of teaching procedures. If it cannot really be determined whether one course of action leads to more output than another, then why stop lecturing?....

2. *Input variability.* Another, possibly unique, property of educational organizations is a very wide variation in input from the environment, particularly in relation to participants and personnel. The range of intellectual ability, interpersonal skill, and knowledge of subject matter among teachers is probably at least as great as that among pupils. This variability causes considerable stress in educational organizations and develops the need to

provide teaching personnel with methods and procedures which are (in effect) teacherproof.

3. *Role performance invisibility*. Classrooms are in effect the production departments of the educational enterprise; in them trainers work. Yet, this role performance is relatively invisible to status equals or superiors. Learners can observe, usually very acutely, the quality of a teacher's execution of his role, but they are not allowed to comment on this, and have few, if any, sanctions to bring to bear. Thus, rewards in the teaching profession seem relatively detached from others' estimates of one's performance; the average teacher gains most satisfaction from intrinsic properties of the role behavior involved. Teaching thus becomes a craft-like occupation rather than a profession, and substitute criteria for teaching effectiveness, such as 'interest of the kids', begin to appear and are used vigorously. Perhaps this is what teachers mean when they say it is not difficult to know when they are doing a good job.

4. *Low interdependence*. A further characteristic of educational organizations, when compared with thing-producing systems, seems to be a relatively low interdependence of parts. Teacher A's failure to teach anything to the participants affects the job-relevant behavior of Teacher B very little—except in a rather diffuse, blaming sense.

This low interdependence has several consequences. First, it tends to reinforce the pyramidal 'man-to-man' style of supervision which Likert and others have shown to be inimical to organizational effectiveness.

The reported stresses and strains in most accounts of team teaching—an attempt to increase interdependence in educational organizations—are mute testimony to the strength with which 'separatist' norms have become institutionalized....

5. *Vulnerability*. Educational institutions are subject to control, criticism, and a wide variety of 'legitimate' demands from the surrounding environment: everyone is a stockholder. To the system inhabitants, the organizational skill seems extremely thin. Many kinds of ingenious defenses are adopted to solve this problem. This state of affairs represents a serious failure of adaptation skills of organizations and tends to reduce autonomy sharply.

6. *Lay-professional control problems*. Many educational institutions are governed by laymen. Even where the board is 'well-trained' and leaves the execution of policy to the administration, notice that the question of educational policy determination still remains a moot one.

And there are internal lay-professional problems as well. In many respects, the administrator may find himself far behind the capabilities of particular trainers (in terms of expert knowledge), and he is in this sense a layman as well. The problems of organizations with high proportions of professionals have been studied vigorously (for example, hospitals and research organizations); I only wish to indicate here that the fruits of such study so far have found little application in educational institutions.

7. *Low technological investment.* Lastly, it seems very clear that the amount of technology per worker in institutions is relatively low. From 60 to 90 per cent of an educational institution's budget ordinarily goes to salary, with a fraction for equipment and materials.... This has consequences: social transactions, rather than sociotechnical transactions, come to be the major mode of organizational production. Because of this, it is possible that education has never made it out of the folk culture stage. And we are back once again to goal ambiguity and its problems.

... in terms of the (ten) dimensions above, the major difficulties to be expected...center around goal focus (as a consequence of goal ambiguity); difficulties in communication adequacy and power equalization stemming from low interdependence, and perhaps most centrally, failures in innovativeness, autonomy, adaptation and problem-solving adequacy, because of vulnerability and lay-professional conflict.

Reading 6.2

Linking the Training System into the Operating System

ROLF P. LYNTON*

For systems in turbulent environments the design, development and operation of linkage mechanisms of appropriate complexity is costly. Decision makers will seek to avoid this investment. Even if they assess the environmental needs correctly, they are inclined to underestimate the response that would be effective and the costs involved in the response. Misjudgment of these costs is frequent among innovators who start their own organizations.

That the development of effective linkage mechanisms is associated with major changes in the system as a whole seems borne out by studies of organizations in a wide variety of settings. From a study of ten cases of organizational development in various settings, Buchanan (1967) established a list of 33 issues arising in each. The one issue that distinguished the seven most successful organizations conspicuously from the three unsuccessful ones was the linkage between the innovative subsystem and the rest of the system. 'In two of the three unsuccessful cases, changes were initiated and progress was being made, only to come to a halt because of action by management.... Steps taken to accomplish linkage were not effective' (Buchanan

* From Rolf P. Lynton, *Administrative Science Quarterly*, 1969, Vol. 14, pp 398–416. Reprinted with permission.

1967: 62). In the successful cases, linkage between people at several levels of the system was established either as part of the change-induction plan or by steps taken early in the program. The linkage was in the form of working in small teams on operating problems or in the form of involving members in large numbers and at several levels during the early stages of identifying the linkage task (Buchanan 1967: 62). The successful organizations differed in the model they used for innovating, in the manner in which the model was introduced into the system, the location of the innovative subsystem in the system, and the time at which various levels of decision makers were involved. They were similar, on the other hand, in the following five aspects (Buchanan 1967: 64):

1. They differentiated the innovative subsystem sharply and formally.
2. In the models they used they found a basis for establishing goals for improvement.
3. The models focused on problem-solving processes.
4. The models led to changes in the kind, distribution and amount of power.
5. The models emphasized norms and skills that facilitated collaboration and problem solving rather than negotiation and bargaining.

It seems that as long as the model in its initial conception allows for these five dimensions, the system can develop the appropriate mechanisms for its singular circumstances and needs. In fact, working out its own distinctively appropriate pattern seems to be essential to effectiveness. The freedom to make changes, and the constraint in using this freedom, seem to stem from two sources. One is the shifting technological and informational needs of the system and the ways in which these can be met, given the resources of the system and the particular environment with which it interacts. The other source is the emotions of the people actually involved in the changes, which the linkage mechanisms are to mediate. Uncertainties from both sources have to be reflected in the openness of linkage mechanisms to further change, that is, their flexibility.

The emotional uncertainties seem the more complex. Sofer (1961) analyzed the emotional demands on linkage mechanisms that occurred in three very different organizations. He found that 'the organization undertakes an emotional division of labor in attitudes towards innovators in just the same way it distributes any other organizational task' (Sofer 1961: 159). Some members will be for the new venture, others against it. 'The relationship (of the innovative subsystem) with colleagues will be uneasy. There occur outbreaks of reciprocal paranoia as well as euphoria.' When people in the innovative subsystem get discouraged and uncertain about whether they can perform the innovative task, they tend to withdraw and to create barriers rather than linkages. Sofer noted some of the mechanisms by which innovators tend to drain off internal tension. They called attention to the limitations under which decision makers expected them to succeed, their 'rigidity,' 'short-sightedness,' 'intolerance' and 'conservatism,' their unwillingness to collaborate, their wish to see the innovation fail. 'All parties will precipitate test cases. These test cases are variously used by all concerned to illustrate those aspects of the total situation that are most favorable to their rationale of the moment' (Sofer 1961: 160). Sofer traced the system of defense by which people in the innovative subsystems sought to protect themselves and to explain their reluctance to devise, use, and strengthen linkage mechanisms (1961: 160–62). The strains in the rest of the system and the ways people express them then tend in turn to isolate the new subsystem further (Burns and Stalker 1961: 171).

In studies of innovation in educational systems, Miles (1964) described how this progressive deterioration of linkage mechanisms made the innovators' fears come true. Support for the innovative subsystem withered, recruitment into it became more difficult, reports of innovative achievements came to lack credibility. Soon the subsystem faced problems of sheer survival (Miles 1964: 654). Under these circumstances intergroup conflict and hostility are very likely to occur, and opposing coalitions develop, with each group magnifying its virtues and the opponents' faults. Such conflict often produced high solidarity *within* the groups. The innovative subsystem, being usually the less powerful, tends to develop substitute satisfactions, like fantasies that some day the others will learn to appreciate them.

Two general conclusions follow. One is that linkage mechanisms need to be flexible and also strong to withstand such strains and such uncertainties. This usually means that they need to be differentiated clearly, be known to have the support of the system's decision makers, and remain highly functional over time. Chin developed the concept of 'intersystem' to describe the linkage mechanisms between two subsystems. 'The intersystem model exaggerates the virtues of autonomy and the limited nature of interdependence of the interactions between the two connected systems' (Bennis *et al.* 1964: 201–14). The intersystem allows linkage to be rooted in another system, and to offer those 'marginal' people who do the linking a base from which to operate and in which to gain and regain perspective and strength.

The second conclusion is simply a forceful reminder that coordination is a heavy cost. This cost may be profitably incurred if, (1) a primary task is clearly differentiated that requires organizational differentiation and, (2) if the new subsystem is maximally autonomous, so that its connections with other subsystems are minimal. In short, the only justification for linkage mechanisms is strict functional interdependence (Kahn *et al.* 1964: 394; Quinn and Mueller 1963: 51). Even if these criteria are rigidly applied, the number of systems that need to design and operate linkage mechanisms will surely increase as more and more decision makers come to recognize the turbulence of the environment.

Reading 6.3

Common Issues in Developing and Managing System Linkages

ROLF P. LYNTON AND JOHN M. THOMAS*

Beyond its use for overview and planning, the classification of linkages has practical values for the detailed designing, management, and evaluation of linkages. It facilitates checking existing linkages for appropriateness to purpose and for mutuality; both are required for effectiveness and stability of each linkage. Beyond this, if linkages are mapped and examined jointly, they reveal unattended or neglected relationships and other aspects of patterns important for institutional policy and planning. Such maps provide valuable data for decisions on institutional leadership, notably governance, internal structure, resource allocation, and operations.

Exhibit 6.4 shows a typical linkage map of a university population centre, with the non-members abstracted into categories (by the centre director).

In the UPP project, comparisons of linkage networks for different purposes typically revealed imbalances of three kinds, each likely to have serious consequences on institutional development if left unattended:

1. Functional Imbalance

Irrespective of the overall density of linkage networks,

a. Functional linkages and enabling linkages for resources predominated.

b. Enabling linkages for legitimization existed in all university programmes but they were few and used very unevenly over time. They were used most at the beginning of the programme, then atrophied within a year; in years 3–4 and 6–7, when crises characteristically occurred in the programmes, they were increased in number and strength and used actively, usually under pressure from the university at large.

c. Normative and diffuse linkages were virtually absent. This particular pattern of imbalance in linkages portends low legitimization and outside support to protect the institution against attack and to support continued innovation. Yet protection was especially important during the early critical

---

* From Dharni P. Sinha (ed.), *Consultants and Consulting Styles* (New Delhi: Vision Books, 1992), pp 91–97.

period in the existence of new and highly experimental programmes of this type, before they were strong enough to deal with their environments on their own terms.

The kinds of questions a consultant using this model could turn the attentions of policy-makers and programme directors to are:

How much support does the population programme have from the top echelon of the university and will this support be permanent? Are there resources to match the new goals, for how long and on what conditions? Since the programme is field-oriented, what support does it have from public agencies and through what mechanisms will this support be maintained?

2. Overload and Conflict

Mapping existing linkages according to their functions also showed strong tendencies to make a few linkages serve many purposes, leading both to overload and conflict. Reliance on a few linkages in itself increased the tendencies of programmes to close themselves off from the rest of the university and from publics outside. For instance, the enabling linkages which some programmes had with a government agency frequently imperilled the quality of their functional relationships with other units of the university. Similarly, diffuse external support for programmes through extensive coverage in public media tended to weaken their legitimization within the university and their ability to mobilize faculty and departmental resources.

To the contrary, multiplicity and separability of linkages seemed to be a valuable principle. A multiplicity of linkages provided safety: a programme did not have all its eggs in one basket. This was extra important for the many programmes which were developing in unpredictably turbulent conditions in the university, at the national level and with respect to international funding.

Separability means that in certain identifiable instances it was important that one linkage should not perform more than one function. In the several cases in which a programme was linked to a single organization for enabling, functional, normative and diffuse purposes, problems and conflicts seemed continuous. Moreover, the conflicts tended to be displaced and to remain unresolved. Enabling organizations and agencies were not *ipso facto* appropriate for functional linkages.

3. Locational Imbalance

Since the university population programmes were field-directed and interdisciplinary, they depended on effective linkages within the university and also with public and private agencies outside the university. Asked which of the nine linkage relationships they found most difficult, all programmes ranked first either the university departments or the national government agencies. Two points of conclusion can be made here. First, the two essential kinds of partners were in conflict and the population programme was caught in the middle; and, second, the middle position was so difficult to maintain that programmes drew closer to either one and experienced difficulty with the other.

This imbalance was touched off most frequetly when programmes engaged in project work and project funding. Several programmes existed wholly on funds from clients for specific items of work, others to a large part. Some programmes had become heavily dependent on one or at the most two major clients, notably, the Planning Council or the Ministry of Health in their country. Others, in an attempt to escape this dependency, had multiplied their work contracts, but at the cost of having to sort out competition between them for faculty time and facilities. Either direction limited the programme's autonomy and hamstrung it in its relations with the university. This particular issue was greatly simplified for programmes which had at least some basic university funds and or programme development funds from elsewhere. For one thing, these programmes were freer to choose the agencies they wanted to relate with outside the university. They commonly chose agencies with missions and styles of working close to their own and in several cases had been able to influence those missions so that the area of congruence was enlarged.

Irrespective of the mode of funding, programmes which had developed their main supports for expansion outside the university invariably experienced serious difficulties within their universities. Funds being available, university administrators had allowed this to occur without anticipating the consequent isolation of the programme inside the university. Some did expect this but were unable to stand against political pressure. Among these programmes were several which, because they looked so productive and enjoyed outside support, attracted foreign funds in large amounts.

The consequences of increasing isolation inside their universities were very similar for strongly outward-oriented programmes. Responding to outside pressures, these programmes decided to expand quickly, but could do so only by employing their own staffs and individuals from various disciplines as needed either on full-time or through other contractual arrangements. They then tended to relate minimally with other units in the university. When two or three years later programmes tried to secure permanent positions in the university for their staff they ran into severe difficulties; and this in turn affected their ability to attract and hold senior staff. Programmes which were largely or wholly dependent on outside funds had additional difficulties trying to balance their work programmes between responding to the needs of outside agencies and carrying out projects by programme faculty. For them, matching goals and activities with funds was therefore a most intricate and also a highly important issue. Mismatches occurred quickly and had long lasting results.

Strong linkage mechanisms inside and outside the university of a 'pooled' pattern[1] were one of three essential safeguards against this. As the field-orientation of a programme made it attractive to public agencies and outside funds, this needed to be counter-balanced by strengthening programme linkages inside the university. The second and third features which effective programmes had in common were a strong explicit and well-publicized programme doctrine and a diversified leadership with notable strength in designing and managing linkages.

Esman defines institutional doctrine as 'the specifications of values, objectives and operational methods underlying social action... a series of themes which project, both within the organization itself and in its external environment, a set of images and expectations of institutional goods and styles of action. Among the sub-variables... are specifically, relationship to (or duration from) existing roles, and relationship to (emerging) societal preferences and priorities.'[2] Prominent in the doctrines of effective programmes in the UPP project were specific statements about the disciplinary composition of the programme, its goals and priorities within and outside the university, joint decision mechanisms (notably for the allocation of funds), and frequent and full reporting of activities to established university bodies. Academic bases for population studies were defined, and the doctrines also specified mechanisms and procedures for settling differences and for securing university wide approval for proposed changes of certain types. Their 'relationship to (emerging) societal preferences and priorities' was characterized by directly involving policy and implementing agencies in discussions and decisions concerning the development of programme activities. Programme activities were seen as 'doctrine translated into action'.[3]

The institution building perspective also highlights certain critical issues associated with the leadership of organization change which can guide consultant planning and intervention. Three leadership issues were prominent in the programmes in the UPP.

1. Significant conflict was generated between the need for leadership to be oriented both to internal policy formation and structure and to the

---

[1] J.D. Thompson, *Organizations in Action* (New York: McGraw-Hill, 1967).

[2] M.J. Esman, "The Institution Building Concepts—An Interim Appraisal" (Pittsburgh: Research Programme in Institution Building, 1967).

[3] H.L. Bumgardner *et al.*, *A Guide to Institutional Building for Team Leaders of Technical Assistance Projects* (Office of International Programmes, North Carolina State University, 1971).

management of external linkages in the institution building typology. The UPP study showed that these two orientations demanded different leadership styles:

> As regards personal style, inside directors tend to be more used to working directly with a few colleagues in well defined roles and with elementary administrative procedures, than indirectly with the larger number which broad programmes bring together. Most try to hang on to their direct individual style in the larger setting and this increases the work load even more. Moreover, this style does not produce the more complex linkages and organizational and administrative decisions on which larger programmes depend.[4]

2. A second issue arose from the need to manage simultaneously organizational or programme 'doctrine', specific programme activities and the co-ordination of structure. Most programmes had difficulty developing leadership which had competence in all three and in integrating them.

3. Providing separately for programme governance and for other aspects of institutional leadership seemed a useful differentiation. This finding reinforces the early, seminal statement of Selznick.[5] In UPP programmes with effective leadership, the structure of governance was derived specifically from the pattern of enabling and normative linkages required by the organization. For example, in inter-disciplinary programmes participating disciplines were included in governance, while in field-oriented programmes agencies in the environment with which a programme collaborated in major lines of activity also participated in the governance of the programme. The UPP study demonstrated that the first key decision taken by the initiators of effective programmes was, in fact, who was to be included in governance.[6] This inclusion decision depended not only on programme boundaries and on linkages with the environment, but was defined by programme doctrine. In turn, a clear, well-communicated doctrine, which reflected the commitment of those included in the governance of the programme, protected the autonomy of the programme.

---

[4] R.P. Lynton, *Institution Building for University Population Programmes: A Short Guide for Policy-Makers* (Chapel Hill: Carolina Population Centre, 1974), pp 73–74.

[5] P. Selznick, *Leadership in Administration* (New York: Harper and Row, 1957).

[6] R.P. Lynton, *Institution Building* (note 4 above).

Reading 6.4

Building a New Institution: Practical Issues

RAVI J. MATTHAI*

A fly sat on the axle wheel of a chariot, and said, 'What a dust do I raise'.

Francis Bacon

This note emphasises problems that arose from the beliefs, attitudes, and behavior patterns which influence the Institute's growth.

Beliefs

For many years the Institute was, perhaps, underorganized. It was believed that the first and most important task was to build a tradition of attitudes. The structure of the Institute was subservient and secondary to this. Whatever organizational system was introduced, it was thought that the community's attitudes would determine whether or not it functioned successfully. The Institute's structure, as a facilitating mechanism, was, in the early years, just enough for the accomplishment of primary tasks. There was a conscious avoidance of seemingly neat but rigid forms. As a result, many aspects of the Institute's operations were relatively unstructured, sometimes to a point of discomfort. But it was hoped that the structures would be created from the development of attitudes, which structures could, as they emerged, be engineered appropriately to form a coherent whole. Such structures that emerged from the community would, it was believed, tend to be self-regulating. With this belief in mind, even detailed integrated planning was sacrificed until, it was felt, attitudes would sustain the creative use of this process.

It was assumed that the Institute's growth depended on the competence, creativity, and initiative of the faculty. Competence would be largely determined through faculty selection and development. If people with a creative potential were selected, it was assumed that they would best express themselves in conditions of free expression, minimum restrictions, and adequate facilities. Initiative, it was thought, would be shown if there was a strong enough motivation, if what came to be called 'academic entrepreneurship' was encouraged and recognized, and if the faculty, as individuals and as a group, developed sufficient confidence in themselves to expose their creations to the world. The faculty's confidence would develop if they were

* From Ravi Matthai, Udai Pareek and T.V. Rao (eds), *Institution Building in Education and Research* (New Delhi: All India Management Association, 1977), pp 69–87.

trusted and confidence was shown in their integrity and work. It would also be affected by the market's acceptance of, demand, and respect for faculty and their output. While on the one hand it was thought that the faculty would build the institution, on the other it was also felt that if, even at the earliest stages, the Institute could gain a fair measure of market acceptance, this would reinforce the confidence of faculty in themselves. The circumstances should be created in which faculty, even if they had not 'made their names', could gain access to the market by virtue of their being members of the IIMA faculty. A community that lacked confidence might build for 'defence' rather than 'attack'. This emphasised the urgency with which it was thought necessary to develop strong boundary relations and the role of Director as the 'gate-keeper' was to transmit to the market his own sense of confidence in faculty capabilities, confidence in the group and in individuals. The messages so transmitted must be in terms of 'us' not 'me' and in terms of the Institute's faculty, not 'my' faculty. This was considered important since the Director's role was to build the Institute and not himself and since it was assumed that the development of faculty confidence would, in the long term, be weakened by an over-personalised institution and by the existence or appearance of faculty dependence on an individual. In some senses, this might be considered presumptuous on the part of the Director, but there were examples in India to serve as warnings of the long-term damage that resulted from such over-personalisation. This, therefore, was one of the dominant considerations in the evolution of the Institute's working environment.

Individuality and the Group

'Creativity' posed a problem. The Institute was concerned with the application of knowledge in the resolution of problems. This implied a considerable emphasis on multi-disciplinary work and hence an emphasis on working in groups. However, it was thought that creativity was primarily an individual characteristic and that group work would only evolve after individuals had progressed towards finding their work identity and had gained sufficient confidence in themselves to trust their peers. In the early years of the Institute, therefore, there was a strong emphasis on faculty individuality. For the faculty, this meant a considerable degree of independence from formal authority in making choices.

If, however, at the same time, the faculty were to develop confidence in building the Institute, in taking initiative to develop new activities and in managing the activities of the Institute, these individuals had to work in operational groups which would be capable of making decisions regarding the activities for which they were responsible. Each activity had a faculty committee with a faculty member as chairman. But in order to create the circumstances in which individuality and free expression would not be circumscribed, the chairmen were given the responsibility for the activity without *de jure* hierarchical authority. The chairman could not dictate decisions to his committee. He had to win over his committee. He could not in any sense give orders to faculty members involved in the activity for which he was responsible. Again, he had to win them over. His responsibility was given by the Director but authority stemmed from his acceptance by his peers.

The problem, therefore, was how, operationally, to reconcile individual creativity with effective group functioning.

The Freedoms

In these circumstances, the vague and much abused notion of 'academic freedom' was introduced. It was viewed as freedom of the faculty to express their opinions without fear of reprisal, freedom to initiate academic activities within the broad objectives of the Institute, freedom of the individual to plan his work to his satisfaction, freedom to innovate according to his creative thinking, freedom of movement to achieve his academic goals, freedom from external pressure, and freedom from the pressure of excessive authority. These are vague phrases, but the attempt was made to translate them into reality.

Freedom of expression in academic work was not a problem. The integrity of the faculty expressed itself in relation to problems discussed in the classroom or analyzed through research. Occasionally an embarrassing situation would arise as a result of faculty severely criticising some part of the Institute's client system. But it was taken for granted that this sort of situation was bound to arise if this freedom were to mean anything. The Director's role was then to reconcile the client system to such free expression on the grounds that the Institute's strength and usefulness would be in the competence and integrity of its faculty. This was vital since a great part of the Institute's strength would come from its equal acceptance by different parts of the client system, e.g., industry, government, and trade unions, whose goals frequently diverged. Freedom of academic expression was therefore consciously linked with building the Institute's image of impartiality. Within the Institute this emphasized faculty integrity, but the faculty's own concern with the client system and their sense of fair play often tempered these expressions with tact and understanding. In the early years, until an adequate level of self-confidence was built, the Director saw his role in terms of partly insulating the internal community from what he believed to be external pressures which were inimical to the Institute's goals and the culture he wished to see develop, whether these pressures were parochial, political, financial or of various vested interests.

However, the more difficult problems arose in relation to meaningful and constructive freedom of expression within the Institute community. This was particularly so in the early years when norms of behavior had not yet evolved into any recognizable form. There were four directions, amongst others, which this expression took—freedom of expression in relation to the constituted authorities (Society, Board of Governors, and the Director), in relation to the organization for academic administration, the non-faculty groups in the community, and in the personal relationships amongst the faculty themselves.

Background

It should be borne in mind that it was in the early years that these problems occurred. The faculty was composed of people with industrial experience, experience in government, with a purely academic experience up to and beyond the Ph.D. level and a very few that combined such backgrounds. An important element that gave cohesiveness to the early faculty was that the first fifteen or so faculty were sent, in small groups, to the International Teachers Programme at the Harvard Business School. The idea was to give them a common learning experience, a common living experience, and a common cultural experience away from the pressures of their place of work....

This strategy in terms of its objective was most successful but the 'follow through' required that this cohesiveness be used to develop an indigenous culture which would typify IIMA. The full-time Director who joined IIMA in August 1965 wondered whether this would create too strong and specific a focus of foreign acculturation and thought that, given the base that had been created, a greater degree of diversity was then desirable. From 1967 the use of the IIP on this basis was discontinued.

In deciding the policy on faculty recruitment from 1966, it was felt that recruitment from academic institutions in India should be minimized. Such local recruitment would merely redistribute existing talent within the country and would not add to the pool of talent available in India. The drive was, therefore, to bring back to India people who were working abroad, either completing their Ph.Ds. or, having done so, were teaching and researching in foreign universities. Many of the faculty so recruited were educated in the basic disciplines...and had had no opportunity to test their interest in 'application'. The motivation and reference groups of these sections of the faculty varied, as did their desire and need to come to grips with the realities of organizational problems....

The faculty development policy aimed at sending existing faculty or potential faculty chosen from the non-faculty research staff of IIMA, the graduating student body of the Institute or from the open market, to Ph.D. programmes in universities in the USA. In some cases, faculty with work experience were sent to the HBS MBA programme and this was the only MBA programme used.

When the effect of these recruitment and development policies began to be felt, a greater diversity in approach, in disciplines, pedagogical preferences, research capabilities, and temperament was injected into the campus community and at the same time faculty saw further avenues for self-development opening.

The faculty was young. The average age would have been in the early thirties. Though, by 1965, all academic activities were being administered by IIMA's own faculty, they were, at the time, as new to these roles as the Director was to his.

Faculty housing was being built on the Institute's 65-acre campus and from 1966 an increasing proportion of faculty moved on to the campus.

Faculty and Institution Building

In the context of such circumstances as existed at the time, it was hoped that the motivation to be creative and to take initiative would be influenced by the faculty feeling that they were in fact playing a part in building the Institute and were simultaneously building themselves, rather than merely carrying out a job which was given to them as paid employees of the Institute.

However, a faculty member's professional satisfaction is derived from his academic output and the recognition of his competence by his students, peers, reference groups, and the Institute. It is understandable, therefore, that he would resist accepting an administrative burden.... Nevertheless, the intention was to get as many faculty as possible involved in academic administration. At the same time, with the encouragement of individuality and free expression, it was thought necessary to convey to the faculty that accepting such administrative positions should be of their own volition and that it was clearly possible for them to reject the Director's request, which they sometimes did, without any fear of recrimination or repercussions. Even those who agreed to undertake these tasks frequently suggested that full-time administrators should be used to take over these positions or, at any rate, the administrative aspects. These suggestions were invariably rejected by the Director in the belief that this involvement of the faculty was vital to the development of faculty attitudes towards institutional tasks. At the most, some administrative assistance was provided. The problem therefore was how to achieve this essential faculty participation in institution building without using the direct force of authority.

The problem of involving faculty in academic administration was made more difficult by faculty concern about the importance given to administrative work in faculty evaluation. Once again, the Director's assurance in faculty meetings that institution building at that stage of the Institute's development was as important as the other academic activities raised three questions asked by the faculty—as to whether this should be so, whether in fact administration was being over-emphasized. Individually also, some faculty members asked the Director for reassurance that their administrative work if well done would be recognized at the time of their evaluation. 'What guarantee is there that I will benefit from those administrative chores?' In the reward and punishment system, the attempt was made to ensure that good academic administration was recognized on par with academic work. However, this in turn caused some resentment on the part of those who disagreed with the policy of equating administrative and academic work....

Administration, Rules, and the Use of Judgement

.... Authority derived from rules might tend to treat them as ends and not means. It was also believed that a creative faculty would be most productive if the emphasis was on their motivation to work rather than on controlling them with rules and regulations. The outcome was that in the early years, except for the rules laid down by the Government of India common to all national educational institutions...few rules were set down in writing. The attitude towards rules, particularly terms of service, was that they were constraints imposed to ensure a basic commonality amongst the national institutes which was considered necessary by the government. The pressure however to adopt more government rules than this unavoidable minimum was resisted. However, the Institute was slow to set down alternative rules of its own. Co-ordination was sought through group discussions in, for example, activity committees and areas. Policy guidelines for faculty activity were laid down by committees but restrictive rules were kept to a minimum. It was hoped that norms of behavior would evolve from such discussions and cooperative management of activities by which faculty would impose upon themselves the behavioral restraint necessary for the accomplishment of institutional tasks.

In this sense, it was also thought that decision-making, particularly in the earliest stages of institutional growth, should not be governed by precedents. The attitude was one of being apprehensive about perpetuating errors of decision-making at a stage when they were bound to occur. This attitude could be expressed in the statement: 'Learn from your errors; don't institutionalize them'. Where the rules, such as they were, hampered the accomplishment of academic tasks, they were broken with little compunction. Such deviations from the rules could only be sanctioned by the Director and this meant that a considerable degree of detail ended up on the Director's table. It also meant that judgement was to be used frequently and that the use of judgement was not to be overwhelmed by the comforting protection of the bureaucratic application of rules.

The three criteria used in the exercise of judgement by the Director were simple. In question form they were:

How important is the related task? Is the deviation necessary for the accomplishment of the task and is it justified? (Sometimes, given the situation at that point of time, the deviation was necessary but might not have been justified due to, for example, a lack of planning. The deviation might have been sanctioned but the reservation would be conveyed to the faculty member.)

Given this attitude, the occasional misuse of such a permissive system did not result in the multiplication of rules, but in the stricter use of judgement in relation to the individual concerned. The aim was to establish relationships of trust and the assumed prerequisite was faculty self-discipline rather than the imposed discipline of authority and regulation. Control was kept as light as possible and exercised primarily through the overall evaluation of an individual and an activity rather than through the minute regulation of each part.

The fact that such a nebulous system functioned is itself a tribute to the integrity, maturity, and motivation of the faculty.

Such a system, however, again focused aggression on the Director since, in the final analysis, it was his judgement that was questioned by those dissatisfied with a decision. These circumstances gave rise to many problems but fortunately none of them were of such a magnitude as to endanger the system. It was not uncommon that such use of judgement was regarded as not being 'objective', and this was perhaps reinforced by the fact that the Director did not explain publicly the apparent discrepancies between individual cases.

The freedom to express aggression against authority was primarily used in three contexts—the corridors, faculty and committee meetings, and in the Director's office. 'Corridor' expressions were heard but not acted upon directly. However, the Director took very seriously expressions at committee meetings or at personal meetings in his office. In an attempt to be 'open-minded', decisions already made by the Director were occasionally reversed by him. However, it was not uncommon for the assertion to be made in the corridors, after an aggressive meeting on personal issues in the Director's office, that if you were aggressive enough with the Director he would 'back down'. Whether or not this was the case, whether aggression paid off or whether there was a genuine desire to be fair-minded, the norm of privacy in relation to such personal issues ensured that the Director could never make a counter-assertion. Perhaps, therefore, encouragement of aggression against authority could be said to have been built into the system. The lack of rules, however, was also found to be uncomfortable. Faculty members wanted to know 'where they stood'. They wanted to know more specifically how to allocate their time between academic activities and how to plan their work such that their plans would be acceptable to the Institute. They wished to know more explicitly their 'rights and obligations', what was permissible and what was not. The suggestion that faculty discuss their doubts with the Director, which they did frequently, was not adequate and not as comfortable as having a written document on which to rely. At a faculty meeting specifically convened to discuss the Institute's academic climate, the view was commonly expressed that there was 'too much freedom', and that there was need to document institutional guidelines and rules. Eventually, in 1971, a note on faculty evaluation was circulated to the faculty.

Individuality and Behavioral Styles in Academic Administration

In these circumstances that led to a somewhat aggressive individuality, the working of academic administrative committees often posed problems. Appointments to all academic administrative positions were made by the Director. The alternative of elections, which was occasionally suggested by faculty, was turned down by the faculty themselves. The Director also opposed the use of 'political democratic' mechanisms in an educational institution.

The norm was suggested, but…did not always work, that committee decisions should be the outcome of discussing the substantive merits of points of view and resolving them in terms of what was best from the Institute's point of view, rather than forcing an issue by a vote. In the early stages, it was common that rigid points of view were held. An impasse was frequently created and the issue was then referred to the Director. Sometimes this was the result of the attitude of a committee member and sometimes of the committee chairman's style of operation. Styles varied widely, from the wholly passive to the overwhelmingly aggressive. Neither extreme worked successfully. The quality of decisions in the former case was often doubtful and the latter extreme, more often that not, resulted in interpersonal crises that necessitated the Director's intervention. Some thought that management required efficiency, and efficiency required speed of decision-making—the frequent analogy of an industrial myth. The chairman was as capable as any member of asserting his point of view, perhaps more so because of his responsibility. Sometimes a different view was regarded as a personal attack and at other times impatience was expressed with the inefficient meanderings of a group of individualistic prima donnas. The emphasis is on 'sometimes'. These situations were a minority and most often committee behavior was remarkably constructive and patient. Initially when such situations occurred, the Director intervened, but later, at the risk of appearing to 'duck' the decision, he forced the issues back to the committee. This had two diverse effects. With smaller committees consensus decisions became the rule and references to the Director for intervention became extremely rare. With large committees consisting of a majority of the faculty, the committees more frequently resorted to voting. But over the years, as the community became more used to the system, the chairmen and members of groups became increasingly sophisticated in dealing with situations that arose from statements which began with phrases such as 'As a matter of principle...' or 'If I may be frank...' or 'With due respect to my colleagues...' which were often a prelude to the introduction of that faculty member's hidden agenda...

Behavioral Styles and Faculty Initiative

The importance of faculty taking the initiative to start new activities and to innovate with regard to existing ones was frequently discussed at meetings and individually with the Director. Generally the ideas put forward were taken seriously and efforts were made to implement them. Whether the idea started with the Director or a faculty member, if a faculty member was interested in it and accepted the responsibility for its implementation, the initiative was left squarely with him. He had the freedom to design the activity, choose his colleagues, establish the necessary boundary relations, and raise resources. It was the deliberate intention of the Director that he should take a back seat and that the faculty member should get the credit and the 'visibility'. Whenever the Director was asked to help in persuading other faculty to participate, or in establishing contacts outside, or in raising resources, he endeavored to play this supportive role but tried to ensure that the faculty member maintained the lead. This, again, placed a heavier burden on the faculty member than if the Director had assumed a greater part of the initiative. It was felt that the concentration of action with the Director would on the one hand inevitably slow down the rate of growth of activities and diminish their effectiveness and, on the other hand, would dampen the initiative of the faculty.

Numerous problems arose. In some cases there was resentment against this burden being placed on faculty shoulders...more serious problems arose when attempts were made to start long-term on-going activities at the Institute in which the faculty members who took the initiative and responsibility showed even the slightest hesitation in regarding their colleagues as peers. Faculty support and participation, vital for long-term institution building activities, were soon lost if the self-assertive leadership style was combined with a possessiveness expressed in references to 'my activity', 'my project', 'my faculty', 'my clients', 'faculty assisting me'.

Planning

A conspicuous gap in the operations of the Institute was the overall planning function. This might be evident from the circumstances described so far.

The two-year post-graduate programme and executive development programmes were planned in advance of the year to which the plan was relevant. Medium- or long-term plans were not made. Research was planned by individuals or by specific project groups.... Consulting, by the nature of the activity, was not planned. Planning across activities was therefore done at two levels. The individual faculty member planned for an academic year in relation to all the activities in which he wished to work or had agreed to get involved. The Director planned the whole Institute for the following year and for five years. These plans, however, were intended, firstly, as a basis for obtaining grants from the government, and, secondly, to serve as his targets for the range and size of academic activities and for faculty, staff, and facility requirements. Such integration of individual plans was done by the Director, but this was inadequate. There was no mechanism for integrated planning between the individual faculty and the Director. The reasons for not acting upon the various suggestions made to appoint a Joint Director or Dean of Planning were: first, that it was felt that in the early stages of the Institute's development there should be no intervening mechanisms between the individual faculty member in terms of his total work and the Director, which mechanism or position could be viewed as a buffer; secondly, that a detailed integrative planning process might inhibit faculty initiative at a time when it was thought to be essential. For this reason, the target-setting five-year plan drawn up by the Director was not communicated to the faculty. Thirdly, it was felt that such planning mechanisms, if they were to be used imaginatively as stimulants and not curbs, should be expressly needed by those whose work was to be planned at a stage of growth when the institution was viable enough in its size and range of activities and in the maturity of attitudes to consider 'consolidation' as an alternative to continued rapid growth.

This need was expressed by the 1971–72 Re-organization Committee and accepted by the faculty. More formal and systematic planning and the organization for it were introduced in late 1972. Unsuccessful attempts were made in the early years to plan research, but today the planning of research is becoming a reality. The Institute continues to grow but in a planned and integrated manner. This process itself, with a mature and confident faculty, will give to academic administrators a surer authority to accomplish their tasks through the clearer acceptance of the process and their roles by their peers.

Reading 6.5

Continuous Improvement Network: The Concept

DAVID H. KIEL

Developing powerful systems to create and harvest good ideas for organizational improvement has been a gift of the total quality management (TQM) movement to organizational life. We may be witnessing the development of a new generation of continuous improvement efforts which focus on a network of organizations rather than a single system.

In benchmarking, a single organization specifies an area for improvement, identifies several organizations that have solved the problem under consideration (so-called 'best of class' operations), studies them systematically, and imports solution elements back into its own system. In a Continuous Improvement Network (CIN), the network of multiple organizations specifies multiple areas for improvement, makes a systematic study of solutions, including experimentation in selected areas, and makes the results readily available to other members of the network for importation into their own organizations.

The composition of a CIN can vary widely. In the United States it could be the 26 plants of one chemical company, the personnel units of a large federal agency, the 400 or so legal services programs of the health departments of 50 states, or it could be some members of a nationwide trade association, or an association of international relief organizations.

The criteria most basic for forming a CIN are the willingness of member organizations to commit time and resources to the enterprise and a degree of similarity enough to permit useful exchange and collaboration. A given CIN may focus on a subset of organizational performance: e.g., marketing, environmental quality management, compensation systems, etc. To be effective, CIN's which are made up of whole organizations will operate a variety of functionally focused networks.

Probably the most successful CIN's will be made up of similar organizations, geographically dispersed, which are non-competitive or cooperative in their function. Such networks would have the most problems in common, will have likely developed differently (which assures variation in their approach to problem-solving), and, being non-competitive, have few barriers to the exchange of information.

CIN: The Value Added

The CIN is an inter-organizational social process methodology. It builds on, and partakes of, some of the positive features of the quality movement. One such feature is a highly organized approach to problem identification and problem-solving. The problem-solving approaches of the quality movement pre-dated Demming and Juran (i.e., force field analysis, brain storming, problem-maps, and statistical process control techniques). However, TQM practitioners organized them into a powerful formal system of problem analysis, supported by simple, yet forceful ideology (e.g., 'The 14 points') and created an organizational superstructure to support the system, (e.g., quality councils, facilitators, quality newsletters, quality societies, etc.). If TQM approaches had not been formalized, universalized, and institutionalized within organizations, the quality movement would not have been able to demonstrate such tangible benefits. The formalization, universalization, and institutionalization of problem-solving approaches has transformed the cultures of the most successful TQM organizations.

The FUTURE MAP is the collective view of the network future based an environmental scan of members which defines the most critical issues and potential responses for the next 3–5 years. More sophisticated CIN's will use a Delphi technique and/or scenario approaches. The FUTURE MAP will contain scenarios composed by members to address critical issues and a variety of scenarios.

The METRICS is a set of carefully crafted agreements for defining and measuring performance in areas identified as priority so CIN members can be confident they are making meaningful comparisons and truly measuring best-in-class performance.

The PROBLEM MAP is an analysis of the typical system member using a variety of analytical tools derived from TQM and other approaches. The purpose of the PROBLEM MAP is to identify and display the most critical interfaces affecting desired system outcomes and indicate where interventions are required for improvement. In a social services CIN, typical problem areas might include client in-take, board training, MIS systems, etc. In an environmental quality CIN, the focus might be on identifying and classifying environmental concerns, maintaining employee involvement, techniques for calculating pay back time for green investments, and the like.

The SOLUTION MAP will show where, in the network of member organizations, units have developed approaches to deal with specific problems identified in the PROBLEM MAP. Most typically these will be situations in which a given plant or agency has undertaken a quality or reengineering program to improve results at that interface (e.g., handling of customer orders, reduction of waste, improving of shipments, decrease in time to perform certain medical or legal procedures, etc.).

The SOLUTION MAP will be a visual representation of the system with numbered and labeled interfaces. These labels will be the references for the story boards of individual improvement projects contributed by the member units to the DATA BASE. Individual quality teams working on an issue will be able to access the story boards of multiple quality teams across the network that have addressed a given issue.

The AGENDA is an evolving document which identifies the most critical unaddressed or emergent problems and opportunities of the member systems in the network.

The PLAN describes how the above agenda's priorities will be addressed. It will identify those units which are undertaking projects to address priority issues, specify contact individuals, and show time tables for completion of specific projects. It will establish interim communications between groups working on similar problems and, to the extent the network itself generates resources, it will allocate those resources to units charged to address most critical problems on behalf of the total network via challenge grants.

The REPORTS will be standard story boards of projects undertaken by individual units, augmented by integrating analyses and comments made by committees who are coordinating the work of several problem-solving groups across units. The reports will be entered into an on-line DATA BASE accessible to network members. REPORTS will also be available on the current results of PROBLEM MAP and FUTURE MAP analyses. REPORTS as a way of transmitting information will be supplemented by site visits, videos, voice mail, and other communication approaches.

The most sophisticated CIN's will codify social process knowledge as well, e.g., failures and successes in implementing improvements. Probably a special report called LESSONS will be required to capture this knowledge and make it accessible to recall and on-going use.

The DATA BASE will contain a record of all the documents that make up the various MAPS, PLANS, and AGENDAS and will be available on-line to network members. The DATA BASE will be continually updated via REPORTS, according to protocols established by the CIN.

At the annual or biannual meeting of CIN representatives the MAPS, the AGENDA and PLAN will be updated, and Network business conducted.

Starting up and Maintaining the CIN

The CIN would be formed in a species of large system meeting, like a Future Search. A series of structured exercises would guide the group in development of the PROBLEM MAP, FUTURE MAP, SOLUTION MAP, AGENDA, and PLAN in that order. The business meeting would identify the tasks to be performed between the meetings of the network and the officers to perform those tasks. The documents generated at the CIN meeting would be distributed to all members of the network.

Like any quality program, the CIN would require an organizational structure, resources to keep going, and on-going training and facilitation. A CIN would need a network administrator responsible for the business of the network and a network coordinating committee which could make program and policy decisions. The coordinating committee would serve in between the network meetings and would probably be an elected body. The network would have by-laws which would define members' rights and responsibilities. The by-laws would control access to the network and establish governance procedures. Just as quality groups have trained facilitators to work with problem-solving teams, the network would require facilitators to manage the sessions at its regular meetings for developing the MAPS, METRICS, the AGENDA, and the PLAN. The network would evolve norms and guidelines for information sharing and visitation within the network. Some CIN's could become non-profit corporations; some could become for-profit corporations.

Applications of the CIN

Professional and trade associations are well positioned to establish functioning CIN's. They already have annual meetings to which representatives of like organizations come. Their purposes include some similar to those of the CIN: to share information, to address common problems, to improve their member organizations. They already perform some of the functions of a CIN: holding workshops on new approaches, discussing future problems, etc. For a large trade association, maintaining one or several CIN's could be a value added service which would disseminate innovations and improvements rapidly throughout association members. For a CIN to be successful, the members of the association would probably need to represent organizations that were not competitive in nature.

Because of their non-competing nature and jurisdictional limitation, governmental units could make wide use of the CIN methodology. A CIN would seem a natural approach within a nation of 50 states. A CIN could be established among any of the bureaucratic divisions of the 50 US state governments, e.g., health departments, revenue services, environmental regulators, commerce departments, corrections departments, etc. Within a state, county level or municipal jurisdictions would seem prime candidates for CIN activity.

Within the non-profit sector, foundations and donor organizations might be likely candidates to develop a CIN, because of their cooperative nature. The CIN could exist among the donor organizations themselves, or among networks of organizations funded by the donors, in order to maximize the benefits from their investments.

Within the for-profit organization, the most likely application of CIN technology is among the units of a large organization with dispersed similar units. Franchise operations of all kinds would seem to be likely beneficiaries of the approach. Networks of utilities and also manufacturing organizations with large numbers of similar plants could benefit. Middle-size organizations with highly differentiated plant structures may not benefit as much because their units may not experience common problems. A for-profit-hospital chain may be a likely beneficiary of the approach. A CIN could serve to intensify and enhance quality programs within national and multi-national organizations by creating a corporate data base to which all quality teams would have access.

Conclusion: The CIN as a Dynamic Force for Organizational Innovation and Renewal

The CIN builds on existing technologies and approaches to formalize shared problem-solving activities of collegial inter-organizational networks. In so doing, it aims at making a quantum leap in the power and effectiveness of that problem-solving activity, even as TQM has dramatically changed the way organizations go about solving problems and making improvements. If CIN's are successful in the private sector, then membership in a CIN will be a crucial aspect of any organization's competitive ability just the way having an effective TQM program is a pre-requisite for successfully doing business in many markets today. In the public sector, CIN's could be engines for innovations in programs and policies across a wide range of problems and activities.

7

Ensuring High Benefits and Continuing Support

The First Cut: Confirming that the Training Itself is Lined Up with the Intent for It

The Second Cut: Attending to Change Patterns over Time

The Third Cut: Ensuring High Impact Organization-wide and in the Larger System

Using Follow-up Data to Revise Training Goals and Policies and to Ensure Continuing Good Fit

Six Generalizations/Maxims from Experience

Making Sure that Training is Worth its Costs

Exhibits
7.1 Impact Outcomes of Program for Management Trainers and Their Indicators

Boxes
7.1 Training Systems Checklist
7.2 Training Objectives Versus Organizational Disposition

Readings
7.1 Utilization-focused Evaluation
7.2 Distractions and Distortions
7.3 Characteristic Impasses and Ways to Manage

... how order emerges at 'the edge of chaos'... is now one of the lodestar concepts in the theory of complex adaptive systems...the boundary between chaos and order is the most fruitful place for complex systems to emerge.

—Thomas Bass

For policy-makers and change managers, the pay-off of any training comes with its contribution to the organization-wide and larger system-wide change strategies that they wanted it for in the first place. Questions of what and how much participants learned in their program, never mind in a particular training session, are for trainers and the training system to assess, and to draw guidance from for future programs.[1] Here we are concerned with what the returning participants can now do that contributes to moving the change strategy forward. This also means combining their enhanced capacities with the many other components that go into making that strategy work and having it all work well together over time. Where training itself fell short of its particular objectives, policy-makers and change managers will also push for improvement in training, no less and no more than they are responsible for ensuring that every other component in the mix contributes its part and that the parts get fitted together to best advantage.

For review now by policy-makers and managers, and modification where indicated, are factors ranging from the original selection of candidates for training and their flow, to the timely arrival of the new equipment they are to work on, the readiness of others to make up the team(s), the updated financial and administrative procedures the teams are to use, and the preparedness of the rest of the organization for the change in general and this next phase in particular. The whole range of factors separately and together is for the board and higher management to review and use to maintain direction and cohesion of effort. And they also assure cost effectiveness—of training just as of the other components of the system-in-change.

This focus, on assessing actual outcomes and on hard-headed decisions to take, is difficult to maintain, and the complex and rapidly changing conditions that prevail in many places make maintaining it steadily more difficult still. So it is tempting to confine attention to training itself, just this one component which is also so much simpler and softer than any other, rather than on all the intricate whole of the many parts. Training becomes an easy target to blame any shortfalls on and to urge to do better, or else. Two of the readings at the end of this chapter recount some of the commonest distortions and distractions at policy-level to avoid and some better ways to manage. And, for a start, Box 7.1 offers a nine-item checklist to help organizations monitor how they are linking training to business results.

---

[1] Evaluating training from the perspective of trainers and their system we deal with in Volume 2 (Chapter 10).

Box 7.1

TRAINING SYSTEMS CHECKLIST

Companies wishing to do a 'reality check' on their training systems should consider a number of questions to ensure that they are linking training with business results:

Is your training linked to your strategic decisions and business goals?
Is it supported by strong leadership?
Does it reflect the needs and values of your company's customers?
Does it communicate your company's values?
Does it help you address customer retention, acquisition, lower costs, less waste, higher speed, and greater innovation?
Does it build on the five core principles of learning?
Is it immediately relevant to your business? Can you clearly map an individual's path toward mastery?
Does the environment empower employees to leverage what they learn?
Does it lead to measurable results?

Conclusion

In a global marketplace where people are often the key to competitive differentiation, the implications for training are clear successes. Today's competitive environment requires a new level of mastery in the skills that directly support business objectives. Our findings show that when the design and implementation of training incorporates the five core principles of learning, it allows people to grow continuously and remain flexible to change. Just as important, effective learning depends on a combination of organizational and individual readiness. Management should actively reinforce and facilitate new learning processes on the job. To learn effectively means that organisational support is not merely present in the training process but is an integral part of the training process.

SOURCE: Forum Issues Special Report prepared and written by Joan L. Bragan, Ed.D, and Jerry A. Johnson, Ph.D., Vice President and Senior Consultant at The Forum Corporation. Every effort has been made to trace the copyright holder(s). In the absence of a reply, permission has been assumed.

For keeping attention in this chapter steadily and practically on policy-making and managing, we will draw repeatedly and in some detail on recent major work in two settings. One is our own work since the 1980s with using training and building indigenous capacity for decentralizing decision-making in Indonesia's nation-wide health services. The other is from current work in nineteen local areas (*thanas*) in Bangladesh which uses management training to make the official family planning program more effective.[2]

---

[2] This is a collaboration between the Government of Bangladesh and the University of North Carolina in Chapel Hill. We have been kindly given access to an early

THE FIRST CUT: CONFIRMING THAT THE TRAINING ITSELF IS LINED UP WITH THE IINTENT FOR IT

The first step, of making sure that the training did what it was set up to do with the participants who took it, is fairly straight forward—the important thing is not to mistake early individual successes for improved performance that will surely last or that these are organizationally significant. Fresh, improved performance of individuals soon after training is simply welcome confirmation that their training was in the intended direction and did set participants up to make a difference. The essential rest remains to be seen, depending as it does on other factors of support for improved performance and making it the new norm.

New and improved technical competencies of individuals show up readily at the workstation. For monitoring less easily visible and countable changes in competencies, we like eliciting incidents from superiors, peers, and subordinates (or, in a family setting, wife or husband, children, neighbors) which show, concretely and in real life situations, how a newly trained person actually handles a situation or two more effectively following training.

Impact evaluation, though, raises such sensitive issues that training systems and work organizations prefer trading impressions and opinions about impact—a very indirect and erratic guide—in preference to collecting hard data about actual performances. This preference for soft data cannot be attributed to excessive methodological difficulties. More likely, the two partners quietly collude because impact is the sum of training plus organizational preparedness and support, and so raises touchy questions about both the system and the organization as well as their collaboration. So the partners reinforce each other's reluctance. In fact, the impact on individual performance, immediate work group, and units can be measured quite economically if a major change strategy is in focus; so also can the impact organization-wide. Measures can also be developed for an organization's growing capacity for further development in the future.

The National Institute for Inservice Training (Pusdiklat) of Indonesia's Ministry of Health had seven objectives for impact evaluation four months

working report on it by Sagar C. Jain, A. Barkat, Kristen Lundeen, A.J. Faisal, Tofayel Ahmed and Sirajul Isal, *Improving Family Program through Management Training: The 3C Paradigm*, 1998.

after its second Advanced Program for Management Trainers (APMT). While that program's impact on current work performance was in central focus, the evaluation scheme referred back to the first program, to future advanced programs, and also to developing future systems capacities for consultation. The objectives were:

1. To have a second round of impact evaluation of APMT-I to assess both stability and snowballing of the changes (benefits) and their synergistic contribution to the benefits from APMT-II.
2. To assess the impact of APMT-II on individuals, systems, and their interlinkages.
3. To assess benefits from the two-week International Mid-Career Program for Developing Individual, Team and Organizational Competencies (Phase 1 of APMT).
4. To assess the impact of APMTs on (a) individuals, (b) organizations, and (c) training strategies and systems as well as major factors contributing to variations in the impact.
5. To assess the impact of APMTs on the effectiveness of building internal consultation resources in the health system.
6. To make suggestions for better utilization of graduates of APMT.
7. To make suggestions for planning the strategy and design of APMT-III.

Creative approaches to the choice of measures and processes for collecting data can make impact evaluation both sound and economical. Indicative sets of impact data can be extracted from routine records, such as production, inspection, and cost figures, and the costs of collecting primary data kept low by judicious sampling of data for indicators that are not usually collected, e.g., process indicators. Exhibit 7.1 shows the impact outcomes and the simple indicators used for evaluating the Advanced Program in Indonesia.

Critical incident methodologies can play an important part in impact evaluation, especially to highlight the range and qualities of change. Each incident describes an actual situation—task, territory, technologies, time; lists the people involved—the participants returned from training and also others involved in the situation; details actions and events in which the participants played a focal role; and assesses consequences. Written, or recorded live in discussion, incidents can be collected from sets of colleagues of the participants at the same, higher, and lower levels in the organization and analyzed to show impact on the planned development(s) for which training was to be used.

Exhibit 7.1
IMPACT OUTCOMES OF PROGRAM FOR MANAGEMENT TRAINERS AND
THEIR INDICATORS

Outcomes	*Indicators*
A. Individual participants only in Phase I:	
1. Personal and interpersonal effectiveness	Initiative taken
	Consideration shown
B. Individual participants in full APMTs:	
1. Personal and interpersonal effectiveness	Initiative taken
	Consideration and help
2. Professional competencies	Training designs
	Training methods used
3. System competencies	More teamwork
C. Organizations sending participants:	
1. Higher credibility of the training function	Competent persons nominated
2. Greater acceptance of APMT alumni	More consultation with them
3. Greater interest in competence development	New training program
4. Greater demand for APMT alumni from outside	Requests received
5. More innovation in training	Analysis of curricula
6. Greater recognition and use of training center	Training center data on programs
7. Stronger training team	Reconstitution of teams
8. Development of training system	Current systems
9. Greater organization-wide learning	Use of experiences
D. The Center (Pusdiklat)	
1. Higher involvement in project activities	More meetings on project issues
2. More open communication	Mutual consultation
3. Increased participation in project inputs	More participation
4. Stronger linkages with provinces	More visits for consultation
5. Establishment of resource network	Intern network
6. Multiplication of gains across provinces or/diffusion function	Inter-province
7. Greater problem-solving actions	More task groups
8. Higher credibility of Pusdiklat in the provinces	More demand by provinces

SOURCE: Pusdiklat, Ministry of Health, Government of Indonesia, 1986.

For example, analysis of critical incidents collected from participants of the second Advanced Program for Management of Trainers in Indonesia, from their superiors, and from their colleagues, indicated signific—
impact on participant interpersonal com—

sensitivity, emotional control, and self-confidence) and also on professional competencies (initiative, collaboration, innovation, and responsibility). Analysis of the same critical incidents also showed impact on four major organizational dimensions: stronger teamwork, higher mutual support, onward team development, and demonstrated initiative. Simple content analysis of critical incidents can also be used to indicate training impact. Grouping such data according to work teams, departments, the organization, and the larger system as a whole can yield information about impact on those systems.

THE SECOND CUT: ATTENDING TO CHANGE PATTERNS OVER TIME

What happens in the following weeks and months to the improved performance of trained people provides early confirmation and alerts one about the organizational aspects of change. Here are four common patterns and some pointers for each of the factors worth high-level attention.

1. If performance stays in the expected range or better and keeps improving with further practice, this means the program was sound, that both participants and their organizations were ready to use the training, and that participants learned enough during training to keep on improving their performance.
2. If performances tend to decline, this means participants and their organizations found the training less useful than expected, or that participants did not have sufficient training during the program and/or support on the job to carry on successfully. But wait, and continue watching, for:
3. If the results show a sharp drop at first and then a rise, this shows that the transfer from training to action was unexpectedly difficult, but that participants and their organizations have overcome the difficulties and are making headway.
4. If the results show a sharp drop and stay down, this means the organizations and/or the participants were not prepared to make the change on the job or that the training objectives were not realistic.

Such results are clearly important to policy-makers as a guide to further action. In most cases, detailed study will be required before strategic difficulties can be located and their strengths assessed. For ‑‑‑nce results (2) and (3) suggest linkage problems in the transiti‑‑

from training to work situations or that training went ahead discon-
nected from progress with other aspects of the change strategy; e.g.,
the expected new equipment or procedures were delayed or altered,
key supporters of change were frustrated and moved away, or the
organizational climate, expected to become supportive meanwhile,
stayed indifferent or even became hostile instead.

THE THIRD CUT: ENSURING HIGH IMPACT ORGANIZATION-WIDE AND IN THE LARGER SYSTEM

In the Bangladesh project of achieving significantly higher results in
the official family planning program through management training
of officers in charge of it in *thanas*, follow-up policies aimed comprehensively 'to monitor progress, to facilitate progress, and to…
strengthen morale'. First-hand acquaintance with these officers had
established that though they occupied a—and maybe *the*—strategic
position in the program, their education and traditional deference to
their medical colleagues kept their effectiveness and morale low.

This is how the Report described them and their state before
training:

1. Despite Bangladesh's success in reducing its fertility in the face of
   abject poverty, pervasive illiteracy and low status of women, there was
   a deeprooted belief that without rapid and significant improvement in
   the socio-economic conditions of people, the fertility cannot be brought
   down without coercion… it was believed that lacking effective authority to hold their subordinates accountable and to obtain needed
   inputs, the thana officers could not do very much to improve the performance of their programs.
2. The TFPOs were mostly educated in social sciences or humanities;
   their formal training in population dynamics and/or management
   tended to be of short duration, fractured and largely didactic and/or
   procedural in nature. Neither they nor their peers and superiors perceived them as having significant management know how. But their
   political skills (exhibited through their trade union actions and similar
   other behaviors) were well recognized.
3. Although gazetted/tenured first class officers of the Government of
   Bangladesh and having an effective trade union of their own, these
   officers tended to be highly prone to status anxiety, especially in relation to Thana Health and Family Planning Officers (who were physicians belonging to the Directorate of Health; TFPOs belonged to the

Directorate of Family Planning) and often in relation to the much younger thana MO-MCH (physicians who also belonged to the Directorate of Family Planning).

4. Those who had had experience in having the TFPOs as trainees, described them as intelligent and politically savvy but generally passive, apathetic, unruly, undisciplined and/or hostile in the classroom.

The training strategy and dominant pedagogical methods had addressed these conditions explicitly and with notable success, and now very broad but also intensive follow-up policies were put in place to sustain the improvements to the maximum.

(Using) ample evidence that new learning tends to steady and significant wash-off starts soon after the trainees return to their jobs (and that) this wash-off takes an accute form when the trainees experience significant operational difficulties in using their new learnings and/or the organizational climate is hostile toward the use of the new learning. This concern led to three important decisions, none of which featured in the initial agreement for mounting the training. These were:

1. Since sustainability of learning requires its continual use over a period of time, it was decided that each trainee will prepare and implement a detailed plan to achieve significant improvement in their programs within a specific period. Further, the trainees will apply all the methods and techniques taught to them in the preparation and implementation of their plans. To give muscle to this decision, it was further decided that these plans would be formally approved by the Government of Bangladesh as the official plans of the participating thanas.

2. To ensure that the trainees do not give up their plans when faced with operational and/or systemic difficulties, a supervised follow-up program was added.

3. To bring prima facie legitimacy and to communicate seriousness of purpose, it was decided that the improvement in the thana programs, reported by the trainees will be formally verified by an independent external organization through detailed field study.

Then, specifically for follow-up, the collaborating agencies instituted four mechanisms.

1. Each trainee submitted a monthly report which consisted of three parts: a daily diary of activities; a summary report on a prescribed form regarding planned activities for the month, specially their status and problems faced/resolved/not resolved; and a copy of the government prescribed MIS form sent each month to the Family Planning Directorate.

2. A follow-up committee consisting of the following was appointed by the Secretary, Health and Population, Government of Bangladesh, to oversee their follow-up:

- Director (Administration), Directorate of Family Planning (Chair)
- Project Director, MIS, Directorate of Family Planning
- Bangladesh Representative, AVSC International
- A representative of USAID, Dhaka
- Director, Training Program
- UNC Training Coordinator in Dhaka

The committee was backed up by a senior staff of the AVSC International as well as the UNC Training Coordinator. They received and acknowledged the reports, prepared summary statements after reviewing the reports, and distributed these to all members of the committee. These summaries focussed on the problems faced by the trainees and their attempts to solve them. (During the training a lot of emphasis was placed on solving their own problems and not relying on their superiors for everything.)

The committee met more or less monthly to review the progress of the trainees and to take appropriate facilitating actions. These actions were limited to those which did not require allotment of additional resources or giving preferential treatment. By and large, the committee tried to improve the flow of supplies and funds by recommending actions by appropriate officials. However, these recommendations were not always effective and were often lost in the bureaucratic shuffle despite direct involvement of Director (Administration) who chaired the Committee and the follow-up by the AVSC/UNC staff. But the important thing was that the trainees knew their work was being watched by their superior officers and other stakeholders. This element of the follow-up was most potent.

3. The third element was site visits by the members of the Follow-up Committee as well as other senior officials of the government and USAID. It was thought that these visits would not only boost the morale of the trainees, but would also generate insight into the modus operandi of the trainees.

4. The last mechanism was the Mid-Term Review Conference. After six months into the follow-up, all trainees together with one official from each thana who played a key role in the implementation of their action plans were invited for a day-long conference in Dhaka to share their progress and experiences and to develop common solutions to the problems faced.

The conference was well attended, including members of the Follow-up Committee and other senior officials of the government and representatives of the donor organizations... (it) resulted in (e.g.) streamlining the procedures for submitting monthly reports... and receiving feedback from the Follow-up Committee... (about) the action taken by the Committee about his/her concern/problem, clarification of the procedure for ensuring regular flow of... supplies (... trainees need to be more proactive in requisitioning and picking up supplies), ensuring needed clinical training (... be more proactive in nominations as well as developing contacts with the training providers), manpower issues (directly contact the Director, Administration)....

Further, since the efforts of the trainees could not succeed without the support of their thana-level colleagues, it was decided to recognize (by an award of a formal certificate) one thana official from each thana who provided the most support,... to be nominated by each trainee.

An important feature of the conference was the presentation and discussion of the mid-term evaluation study prepared by the MIS Unit (which confirmed) that (1) the baseline as well as the progress reported by the trainees were essentially correct, and (2) given their progress to date, the goals set by the trainees were quite realistic....

This management training project had aimed 'to achieve at least 4 percentage points improvement in the contraceptive prevalence rate (CPR).... In the preparation of their plans, the trainees had set much higher goals, which averaged to 8 points.' With all statistical adjustments made, the increase in the first five months averaged 3.99 points, i.e., 9.6 points annually, if maintained.

USING FOLLOW-UP DATA TO REVISE TRAINING GOALS AND POLICIES AND TO ENSURE CONTINUING GOOD FIT

Occasionally, proper systematic follow-up reveals wide discrepancies between plans and outcomes; fears that it might do so is exactly what leads diverse partners in training to collude to minimize it, each for their own reasons. Starving follow-up of funds is usually easiest; so also is giving it low status and priority or doubting its technical feasibility to tell anything not known already or of practical use in complex situations.

Box 7.2 summarizes the experience in a large US corporation where follow-up did reveal a major misfit, though this major training program had met its immediate objectives well. It was only from the quite conflicting reactions to the newly trained supervisors, that their managers and then policy-makers realized their quite inadequate appreciation of the sharply differing views workers had of the training strategy and design they had agreed and set out on and how the supervisors might also misuse their training. The ommission of so important a constituency—the supervised—in the formulation of training plans and presumably of the change strategy before that warrants most urgent consideration at this point and the determination to rectify this error quickly, to limit further damage and, if possible, reverse the festering and spreading that this follow-up revealed.

Box 7.2

TRAINING OBJECTIVES VERSUS ORGANIZATIONAL DISPOSITION

An evaluation study of a supervisory training program in a large American company shows clearly how a major discrepancy can arise between the objectives of the program and the training needs and possibilities on the job. The objectives of the program were in the general area of improving human relations among the workers and between workers and management. Specific objectives included reducing conflict and promoting greater job satisfaction. By these routes greater efficiency was to be achieved. Foremen were to be the change agents for these improvements. The program was to train them for this function.

Preliminary studies established two clusters of supervisor behavior which could serve to evaluate the training in terms of its objectives. One cluster included kinds of behavior that could be classified as 'considerate' attention to workers as listening to personal problems, helping, and the like. The other consisted of behavior that stressed formal relations, written rules, and keeping to production schedules. The authors formulated these objectives into two operational criteria. One they called 'consideration'; the opposite they called 'initiating structure'. Factorially sound and highly reliable instruments were developed for measuring leadership attitudes and behavior in terms of consideration and initiating structure.

From these instruments, applied before and after residential training, clearly favorable training results were established. The foremen showed significant decreases in initiating structure and corresponding increases in considerate attitudes. But when the same instruments were used again later, after the foremen had returned to work, they revealed the opposite result: trained foremen tended to be lower in consideration and higher in initiating structure than did the untrained foremen. A check with workers under these foremen confirmed these results. Clearly the effects of this human relations program were not stable.

The general interpretation of these results was that the program succeeded in making the foremen more considerate but that it at the same time separated them sharply from the workers. The foremen themselves became more aware of belonging to the management. Singled out for special training in a program

Box 7.2 contd...

that was obviously expensive, they concluded that they had definitely crossed over to the other side. Certainly the workers saw this as the main meaning of the supervisory training program. The result was that the more considerate attitudes that showed up in the immediate posttraining questionnaire were off-set by the foremen's tendency back at work to assume more determined leadership roles. The discrepancy between these two evaluations at the end of the program and later on the job illustrates well the danger of relying only on the first when the acid test of effective training is the second.

The authors then correlated the 'contradictory' results with the 'climate' set up by the foremen's superiors. The correlation was direct: trained foremen who continued to show more 'considerate' attitudes on the job were those whose superiors were 'considerate'. The others dropped the considerate attitudes they had gained in the training program in order to conform with superiors who were strong in initiating structure. The implication of this for a more effective training strategy would be to provide training for the foremen's superiors and perhaps for *their* superiors also.

The authors also took a second look at the training needs of different jobs in order to establish whether more considerate attitudes in fact produced greater efficiency. This reexamination led to a useful distinction. In production divisions where meeting time schedules and production targets produced great stress, foremen with the highest proficiency ratings showed more initiation of structure. In the service divisions, on the other hand, where these stresses were not so prominent, the higher proficiency ratings went with more consideration. This finding suggested differentiating between training objectives for foremen in production and service departments and changing the criteria for selecting participants.

The results have wider implications. They call for formulation separately of long-range and short-range objectives of training. The relative importance of work satisfaction, freedom from conflict, speedy technological change and immediate efficiency need to be decided in the work organization. 'Perhaps immediate efficiency', the authors conclude, 'may not be so important as a long-time balance between efficiency and morale.'

Source: Summarized from Edwin A. Fleishman, Edwin F. Harris, and Harold E. Burtt, *Leadership and Supervision in Industry* (Columbus, Ohio: The Ohio State University, 1955).

More commonly, where basically sound training policies are in place and strategies under way, follow-up results are best used for identifying particular aspects that need adjusting in the light of experience or need experimenting with more till the results are better.

Back to square one is quite commonly where follow-up results should lead: the *reconceptualization of the change and the priorities* for it (perhaps in the light of turbulent conditions); the *composition of stakeholder groups* to discuss and agree on change goals, strategies, and training plans; and, very often, to taking another look at the *future tasks* for which training is to prepare people, and also the *capacities of the organization* and the larger system for changing, soon and again and again.

Faulty *task analyses* at the beginning are often at the bottom of difficulties that persist long after, less often on technical grounds and more often because, conceived too narrowly, they excluded essential context—social and organizational context most likely. Technical changes are usually well tracked and accommodated without question, but not so changes in the roles and relationships essential to performance on new lines.

Or, *selection* for training ran counter to prevailing custom and training—and its participants lost out. Official agencies commonly suffer this difficulty. Officers are sent for specialized training, only to find on their return that they have been assigned to a different position and perhaps to another agency, place, and sector altogether. Considering government officers to be interchangeable and so able to turn their hands to virtually anything can lead to such frequent moves that no task analysis or training could keep up with their future work, and contextual considerations can only remain general at best.

Follow-up too may fall short of plans. In the Bangladesh project site visits by members of the Follow-up Committee as well as other senior officials of the government and the international funding agencies were instituted. Unfortunately, this element of the follow-up fell far short of the original intent. The primary contributing factors were: a lack of full appreciation of this activity, inability to make time, and inadequate budget. As a result it did not become an organized and regular activity. Very few trainees were visited and the visits did not always generate the desired effect because the visitors were not fully sensitive to the strategy adopted for the training. To make up for the site visits, the Training Director wrote several inspirational letters to the trainees, but they were a poor substitute for face-to-face interaction.

SIX GENERALIZATIONS/MAXIMS FROM EXPERIENCE

For playing their proper part in ameliorating shortfalls, experience strongly suggests six generalizations for policy-makers to use as virtual maxims. First, use hard data of actual performance and its fit with change plans, and make the training system responsible for providing them; its additional contact with operations that collecting follow-up data calls for will itself strengthen that strategic relationship and also serve to check and fine-tune training. The next chapters will consider systematically the role and relationship changes that better training calls for from all partners.

Second, attend to small misfits as well as large ones: mere hints of data may, like tips of icebergs, indicate large, festering problems below the surface, too difficult to express openly. This is commonly the case where relationships are closest, as in families and neighborhoods, and in companies with long traditions of inclusion and exclusion. A constituency left out of initial meetings or not heard there may turn out to have a crucial role in effecting change (as workers on the floor did in the example in Box 7.2 and as clients of service programs, women, and the poor generally do in very many well-intended and otherwise well-designed change efforts). Follow-up offers a second alert to absences or the low voice of strategic partners, and to hesitations and misfits that hide large predicaments and issues waiting for resolution or, at least, proper appreciation.

Third, whether the alert from follow-up is small or large, trace discrepancies to wherever the data lead.

Fourth, surface, publicize and reward the good results that follow-up reveals with at least as much regularity and enthusiasm as remedial action receives for mending shortfalls and preventing future disappointments.

The last two generalizations point to dimensions easily hidden by immediately pressing issues and other ready temptations to act, and to act decisively and quickly. They concern policy-makers most directly and inescapably. So the fifth maxim is to look for and insist on finding in the follow-up clear indications that training is also building up the numbers and organizational capacities the overall, longer-term change plans call for. That check then includes the service personnel (and their supervisors and managers) 'behind' the more readily visible operating personnel (and *their* supervisors and managers), and, encompassing all, the capacity of the training system itself.

And the sixth maxim, a reminder of the policy-makers' proper responsibilities for how the training system works, is to avoid micromanaging affairs there—even the appearance of it. The agreed policies and strategies provide the training system with the guidelines for its performance follow-ups, including performance on budgets;

provide the data for assessing its workings and also with pointers to areas for improvement as well as adjustments in plans and operations needed for meeting changed conditions. The leadership of the training system itself has the responsibility to work out all these; the policy-makers' is to hold it accountable for doing so and to offer and be available to help with that. To maintain and also strengthen the essential innovative function of the training system, policy-makers stand back, and so protect its freedom to work things out in its best way. In line with standing apart from operations there, they also hold the leadership accountable for those operations and make sure of adequate leadership of the system into the future.

MAKING SURE THAT TRAINING IS WORTH ITS COSTS

Training strategies and programs are instituted to yield benefits in excess of costs, that is, bring net benefits to the organization, the larger system, and to general development. However crude and nonspecific the calculation on which a strategy was originally approved and funded, policy-makers and providers of resources expect to be convinced soon after its completion that the training achieved the goals defined, and kept its costs within the limits set for it. Careful housekeeping and accounting of training expenditure are important, and definitely the responsibility of the training system to document. But evaluating the worthwhileness of training involves far more.

Much more difficult to assess are two other sources of cost/benefit consequences which are essentially related to training outcomes but arise outside training *per se*. One of these is the costs of developing the other components for the changes in which the newly trained people are to be used. These other components—technical, managerial, organizational—are usually complex and intricately interrelated, and estimating their costs accurately in advance is very difficult. And even well-calculated training decisions are subject to sudden shifts in general conditions and often invalidated. In the early 1980s, for instance, the sharp escalation in costs of investing in new technologies and expansion led in many countries to drastic revisions in training plans that were not related to the quality of training or its specific costs. Other contextual costs had simply become too high to continue developments at the originally planned speed and scale that training was to serve; many programs were cancelled altogether and the costs already incurred written off. Estimates of these kinds of costs, their reassessment in terms of later eventualities, and revisions in training plans are all in the domain of policy-makers. The collapse of East Asian economies in 1998 led to even more drastic upsets, and to precipitous and often crude budget cuts.

Also hazardous to assess, monitor, and adjust expenditure for which policy-makers are responsible is the rather different dimension of the adequacy of training plans, programs, and performance in the light of longer-term developments, e.g., in technologies, scale and location of services, or in building the basic capacities for undergirding the next strategic steps in development. The computer 'revolution' is a dramatic case in point and it continues to be revolutionary and dramatic with no end in sight. Cost estimates to take account of such large unfoldings as well as keeping pace as best one may with forward looking training strategies and designs can only be very rough and eventual benefits mere conjecture. In past decades, the rapid expansion of training and its rising costs often crowded longer-term needs off-stage, with the result that training systems have again and again been pressured into offering 'crash' programs to catch up with needs only lately recognized. The costs of such programs, far higher than warranted in the normal course of events and often distorting the cost of regular training programs running concurrently, should be debited to policy-making, often myopic, true, but often also truly hazardous. But the training system is usually the scapegoat: its performance 'fell below par'. In projecting future needs, suggesting appropriate strategies to meet them, and evaluating the contributions made by training persons and institutions expert in developing new technologies and visualizing 'futures' might well be valuable contributors. An additional constituency important to include in policy formulation?

Unhappily, discrepancies and misfits between training plans and performance hit hardest where they are also the most difficult to resolve, notably in countries in rapid development where resources are also scarcest and ought to be used to best effect at least cost. Training needs in those countries are especially difficult to define, let alone keep up-to-date and embodied in organizational policies. Well-designed and operational follow-up and revision procedures are then particularly important to help bridge the gaps that surely occur between needs and policies, and between training objectives and training needs.

To bridge a gap of any sort, something has first to exist on the other side. It is the policy-makers' responsibility to see that it does. Instead, we have seen training systems struggling to evolve sufficiently clear training objectives out of inadequately defined needs. Either of two results has invariably followed this confusion of responsibilities. In some cases, where the system persisted with pushing and making do, its strategic relationship with the organization deteriorated fast. By doing this, the system got caught in virtual quicksand: every effort later to put the relationship on a sounder footing sunk training further. Its every move led to accusations that it had usurped the proper functions of others (and higher ups) and kept on overstepping its responsibilities. If it then protested that it had work to do and could not mark time (indefinitely) till policy-makers caught up with responsibilities they had neglected, that touched off infighting and neither improved training nor created more solid bases for it.

In other cases, the training system has taken an early hint and withdrawn from any attempt to evaluate overall training goals and has limited its evaluation instead to meeting the training objectives as stated on paper within the confines of formal programs. The question of their efficacy for the participants' lives and their organizations was left to *them* to pursue or not, as they wished. The usual result of this very understandable reaction is uncertainty and low morale in the training system. They can never be sure that their devoted and diligent efforts have had any value in practice.

For giving the complexities and possible eventualities their due—but no more—and recapturing the elation properly accorded to well-focussed training, the Bangladesh project reviewed role clarity and role performance again through highlighting the actual, practical issues to be worked on and trained for. This showed with fresh clarity that training, when focussed on plausible, practical tasks and issues, can even be a lead factor in improving organizational and system performance, with policy-makers and change managers in their proper roles, and trainers, principals, and administrators of their system in theirs. Top level concern for this issue tends to bring a high degree of seriousness of purpose in role perception. Similarly, a high degree of commitment to deal with the issue tends to produce a high degree of role commitment: and a high degree of competence in handling the issue then tends to create confidence regarding role competency. This almost one-to-one relationship between role-behavior and issue-related behavior indicates that by shifting focus from role to issue we can avoid the minefield of emotionality and still achieve our aim.

Concern, Commitment, and *Competence* (the 3Cs, in short) are interactive in their relationship with each other. A high level of concern tends to breed commitment, and a high level of commitment tends to motivate the person to acquire the needed competence. The reverse is also true. A perception of a high level of competence in oneself tends to encourage the person to come forward to take problems in hand and to act on them. Such interactivity may not be found in all cases and in all situations, because this interactivity is not automatic. For it to take place, a catalytic event is necessary. Sometimes, such events happen on their own, but they can also be generated.

Reading 7.1

Utilization-focused Evaluation

M.Q. PATTON*

Utilization-focused evaluation is not a formal model or recipe for how to conduct evaluative research. Rather, it is an approach, an orientation, and a set of options. The active-reactive-adaptive evaluator chooses from among these options as he or she works with decision-makers and information users throughout the evaluation process. There is no formula guaranteeing success in this approach—indeed, the criteria for success are variable. Utilization means different things to different people in different settings, and is an issue subject to negotiation between evaluators and decision-makers.

The outline that follows pulls together and organizes some of the critical elements and considerations in utilization-focused evaluation. This outline is not meant as a recipe, but only as a brief overview of some of the major points made above.

There are only two fundamental requirements in this approach; everything else is a matter for negotiation, adaptation, selection, and matching. First, relevant decision-makers and information users must be identified and organized—real, visible, specific, and caring human beings, not ephemeral,

*From M.Q. Patton, *Utilization-Focused Evaluation* (Newbury Park: Sage, 1978), pp 284–88.

general, and abstract 'audiences', organizations, or agencies. Second, evaluators must work actively, reactively, and adaptively with these identified decision-makers and information users to make all other decisions about the evaluation—decisions about research focus, design methods, anlaysis, interpretation, and dissemination.

An Outline of the Utilization-focused Approach to Evaluation

I. *Identification and Organization of Relevant Decision-makers and Information Users*

A. Criteria for Identification: The Personal Factor

1. People who can use information.
2. People to whom information makes a difference.
3. People who have questions they want to have answered.
4. People who care about and are willing to share responsibility for the evaluation and its utilization.

B. Criteria for Organization

1. Provision can be made for continuous direct contact between evaluators and decision-makers for information users.
2. The organized group is small enough to be active, hard working, and decision-oriented (my own preference is for a task force of fewer than five, and certainly fewer than ten, people).
3. The members of the group are willing to make a heavy time commitment to the evaluation (the actual amount of time depends on the size of the group, the size and scope of the evaluation, and the members' ability to work together).

II. *The Relevant Evaluation Questions are Identified and Focused*

A. Criteria for Identification of Questions

1. The members of the evaluation task force (i.e., identified and organized decision-makers, information users, and evaluators) agree on the purpose(s) and emphasis of the evaluation. Options include:
   (a) Information for program improvement (formative evaluation);
   (b) Information about continuation of the program (summative evaluation); or
   (c) Both formative and summative evaluations but with emphasis on one or the other (equality of emphasis is not likely in practice when a single evaluation is involved).
2. The members of the task force agree on which components and basic activities of the program will be the subject of the evaluation (the point here is simply to delineate what aspects of the program are to be discussed in detail as specific evaluation questions are focused).

B. Alternative Approaches for Focusing Evaluation Questions
1. The evaluation question can be framed in terms of the program's mission statement, goals and objectives.
    (a) Evaluators must be active-reactive-adaptive in goals clarification exercises, realizing that the appropriateness of generating clear, specific, measurable goals varies depend upon the nature of the organization and the purpose of the evaluation;
    (b) Goals clarification provides direction in determining what information is needed and wanted—goals do not automatically determine the content and focus of the evaluation which depend on what task force members want to know;
    (c) Goals are prioritized using the criterion of information need, not just that of relative importance to program.
2. The evaluation question can be framed in terms of program implementation. Options here include:
    (a) Effort evaluation;
    (b) Process evaluation; and
    (c) The treatment identification approach.
3. The evaluation question can be framed in terms of the program's theory of action.
    (a) A hierarchy of objectives can be constructed to delineate the program's theory of action, wherein attainment of each lower level objective is assumed necessary for attainment of each higher level objective;
    (b) The evaluation might focus on any two or more causal connections in a theory of action;
    (c) The theories or causal linkages tested in the evaluation are those believed relevant by evaluation task force members; and
    (d) The evaluation question links program implementation to program outcomes, i.e., determines the extent to which observed outcomes are attributable to program activities.
4. The evaluation question can be framed in terms of the point in the life of the program when the evaluation takes place. Different questions are relevant at different stages of program development.
5. The evaluation question is framed in the context of the organizational dynamics of the program. Different types of organizations use different types of information and need different types of evaluation. Programs vary in organizational terms along with the following dimensions:
    (a) The degree to which the environment is certain and stable versus uncertain and dynamic;
    (b) The degree to which the program can be characterized as an open or closed system; and

(c) The degree to which a rational goal maximization model, an optimizing systems model or an incremental gains model best describes decision-making processes.

6. The active-reactive-adaptive evaluator works with decision-makers and information users to find the right evaluation question(s). The right question from a utilization point of view has several characteristics:
   (a) It is possible to bring data to bear on the question;
   (b) There is more than one possible answer to the question, i.e., the answer is not predetermined or 'loaded' by the phrasing of the question;
   (c) The identified decision-makers want information to help answer the question;
   (d) The identified decision-makers feel they need information to help them answer the question;
   (e) The identified and organized decision-makers and information users want to answer the question for themselves, not just for someone else;
   (f) The decision-makers can indicate how they would use the answer to the question, i.e., they can specify the relevance of an answer for their program.

7. As the evaluation question is focused, the fundamental, ever-present questions that underlie all other issues are: What difference would it make to have this information? How would the information be used and how would it be useful?

III. Evaluation Methods are Selected that Generate Useful Information for Identified and Organized Decision-makers and Information Users

A. Strengths and weaknesses of alternative methodological paradigms are considered in the search for methods that are appropriate to the nature of the evaluation question. Options include consideration of:
   1. Quantitative and qualitative methods.
   2. Hypothetico-deductive objectivity or subjectivity versus holistic-inductive objectivity or subjectivity.
   3. Distance from, versus closeness to, the data.
   4. Fixed versus dynamic designs.
   5. Relative emphases on reliability or validity.
   6. Holistic or component units of analysis.
   7. Inductive versus deductive procedures.

B. Decision and measurement decisions are shared by evaluators and decision-makers to increase information users' understanding of, belief in, and commitment to evaluation data.
   1. Variables are operationalized in ways that make sense to those who will use the data; face validity, as judged by decision-makers and

information users, is an important instrumentation criterion in evaluation-measurement.

2. Evaluation designs are selected that are credible to decision-makers, information users, and evaluators.

3. Major concepts and units of analysis are defined so as to be relevant to decision-makers and information users; the long-term relevance of definitions and units of analysis are considered to increase the potential for continuous, longitudinal evaluation (where appropriate).

4. Multiple methods are used and multiple measures employed as much as possible to increase the believability of findings.

5. Decision-makers and information users are involved in continuous methods, design, measurement, and basic data gathering decisions as changed circumstances, resources, and timeliness force changes in methods. Recognizing that initial proposals are poor predictors of final designs, active-reactive-adaptive evaluators seek involvement of relevant decision-makers in design and measurement questions as they arise.

6. Decision-makers weigh with evaluators the methodological constraints introduced by limited resources, time deadlines, and data accessibility problems. All task force members must be highly knowledgeable about the strengths and weaknesses of data collection procedures.

7. The utilization assumption guiding methods discussion is that it is better to have an approximate and highly probabilistic answer to the right question than a solid and relatively certain answer to the wrong question.

IV. Decision-makers and Information Users Participate with Evaluators in Data Analysis and Data Interpretation

A. Data analysis is separated from data interpretation so that decision-makers can work with the data without biases introduced by the evaluators' conclusions.

B. Standards of desirability are established before data analysis to guide data interpretation; the nature of the standards of desirability will vary along a continuum from highly crystallized to highly ambiguous.

C. Data analysis is presented in a form that makes sense to decision-makers and information users. Decision-makers are given an opportunity to struggle with the data as they become available, so that surprises are avoided.

D. Evaluators work with decision-makers and information users to make full use of the data.

1. Realizing that 'positive' and 'negative' are perceptual labels, the responsive evaluator avoids characterizing results in such monolithic terms. Most studies include both somewhat positive and somewhat negative

findings, depending upon one's point of view. Analysis and interpretation focus on specific results, relationships, and implications rather than general characterizations of the program.

   2. Both strengths and weaknesses of the data are made clear and explicit.

E. Evaluators work with decision-makers and information users to develop specific plans for action and utilization based upon evaluation findings and interpretation.

   1. Evaluation ultimately necessitates making leaps from data to judgement and from analysis to action.

   2. Utilization-focused data analysis and interpretation includes the judgements, conclusions, and recommendations of both evaluators and decision-makers.

V. *Evaluators and Decision-makers Negotiate and Cooperate in Dissemination Efforts*

A. Dissemination of findings is only one aspect of evaluation utilization, and a minor aspect in many cases. The primary utilization target consists of relevant decision-makers and information users identified and organized during the first step in the evaluation process.

B. Dissemination takes a variety of forms for different audiences and different purposes.

C. Throughout dissemination efforts, both evaluators and decision-makers take responsibility for the evaluation from initial conceptualization to final data analysis and interpretation. Options include:

   1. Both evaluators and decision-makers are present at dissemination presentations; and

   2. Both evaluators and those for whom the evaluation was conducted are identified in all reports and presentations.

Reading 7.2

Distractions and Distortions

ARTURO ISRAEL*

Since the mid-1970s, the increased interest in monitoring and evaluation has pushed managers toward greater concentration on measurable aspects—...effects on management or on operations are unclear, as is the extent to

*From Arturo Israel, *Institutional Development: Incentives to Performance* (Published for The World Bank by The Johns Hopkins University Press, Baltimore, 1987), pp 162–63.

which they have diverted management's attention to inputs to the neglect of basic objectives. A detailed evaluation of monitoring and evaluation systems would probably find they have done little to improve the quality of decision-making by management.... [In] the not uncommon situation, in which managers do not know and are not interested in learning how to use their monitoring and evaluation system or any other management information system available, the systems...generate no benefit. The availability of computers, however, generates a demand for information. Scarce, skilled personnel devote their time to gathering data and writing reports instead of working directly in operations. Data gathering is a bottomless pit which, if unchecked, can absorb an inordinate amount of scarce resources for no useful purpose.... The dilemma is that quantitative techniques are the most direct and obvious method of stimulating, at least partially, the discipline of specificity, but they are not automatically useful, and there is a good chance that they might have a negative effect. The introduction of these techniques should proceed with extreme caution.... Managers should be encouraged to define as early as possible the information that they are most likely to use, and the institution should adapt the choice of techniques to those requirements. Managers or professional staff should periodically review the use... reorientation in their application may well be needed so that the techniques are used to measure effects instead of inputs.

Beyond this initial point, the analysis becomes increasingly complex because a judgement about which techniques to use is contingent on many variables. One is the distinction between programmed and unprogrammed decisions. Programmed decisions, typically, rely on quantitative techniques, but unprogrammed decision-making requires judgements for which only a limited amount of quantitative data is actually useful. How does one give this quantitative input only the proper weight and not more?...in high-specificity activities the relationship between programmed and unprogrammed decisions is like an inverse pyramid, in which the highest proportion of unprogrammed decisions is at the top and the lowest, at the bottom. In people-oriented activities, the shape changes into a rectangle because the proportion of unprogrammed decisions *should* increase at the lower levels.

In low-specificity activities that provide services that are very decentralized, and have low-level staff scattered over wide geographical areas, it is necessary for the management system to include a strong set of internalized norms because of the latitude that field staff have in making day-to-day decisions. Every day, field workers face complex situations with little managerial supervision or control and few mechanisms for communication. The quality of their performance will depend on their having internalized the 'right' values and learned how their discretionary powers should be applied. In this respect, internalized norms are a surrogate for specificity and can ensure an adequate institutional performance. In order for staff to internalize the institutional norms, there need to be standardized rules that have been tailor-made for the activity.

Reading 7.3

Characteristic Impasses and Ways to Manage

PAUL C. NUTT*

Figure 1 illustrates two ways that the evaluation process can be cut short. Sponsors and evaluators who attempt short cuts often exhibit stereotyped behaviour which will be referred to as 'model mania' and 'data mania'. Each creates problems which limit the effectiveness of an evaluation.

Figure 1
SOME TRUNCATED EVALUATION PROCESSES

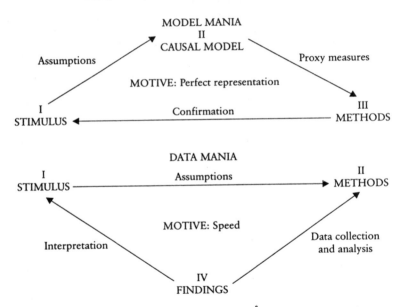

Reprinted with permission from P.C. Nutt, 'On Managed Evaluation Processes', *Technological Forecasting and Social Change*, Vol. 17, No. 4 (1980).

*From Paul C. Nutt, *Evaluation Concepts and Methods: Shaping Policy for the Health Administrator* (Bridgeport: Robert B. Luce).

Model Mania

The ideal evaluation process can be shortened by following an 'assumption-measures-confirmation' path. The motive behind this process is precision in the representation of the evaluation problem provided by the causal model. It is termed model mania because the causal model and the proposed method of evaluation are repeatedly tested against perceived reality.

Model mania occurs when causal models are very difficult to construct or when the model proves to be contentious, raising many controversial questions. For example, a state mental health department with twenty or so custodial institutions sought to develop an evaluation scheme to measure the effectiveness of its institutional administrators. The task of devising a causal model for the process of mental health administration proved to be difficult. Each proposed model provided a unique conception of the administrator's role, which suggested a particular set of measures. Each of the models proved to be unacceptable to particular mental health reference groups. Cost and efficiency measures were criticized by psychiatrists and psychologists who treat patients. Quality care measures were seen as vague and nondiagnostic and thus unacceptable to executives in the state department of mental health. The controversy led to many changes in the model in their attempts to find one that matched the implicit perceptions of the sponsor. In short, model mania led to no appreciable action in assessing the managerial competence in the institutions.

Evaluation that is focused on vague questions like measuring care quality in a hospital, or controversial issues such as negative income tax evaluation, often results in iterative model building where model construction becomes an end in itself.

Data Mania

The evaluation process can also be shortened by following an assumption-data-interpretation path. It is termed data mania because a preference for data supersedes all other considerations. The motive fuelling this process is speed.

Data mania stems from gathering data with little (if any) notion of causality and from ritualistic data accumulations. For instance, the health industry has lamented the lack of data to the point where legislation often mandates certain types of data accumulation. A recent example of data mania is the Health Planning and Resource Development Act of 1975, which requires a careful inventory of all health delivery resources. Apparently, the resource profile is thought to have diagnostic value, helping planning agencies identify deficiencies in patterns of care delivery.

Sponsor and Evaluator Preferences

Figure 2 provides a schematic representation of sponsor and evaluator behavior when conducting an evaluation. The sponsor dominates the left side of the diagram. Administrators, who often become the sponsors of evaluation efforts, are constantly sifting and winnowing potential evaluation problems. When the needs for information exceed some threshold, the sponsor can allocate resources to initiate an evaluation project. The evaluator controls Stage III, methodology, in the same way the sponsor controls Stage I, the stimulus. The sponsor is unlikely to have up-to-date know-how of evaluation methods. Sponsors and evaluators share control over the development of causal models and the findings. The dialogue between evaluators and sponsors in Stage II (model formation) and Stage IV (documentation of results) leads to success or failure for the project.

Figure 2
BEHAVIORALLY BASED EVALUATION PROCESSES

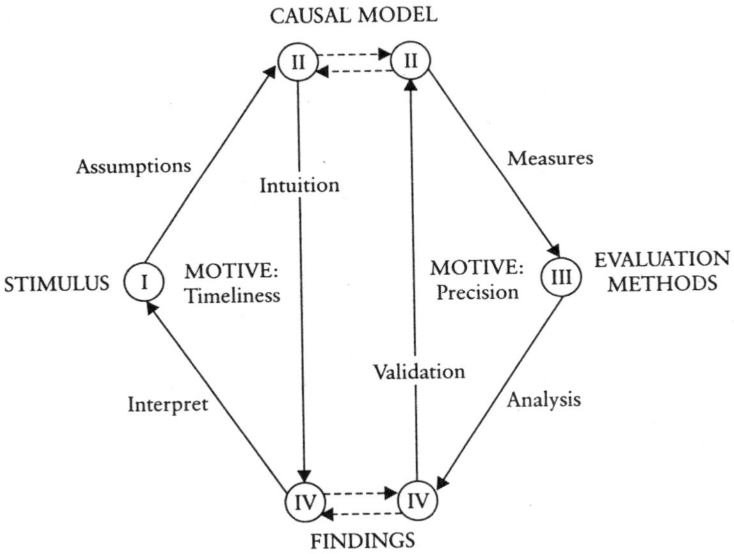

Reprinted with permission from P.C. Nutt, 'On Managed Evaluation Processes', *Technological Forecasting and Social Change*, Vol. 17, No. 4 (1980).

Preferred Paths

The sponsor's preferred path leads to a 'stimulus-model-results' evaluation process, as shown in Figure 2. The sponsor makes assumptions in order to build the causal model and uses the model to visualize ways to overcome problems implicit in the stimulus. Their motive is timeliness; a detailed investigation is perceived to take too long. Churchman points out that managers often believe they should be able to tease out findings without the expense and frustration of formal data collection. The manager examines his causal model, may get the opinions of staff and peers, and then draws conclusions without the aid of tiresome academic fumbling. Administrators rich in experience believe they can draw on this experience to overcome the need for many evaluation projects.

Improving the Evaluation Dialogue

Sponsors and evaluators adopt distinct paths because they have distinct roles and skills. Sponsors must excel in diagnostic skills (deciding when additional evaluation information can materially aid the organization is particularly important). Methodological skills are the forte of the evaluator, so these skills are stressed. Neither skill can supplant the other.

Evaluators attempt to validate, using a model. The results may lack relevance because they were not exposed to the forces motivating the evaluation. Validation does not occur unless the findings are interpreted in terms of the sponsor's needs. Validation using a model leads to stacks of unread consultant and staff reports. Often, relevant and thought-provoking information fails to influence decisions in organizations because its validation lacked field testing and because the information was not carefully interpreted to the sponsor.

Sponsors can rely too often on their intuition. Churchman contends that a strict reliance on intuition leads to dogmatic managers. They become professional skeptics who contend evaluation has little chance of illuminating complex issues, and relativists who believe that a mosaic of obscure contingencies dictate the success of interventions. These and other manifestations of the practical school dominate many policy-level positions in organizations. Unfortunately, many problems are counter-intuitive.

Remedies to these problems lie in the dialogue that occurs in Stages II and IV. To illustrate, the causal model may be developed jointly by the sponsor and evaluator, as shown in Figure 3. Both can educate. The evaluator learns more about the motivations behind the study and the necessity of key assumptions. The evaluator may be able to relax constraints by pointing out how evaluation methods with greater power can be used when certain assumptions are changed. This dialogue aids the evaluator and sponsor to enrich the causal model, trimming out restrictive assumptions and devising measurable program and performance factors.

Sponsor-evaluator dialogue is also essential in explaining the meaning of evaluation findings, also illustrated in Figure 3. Evaluators can aid sponsors by fully exploring the implications of the evaluation information. Reports or presentations should be jointly developed to describe policy guides and to provide the sponsor with an interpretation, a story, or an anecdote that can be used to illustrate key points. The evaluators must help the sponsor understand the limitations of the evaluation's conclusion-drawing power.

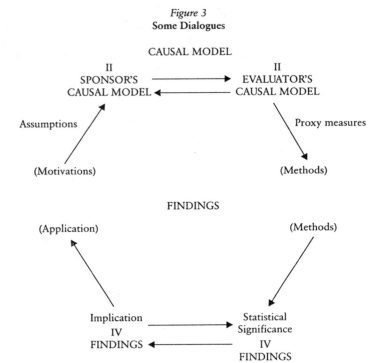

Figure 3
Some Dialogues

CAUSAL MODEL

Reprinted with permission from P.C. Nutt, 'On Managed Evaluation Processes', *Technological Forecasting and Social Change*, Vol. 17, No. 4 (1980).

The sponsor aids the evaluator by reemphasizing the motivation for the study and how the information will be used. Again, this dialogue permits the sponsor to make full and complete use of the evaluation information.

Managing the Evaluation Process
Avoiding Evaluation

The threatening nature of evaluation sets it apart from many other collaborative staff-administrator activities. When an evaluation is conducted, someone may lose, and lose badly, if the results do not support the predictions, programs, or commitments of an organization's power figures. Survival, stability, and growth are goals that often dominate the work world of administrators. Evaluation focuses on past accomplishments and may turn them into deficits. For these reasons, administrators attempting to advance or maintain their power position against the intrusion of competitors often resist evaluation. In other instances, programs become highly entrenched and, as Suchman points out, are based upon a large collection of inadequately tested assumptions and defended by staff and field personnel with strong vested interests in the continuation of the program as it is. Testimonials and assurances of success are periodically demanded from program administrators, forcing the administrator into a total program commitment. Such commitments entice the administrators, and others with vested interests in the programs, to avoid evaluation, fearing its findings.

To avoid evaluation, administrators often engage in rationalization, including the following:

1. *Alleging long range effects*: A prediction is made that the effects of a program will not show up for some time, making longitudinal studies essential. For instance, a major university conducted a pilot test of a suicide prevention program using a computer interview. The preliminary evaluation suggested that the interview was more effective than the psychiatrists. The results were put away for five years, to determine its 'long-term effects'.

2. *Contending important effects resist measurement*: A contention is often made that instruments cannot detect program effects. The program is described as having subtle, general, or small effects that will evade detection by anything but very costly evaluation and that evaluation funds could be better used to deliver program services.... Those attempting quality-of-care studies of nursing are confronted with claims that even unobtrusive measures will [somehow] disturb the patient care process and that 'tender, loving care' is not measurable anyway.

3. *Refusing to withhold services*: Experimental and control groups may be called unreasonable because they withhold services from the needy....

Pseudoevaluation

... When evaluation can no longer be resisted, or when these rationalizations have been dismissed, those with vested interests often engage in pseudoevaluation. Pseudoevaluation is carried out to manage the evaluation process so that a thoughtful assessment of a program is impossible. Some evaluation abuses... are listed below:

1. *Eyewash*: An attempt to justify a weak or bad program by focusing evaluation on these aspects of the program expected to fare well. Referring to Figure 35 the sponsor makes assumptions and suggests causal relations that he suspects (or knows) will provide findings supportive of the program.

2. *Whitewash*: Covering up the prospect of program failure by soliciting testimonials to distract evaluation efforts. The left-hand loop in Figure 2, embracing the assumption-intuition-interpretation activities by sponsors, can be used to whitewash. Accreditation teams for hospitals and academic programs often act on testimonials in the form of reports and presentations which extol their virtues, and not on formal performance measures.... The testimonial is hoped to close the link between assumptions and interpretation.

Whitewash is often successful because requests to evaluate, like the continuing education example, are proforma: a serious attempt at assessment is not expected. In other cases, program failures are covered up by elaborate reasoning stemming from intuitive assessments and by favorable comments in or out of context.

3. *Submarine*: Attempt to eliminate or destroy a good program. Submarining often stems from administrative in-fighting over rights to succession on turf. Again, the left hand side of Figure 1 is used, but in this case negative information is posited or solicited. Objective evaluation is avoided as it may reveal positive program features.... For example, the programs, missions, and guideliners of Regional Medical Programs were altered by administrative edicts so frequently and pervasively that... the Regional Medical Programs were phased out because 'they failed to settle on a mission'.

4. *Posture*: Using evaluation as a gesture to create the aura of scientific objectivity. The sponsor looks good when his/her organization or unit sponsors self-assessment or appears forward-looking when new opportunities are being carefully examined. The sponsor encourages the evaluator to move through all stages (Figure 3) but withholds resources and personal sanction. No results are expected or even desired.... Activities labelled 'fact finding' in public agencies often signal this type of evaluation.

5. *Substitution*: Shifting attention to less relevant, or defensible, aspects of a program to disguise failure. All stages in Figure 3 are covered but the interpretation activity is selective, reporting only positive program features. These tactics are often attempted with varying success.

6. *Delay*: Postponement tactics can be used to thwart evaluation. The scope of the project can be studied at length and then restudied to point out to those pushing for evaluation that a proper study takes time. After repeated failure to build a model, a case can be made that evaluation just isn't worth the effort.... Delay is probably the most common form of pseudoevaluation, and is often signalled by task forces, elaborate agendas, and the sudden emergence of a preference for group decision-making in otherwise autocratic administrators.

7. *Reconstruction*: Attempts can be made to piece together programs in the light of beneficial changes in performance indicators. The causal model is built to reflect the performance data. For instance, a Blue Cross organization mounted a variety of cost containment programs in response to a state's legislative mandates. First, one intervention is attempted and then another, with the last intervention often based on a spin-off of the previous program. If costs begin to show a measurable decline, a frantic search for a causal agent is mounted to reconstruct the program.

8. *Inadvertent programs*: Data found to verify the beneficial effects of inadvertent interventions can be relabelled as planned interventions to enhance the prestige of administrators. A causal relationship is discovered,

following a routine performance audit. Serendipitous outcomes often stimulate data collection, to refine the effectiveness measures and to isolate a defensible causal agent, under the administrator's control. The sponsor verifies the veracity of the data, and then frames an evaluation question which the data can confirm. The process has but one step: intuition....

9. *Hand-picked panels*: Site visit teams are often used to evaluate programs. Outsiders often set up expectations based on experiences that are not transferable. By selecting a site visit team whose experiences, and thus biases and expectations, are similar to those operating in the program, the program can be sanctified. Or to eliminate an unwanted program, a site team may be selected, whose members are likely to be hostile to the practices of the program....

10. *Fixed indices*: Evaluation sponsors dictate criteria and criteria weights. Measures of the criteria are fixed to steer the evaluator toward issues the sponsor wants considered. The sponsor restricts the evaluator's scope of inquiry by dictating the measures and by restricting the evaluator's role in interpreting the results (see Figure 3). Interpretation is reserved for the sponsor and no dialogue is permitted (see Figure 1).... Well-endowed hospitals, for instance, publicize those indices that measure institutional solvency. Fixed indices are also used to make a point. When pupil-teacher ratios are falling, school systems compare them to other schools to justify budget increases.

Fuzzy Interpretations

As a last resort, sponsors may develop tactics to aid them in explaining away negative findings, should they occur. The results are made fuzzy to raise questions which may discredit the findings. Suchman contends that even well-conducted evaluation projects can be rendered suspect when someone in a position of power makes one of several claims. These include the following:

1. *Alleging a poorly selected target group*: The effects of the program were claimed to be understated because those who could benefit most from the services, or respond best to the intervention, did not participate in the study. In short, a biased source of the target group is alleged. Randomization makes this claim implausible but the benefits of randomization are seldom understood, so it can be alleged anyway. A variant on this theme is to claim that those needing the services were in the control group. Again, randomization will make this claim implausible.

2. *Claims of concentrated effects*: Some service recipients improved immensely, but the claim is made that these benefits were washed out by those who did not need the services. The selective effect argument is difficult to combat unless individual cases can be traced to isolate high benefiting participants.

3. *Claims of faulty program mechanisms*: A more intensive program is advanced as necessary to produce positive results. This claim was advanced

by Head Start advocates, who were able to initiate 'follow through', a program designed to work with low income children after they began grade school.

4. *Claim of bias*: All sorts of claims can be made which imply bias. Contending that control groups were improperly selected, measures were taken without reliability checks, and the wrong measurements were used, can discredit evaluation findings. The 'Hawthorne Effect' (people responding to the evaluation situation, not the program) can always be alleged because the Hawthorne had taken on the status of an empirical law.

8

PARTNERS: MANAGERS IN TRAINING AND TRAINING IN MANAGEMENT

Partnering: The Quality Spectrum
  Hostile to Reluctant
  Critical to Skeptical
  Supportive but Little Involved
  Active Support and Championing
  Champion to Full Partner

Managers as Partners at Different Stages of Training
  In the Pre-training Stage
  While Participants are in Training
  For Follow-up

And Training: From Special Resource to General Partner

Exhibits
8.1 From Change Strategy to Training Programs: Partnering at Eight Stages
8.2 Main Training Roles and Related Competencies

Boxes
8.1 Training Functions for Organizational Effectiveness
8.2 Making HR a Business Partner
8.3 Fifteen-item Agenda for HRD Professionals with Policy-makers and Change Managers

---

Companies that are able to align human resources with organisational vision and objectives will establish competitive edge. Willingness to constantly evaluate and measure the degree of alignment will maintain that edge.

—Lisa Smith

Training and development professionals must transform themselves into savvy, knowledgeable business people who...also understand the overall framework in which their (organisation) operates.

Only with this understanding can (they) gain the credibility to access the decision-making inside...(and) help develop the kind of organisation-wide environment that recognises the training professional as a major player on the organisational field.

—A.P. Carnevale et al.

Fast changing, turbulent times escalate pressures to learn and readiness to relearn: to learn more, faster, and in any and all settings and ways to be had. Needs and means spell each other in this surge for learning. On and on. So, with no end to it in sight, conserving effort is essential too: pacing as for a marathon, not for occasional spurts followed by exhaustion.

Knowingly or not, we are each other's helpers in this, casting each other as model, mask, warning, encourager, guru, hinderer—the kaleidoscopic constantly changing cast of others we use for our learning. Add awareness, intent, and good practice and we become the 'mobile training units' to be routinely included in job descriptions for managers.[1] Formal training, its proliferation, galloping technical sophistication, and developing training systems are elaborations on this simple truth of having to learn more and faster and without end—the means reliably on call to respond better to greater needs.

Their high position, seniority, and prominence assure policy-makers high influence as 'trainers', in the ways they behave when carrying out their responsibilities and also in their personal contacts. It is they too who create the settings for formally designated training to help their organization cope and keep coping in these times. With sights raised to encompass the full extent of the environment the organization has to concern itself with, now and in the foreseeable future, policy-makers assess the order and kinds of transformation the organization must make in its life-blood connections with its world and internally, set change strategies going for this, and monitor and modify them to keep them on track. With transforming itself, the organization then changes its environment in turn, and so also the setting that makes for other organizations. These make up the set of crucial functions for which we have kept policy-makers most steadily in focus in this volume so far: their role, range of responsibilities and, where possible, their options.

[1] See, e.g., Ken Blanchard, "Leaders as Trainers" in *Executive Excellence*, July 1998, pp 6–7.

In addressing this volume to 'change managers' as well we have side-stepped a distinction which now needs drawing. On a traditional up-and-down organization chart, they would be on the level below policy-makers, that is, they work within limits and on lines set by those higher up (or, on the less obviously hierarchical charts, by those in the inner circle). Within their scope—the unit, area, specialist function, particular assignment—managers too make policies (= goals and rules) and institute change strategies (= resource allocations, novel arrangements and processes, time frames). We have paired them with policy-makers also because of their intimate involvement in organization-wide change, often right from the beginning. Many wear both hats, one to make overall policies and the other to take charge of implementing them in their division or other part. And policy-makers routinely draw in top managers, too, for counsel—formally and informally, face-to-face and via the data and recommendations they provide, on request, and also initiated by *them.* Maintaining the proper, broad, overall perspective and addressing all who worked it out and have to use it is what we had most in mind in addressing this volume to both.

Now we want to focus on the change manager in particular, on *that* role and set of functions, no matter where the person who has them sits in the organization or system. We want to map and rehearse what partnering with training and the training system means in that role and what particular functions managers have at various stages of program development and follow-up.

Exhibit 8.1 shows change managers partnering with their colleagues in the training system. This segment is taken from planning a training program, from identifying new competencies (and other resources) needed for implementing a change strategy to selecting participants for training to acquire them.

The segment starts with the managers clarifying, in the first place for themselves, what a change strategy in view might require by way of manpower development, e.g., new technical competencies, more people, working in teams, frequently changing tasks, and then they invite their partners in training to react, out of *their* expertise. A fresh view and double checking the estimates so far may be welcome. Specifically needed next is clarity as to the part(s) training could (and could not) take on, what going ahead with it so would take by way of time, funds, etc. (and associated dislocations), and what are

Exhibit 8.1
FROM CHANGE STRATEGY TO TRAINING PROGRAMS:
PARTNERING AT EIGHT STAGES

The Work Organization	The Training System
1. Decides on a change. Specifies inputs required, including new knowledge, understanding, skills.	2. Responds by specifying what can be acquired through training.
3. Studies who exactly is involved— numbers and levels—and when, all this in relation to other inputs, for example, technological, financial, and organizational.	4. Offers help in working out minimum concentrations of trained personnel required for change.
	5. Works out and communicates training specifications, for example, kinds and duration of training for different people— sequences, follow-up services, and contributions required from the organization and other agencies.
6. Decides to go ahead.	7. Collaborates with the work organization in drawing up a training plan for implementation.
8. Selects participants, schedules inputs.	Collaborates in selecting individuals for particular kinds of training and in providing needed program(s) and places.

alternative training strategies and programs worth considering with their likely costs. Considering these questions and shaping plans to suit local practicalities may take a series of meetings interspersed with revisions by each partner. This segment of eight stages ends with training plans agreed and managers detailing participants to go for training.

Clarity, about each other's expertise and also about which partner is responsible at any stage for decisions and actions—and consequences—makes for good partnering. Easy collaboration across these boundaries marks organizations with well-functioning cultures. To push the partners to work out this clarity through increasingly consistent practice and also make it well-understood in the organization and larger system is an important contribution for policy-makers to make.

Most supportive is clarity about which partner policy-makers will hold accountable for training outcomes. Holding change managers accountable for the progress they are making with the manpower component of change strategies is quite correct, if training in fact did its part as promised. Managers quite rightly expect their training partners to come clean about what they can and cannot agree to do and about what proper doing will cost. And they are entitled to their expert assistance again when preparing for the newly trained participants' return and related changes.

PARTNERING: THE QUALITY SPECTRUM

In practice, the quality of partnering varies from zero, and even hostility, to active sharing in each other's functions.

Hostile to Reluctant

That training upsets things, is a lot of trouble and brings more, fuels active hostility to it from many managers; that training is a waste of time—the more common view—often springs from past disappointment and lingering ill repute.

Only policy-makers determined on change can turn active hostility aside and insist that managers engage with training in essential partnering. With consistent backing from them, and trainers crediting managers with large parts of any success, effective partnering then has good chances of developing.

Historical disappointment with training is subtler and usually takes longer to displace because their, training partners then want to play things very safe: to avoid outcomes falling short—again—and so reinforcing the low reputation, training partners may put forward only standard, middling designs and methods and, to make doubly safe, escalate staff, time, and other resource requirements for them; this when managers are actually looking for quite fresh approaches and hope against hope that their partners here have a new face.

Abolishing training, the logical step from such pervasive disenchantment, only the fewest organizations would even consider practical. No self-respecting organization these days is without training clearly identified, and funding agencies require it. So training continues even in quite unfavorable settings, but for window dressing and ritual. For any training 'for real', managers then take their chances outside, they outsource it.

We ourselves have experienced well-functioning training getting almost washed out when a chief executive took charge who abhorred change. Some programs he cancelled directly, others he disabled by re-assigning key trainers. Morale plummeted. Yet, in public utterances, he championed training all along.

Training cannot develop against pervasive hostility and indifference; so low-key, low-risk programs may well exhaust possibilities to keep it alive within a hostile or even indifferent organization. Using all opportunities to open the organization more to the outside world in hopes of uncompromised mind-changing encounters with training successes elsewhere is a second safe line of action. Outsourcing training is one such opportunity.

Critical to Skeptical

These only barely more positive attitudes actually present fertile ground for increasingly close and effective collaboration. Managers who approach training with these are often quite ready to be convinced of the worthwhileness of training, only they want to see solid evidence first. And their partners should welcome this condition along with the readiness, for that sets the stage well for effective collaboration.

In Indonesia as consultants to help a Province improve its training function, we found all levels of the training system thoroughly demoralised. Its head, who also directed all planning, routinely kept training near the bottom of resource allocations. When trainers then used these resources for a concentrated program to upgrade District heads and went about planning this together with them and plausibly altogether, and the program then also met its goals and led to very desirable changes in their practice, he set out to revise his view of training. He himself joined the next program, and redesigned the Provincial planning process as his project. A strong, competent and well regarded person himself, he readily looked at fresh evidence about training and what it could accomplish if prepared and done well. From downgrading training across the board, he changed to [being a] strong, active supporter of all training that passed his critical assessment, and championed high-quality training too at national level.

Directly, possibly as a test case, managers want to see trainers propose strategies and program designs and also modify them in discussion, till they clearly address the key needs the managers see, and do so in ways and within limits that are realistically feasible. As they work away at that, the partners not only create a specific program of promise, they also strengthen their partnering and make it reliable and enjoyable—something to keep up gladly.

Supportive but Little Involved

Many managers, maybe most, support training and partner it without thinking about it much or examining its impact regularly or critically. They expect their training colleagues to get on with it and keep it going. As for themselves, they answer questions, sign off on programs and participants, and generally collaborate in reviews and forward programming. Training has been helpful in the past, they expect that to continue, nothing they hear about informally makes them doubt it, and policy-makers back it. All that is good enough; they can devote their time to their other responsibilities.

> This pretty well describes the support the Health Secretary in an Indian State gave training. He knew the head of the apex training institute for the State and his consultant and their high reputations and backed them wholeheartedly, and his backing disposed managers at all levels of the system to support training. As chair of the committee charged with training, he routinely led the formal acceptance of reports from the training institute and system and the plans and budget for them.

Where training is well established and programs pretty routine and effective, this well-wishing, low-energy degree of support may suffice, but not for new and innovative training to back major change strategies. The onward experience in this instance confirmed this important limitation. When this secretary was promoted to another state, his replacement countermanded or undercut all change strategies, sidelined training, and cut training budgets. The head of the central training institute was dismissed and with that the consulting also discontinued. All further development of the training system across the state was put on hold. Conclusion: high innovation gains safety with high involvement of key managers.

Active Support and Championing

This usually grows along with the realization that managers themselves own training, not merely as the clients who acquire it but as fully in-charge of having training meet the purpose(s) they set.

Preparation and follow-up are the most obvious and legitimate stages for managers to participate powerfully in that role. Through active participation together with training professionals they come to assess situations, opportunities, and options more truly and, also importantly, to know they do; and they also gain new credibility with these partners.

> An Under-secretary in [the] State government had responsibility for training in his varied set of duties. He gave it time and attention, critically studied proposals that reached him and became convinced that training warranted higher budgets and visibility. He checked this out with administrators under him, identified bottlenecks to loosen or bypass and confirmed his impression that, even as it was, training effectively helped field and other staff improve their performance significantly. He let it be known that he was open to proposals to enlarge ongoing programs and to new innovative programs as well. And he assured the training system of the additional support it would need. His support was infectious. Participant numbers increased with the very next programs, the training system grew, spread and diversified, and new programs got under way.

Champions to Full Partner

Closest partnering comes with managers actually acquiring competencies in training and joining training teams from time-to-time as colleagues, in *their* role. Many training competencies enhance management competencies as well, such as active listening and noticing incipient learning and how best to help bring it out. The direct contribution managers can make as colleagues in training, with their direct all-round and detailed knowledge of the actual work settings that training and newly trained participants are to improve, needs no spelling out here.

Of greatest lasting value to the organization of this closest, collegiate partnering is likely to be the managers' shift of perspective, from habitually focusing on pretty direct action-with-intended-results to focusing on capacity-building; often less specific but lasting, this shift which is so important for higher management and policy-making. Switching to short and long timeframes at will is a far-reaching competence, beyond even the ability to see things from the various angles different specializations in management bring.

With developing people moving ever higher on management agendas, trying to make frequent changing easier as turbulent times demand, and developing competencies in training along with others in a manager's set—this closest partnering with training has extra great promise. This is the shift that the provincial director made when, persuaded that *some* kinds of training were indeed useful and worth promoting. He used his opportunity as participant to design a training module for his planning responsibilities and then spread the use of it throughout the province.

Among the most highly people-centered organizations, a several years' assignment to training responsibilities has become a step to the highest promotion. Managers making themselves flexibly available as resource persons in training has become common—and even more common, unfortunately, its travesty, as guest lecturers-on-call to fill gaps in the program at a moment's notice or for show. Corresponding shifts from training to management are also becoming more common and have corresponding benefits. Actual experience as a manager, with responsibilities for getting results, enhances trainers' appreciation and feel for the actual settings in which training is to produce new growth.

MANAGERS AS PARTNERS AT DIFFERENT STAGES OF TRAINING

As managers, concentrated partnering is greatly and most obviously necessary at the pre- and posttraining stages, when managers must make sure that training as planned takes proper account of the day-to-day practicalities of the tasks, settings and people, and then also bridges well to the changes the strategy aims at. To this, managers bring their long familiarity and effective habits to date, and detailed working knowledge of the tasks and conditions and people available to train. They then release some for training first and hold back others for later. And it is they who plan and arrange the changes to give training fullest scope afterwards—in the tasks, assignments, and work organization they control directly and also in outside services to support it. Managers contribute too while training is going on, by showing continuing interest in it and encouraging positive anticipations all round. Active partnering at home during the training phase is especially valuable early to get major change strategies well under way, and for training programs that takes colleagues offsite for days or weeks and count on others to cope without them.

In the Pre-training Stage

To Clarify Training Objectives and the New Tasks and Settings for Participants following Training

This is where rigor is most needed and where it is also most lacking. Most task descriptions are far too general, incomplete in content, and almost devoid of context to draw clear job descriptions from. Specifications for training based on them can be no better. And no amount of protesting by old timers that they already know all that's worth knowing can make up for these defects and deficiencies.

> Most job descriptions for sales personnel and extension officers show these weaknesses. Contact with customers and clients, the primary setting to be competent in, is assumed altogether or left unexamined and unspecified. Yet, experience tells that this is the very area in which better selection and then training is most required.

Only looking again, detailed study and full, accurate descriptions can make up the answer, even when this involves a good deal of trouble and often delay. For changed tasks and settings, familiarity and habits would not be good enough in any case. Upgrading the prevailing standards and making *operational* descriptions the norm become essential for planning the new tasks and for dividing them into jobs and settings that suitably selected and trained people can actually do well in.

For completing descriptions of task and jobs and pinpointing the crucial elements of content and setting in enough detail, managers find questioning by people with training in mind very helpful. Often trying too, as the testers persist in their checking and double-checking. Managers can call a halt when further detailing would exceed practical implications, at least for now, till other changes come on-line.

At least, all the efforts to perfect task and job descriptions do double and treble duty. The same detailed descriptions serve next for identifying and selecting suitable participants, and then again for quantifying and phasing-in the associated changes for making the training count in the strategy, such as rearranging workstations; revising roles, assignments and organization; and ensuring wider organizational support. Numbers, sequences, and combinations of people to train will also become clearer in the course of all this. Many practical overall manpower plans for implementing change strategies have been developed from such practical, meticulous, laborious beginnings.

Participant Selection

The to-be-changed tasks and settings are the touchstone here, and selecting suitable people to be trained for them the first cut. Managers partnering with trainers take things this far. For the two onward steps, to selecting and releasing particular people now on board or recruiting new people, managers do well to draw in their own staff and colleagues. It is as if managers and trainers together have set the stage for the particular training, just as policy-makers had set the stage earlier for the change strategy. Now, some additional groups come on stage, next some individual players as well. Their active involvement at proper times is immediately practical. It is also important symbolically, in communicating the calm, good order and personal consideration in the organization that best sustain readiness for change.

First to involve are all who are to keep things going—in the family or neighborhood or on the floor office or aisle—while the select few go ahead with training and pioneering the changed tasks, etc.; they too receive the newcomers. To involve them in working this out, through all detailed complexities, can make all the difference to how training is viewed and how trained people will be received back. For training and the larger change to which it also points to gain widespread credibility, those managers do well who make sure that the candidates they have in mind for training are suitable too in the eyes of people they most directly work with. Disagreement on this score is costly and often runs amok.

Finally, the candidates themselves: some may jump at the opportunity for training and the changes to which it will lead, others hesitate and are inclined to turn it down. Also, candidates react differently to the arrangements offered.

Two examples: to one candidate the detailed organizational care for travel, and personal and family details indicate high regard and order to rely on while away, while another feels belittled rather than elated by the same arrangements as if he could not look after such things himself. In the manager's view, offering to send someone for training at a high fee shows high importance, of this training and this candidate for it, but the candidate may fear that accepting the offer will commit to this work and this organization more than he or she is ready to, or even that the high fee just shows how very much the organization and this manager in particular want him or her out of the way so that they can get on with the changes he or she is against.

Managers who do well work out best possibilities together with the candidates. Most often particular details are most at stake, like timing, reluctance to be first, or fear of losing best colleagues.

Getting the Settings Ready for New Task Performance

Planning and making a start with getting associated changes ready in time for participants to put their training to good use as soon as they return is the best contribution managers can make at this stage. This communicates better than anything else that all, they themselves and the whole organization, mean what they keep saying about how vital change is and the training for it.

Often the changes required are quite minor, such as expediting supplies to keep pace with expected increases in production, and modifications of the division of work may be worked out by the work group with little or no special assistance. When training is linked to product changes, major expansion, and reorganization, or to new technologies, changes on which effective training depends are likely to be major. If the required changes are likely to take long and are somewhat uncertain, e.g., modification of buildings, acquisition of new equipment, or protracted negotiations within or outside the organization, either training should be delayed or these realities built into the participants' expectations.

Perhaps the main objective of further management action at this stage is to ensure that participants' expectations are realistic in terms of the training they receive and its potential application afterwards. About the training itself, organizations can secure information, put the participants in direct touch with the institution and encourage their contacting others in the organization or locality who have participated earlier in similar training. The minimum condition is simply some preparatory time; this is mentioned because participants do sometimes arrive for training having first heard about the training program and their going to it by telegram the previous day. Other organizations to the contrary make a point of involving participants actively, right to the time they leave for training, i.e., in preparing the changes essential for using their training and sending them off well acquainted with plans for the rest.

While Participants are in Training

Getting the associated changes ready continues—this is quite generally true for organizations who have started their change strategies with real promise. What even they commonly miss is to keep their absent participants informed and aware of this. Yet, at this stage too, partnering has personal as well as organizational dimensions. Staying in touch with participants who are away for training is more than courteous; it is important to the outcome.

Out of sight, out of mind. In most organizations we know, the participants' departure for full-time training and even their starting a program locally and part-time, signals time to take a break: managers can now forget them till the training ends and they return with the expected results. That this neglect can interfere seriously with the training itself they may never learn. Unresolved questions about how things are at home or office distract participants from learning what they came for, and active worrying does worse. And memories of neglect often become lasting resentment, at family members and also at the organization and its managers.

Damage control, or better, damage prevention, is the prescription. Foreseeable causes to worry are best surfaced in discussions before training and minded in taking training decisions, notably about timing. Then, continuing contact during training requires drawing a nice line: too much contact would convey mechanical rather than genuine interest, and encouraging participants to share as they learn may come through as pressure or as a check—itself belittling—on whether they are working hard enough.

Keeping *some* information flowing, especially about progress with making the associated changes, will limit the wondering on that score at least and help make exhaustion and discomforts worthwhile. Participants learn more and better with assurances from time-to-time that their families and personal affairs back home continue well enough, and will also remember more.

For Follow-up

At best, all changes in tasks and settings have been effected and are ready for the participants when they return. Second best is to have plausible explanations ready to offer them for any shortfall and clear indications for when they will come on-line and for how to put the training to best use meanwhile. Reaffirming by all possible means that organizational change continues high on managers' agendas pays off most handsomely at this transition from training to back home. Participants who return after a long time away, need sheer time to settle in again. Next, scheduled but perhaps best for a week or two ahead, can come one or more meetings with colleagues in which they share experiences and thoughts from their training and answer questions. Settling in, back home, is done best in terms of what's new, the ahead that is now unfolding.

Instead, returning participants are often left to manage the transition by themselves and against contrary signals. With nothing said, they take the settling-in time they need but surreptitiously, and feel awkward and guilty about it. Finding work piled up and awaiting their return shows nicely how indispensible they are—in terms of the past that is: training aside, they should step right back into the same rut. Whatever anyone said or says, in fact no one, not colleagues or management, had stepped in and smoothed the way to the new.

Even aside from what actions and inactions of managers mean for personal goodwill and organizational climate in general, cost considerations alone counsel high cost-benefits for investing care and time at this stage. Certainly, for residential training, costs quickly mount high. For a young executive away for a three months' program in-country, direct costs alone may be $15,000 equivalent or more plus travel and loss of his or her work (namely, $6,000 for continuing salary and benefits + $4,000 program fee + hotel etc.). Additional costs will have been incurred as well in making the changes in tasks and settings that the training is preparation for, even before participants return. Compared with these substantial outlays up-front, managers' efforts are quickly cost effective when they smoothen the participants' transition back from training so they can concentrate their efforts on putting their training to best use quickly, and so play their part in pushing the change strategy ahead.

Box 8.1 shows the roles of line managers and of HRD in keeping training aligned with operations. Back to the quote at the head of this chapter and generalizing it further: '(Organizations) that are able to align human resources with organisational vision and objectives will establish a competitive edge. Willing to constantly evaluate the alignment (and modify it to keep it tight) will maintain that edge.' Box 8.2 lists recommendations for doing this.

AND TRAINING: FROM SPECIAL RESOURCE TO GENERAL PARTNER

Much of the partnering that this chapter has been about managers are inclined to regard as old hat, something they have done all along.

Box 8.1

TRAINING FUNCTIONS FOR ORGANIZATIONAL EFFECTIVENESS

Line Manager	*HRD Department*
1. Analyzes each employee's role and lists detailed functions to be performed, outlining managerial, technical, and behavioral capabilities required.	1. Designs systems to identify training needs.
	2. Collects information about training needs from line managers.
	3. Keeps up to date on trends in training.
2. Identifies training needs of each employee in terms of relevant functions and communicates these to HRD department.	4. Collects information about available training programs.
3. Encourages employees, provides opportunities to take responsibility and initiative and to learn on the job.	5. Disseminates information about training opportunities to line managers.
	6. Analyzes training needs and plans in-house training.
4. Provides continuous coaching and helps employees to develop problem-solving skills.	7. Managers training production (functions and facilities).
5. Sponsors subordinates for training with HRD department.	
6. Obtains feedback from subordinates about capabilities acquired during training, discusses opportunities for trying out what they have learned, provides such opportunities.	
7. Institutes group discussions, etc., to help subordinates learn to work as a team.	

SOURCE: J.W. Pfiffer and L.D. Goodstein (eds), *The 1984 Annual: Developing Human Resources* (San Diego: San Diego University Press, 1984), p. 165.

Well yes, setting it all out so systematically is quite interesting and could save time and energy. And, yes too, times are changing, and, I admit, doing what I/we have always done works quite erratically now—well enough sometimes and not well at all at others—and, no, I cannot tell why. Truth to tell, I am pretty sure that isn't going to be nearly good enough for managing in future, with all the changes and uncertainties ahead.

So, practical people that we are, better get some more training is the obvious response; and for newcomers, still heading into careers,

Box 8.2

MAKING HR A BUSINESS PARTNER

1. Train HR people in business to get wholistic business perspectives.
2. Get involved in larger organisational issues and handle co-ordination at that level.
3. Align HR strategies with business strategies.
4. Keep in mind business strategy while designing training programmes.
5. Convene business strategies forums, hold strategic discussion meetings, and prepare discussion paper.
6. Initiate process of discussion on strategy formulation from the frontline upward.
7. Help in searching state of the art practices for the business team.

SOURCE: From an HR Group of Turner-Morrsion, July 1998.

it is to add an MBA to the engineering or social work or whatever other professional degree they have even before entering. If the trainers are any good, that should take care of the problem. The explosive proliferation world-wide of training programs and of management schools tells how pervasive the nagging anxieties are and how they reverberate through whole societies and keep escalating—about inadequacies to cope, about being unable to manage with a sure enough touch, about doing oneself justice, about facing a whole life with reasonable equanimity. And that the same people turn up for training again and again, as if on a regular diet or fix, tells that training, bought like a prescription, produces only passing relief at best but does not change the worrying condition. For better and more lasting effect, managers may really have to look at training differently, give it a different position in their scheme of things. Which would be in line, of course, with the basic theme of this whole book.

This shift is away from treating training as a resource only, first and last—on call for filling particular gaps in knowledge, skill or even in a generalized competence-like thinking ahead or salesmanship—towards involving the training system in mapping and preparing the organizational context and the change strategies themselves, to which specific training will then make its contribution. Drawing training that much closer and involving its leadership directly in what is traditional managers' and even policy-makers' business means regarding and treating it more like a partner in a joint endeavor.

For organizations with long traditions, this upgrading may be quite a jolt. Upgrading the general Human Resource Development function instead—not alongside but instead of training—may be easier to accept. That would show more regard for the people component in the organization's life and purpose and be more welcome and probably timely in all places these days anyway. Without more clarity about what is really at stake here, upgrading HRD in general risks losing sight of the particular innovative, cutting edge function which is the one that needs highlighting most. And *that* is training's essential contribution. At issue is to give new prominence to this innovative function in particular, and to build it best into the structure and normal ways of the organization and larger system for the future.

Making this move now has good company. It goes along well with steps everywhere to flatten organizational hierarchies and encourage flexible collegial relations, and to engage much more actively with the environment where relating as peers is essential anyway. This is simply best preparation for steering organizations in turbulent conditions. So, unfamiliar though it may be, partnering, of managers with training and also of training with management, looks clearly the best way to go.

As partners in designing change strategies and also in keeping it on course, managers can routinely expect training to come up with methodological and procedural contributions, e.g., ways of interrelating strategic components, estimates of time and other resources some step will take, and indicators to recognize changes accomplished or lagging. Quite likely they will find comments and views from the training perspective useful from time-to-time to sharpen or round out managerial thinking, and ask for them if the training leadership has not offered them of their own accord. Ignorant of, and certainly less committed to, established orthodoxies of business or of running the organization, training partners often come up with refreshingly innovative, creative thoughts on long-time and often festering issues. For other purposes it is important that the training leadership become acquainted first-hand with points of view characteristic for managers. For trainers to step into management positions and for set times become management colleagues on managerial tasks adds credibility along with more intimate knowledge of work in that role, just as does managers taking on training functions and partnering training at its closest as colleagues.

Partnering managers spawns additional roles for training professionals. Trainers who are normally busy in sessions and program

Exhibit 8.2
MAIN TRAINING ROLES AND RELATED COMPETENCIES

Concern	Perspective	Focus	Objective	Posture on Strategy	Main Role	Needed Competency
Content	Operational	Current role	Role effectiveness	Implement	Training	Technical expertise
Content	Strategic	Multiple roles	Role flexibility	Input	Research coaching and counselling	Organizational awareness and research competency
Process	Operational	Teams	Synergy	Help	Consulting	Strategic awareness and consultancy competency
Process	Strategic	Leadership	Transformation	Partner	Change management	Business knowledge

Box 8.3

FIFTEEN-ITEM AGENDA FOR HRD PROFESSIONALS WITH
POLICY-MAKERS AND CHANGE MANAGERS*

1. Foster acceptance and understanding of constant change.
2. Develop culture of continuous improvement and learning.
3. Strategic planning at *all* levels.
4. Structure the organisation to enhance adaptive capacities.
5. Create new communications networks.
6. Create organisational capacity for anticipating and responding to change.
7. Help executives select and sponsor desirable changes.
8. Improve change tactics of executives and managers.
9. Update team development concepts.
10. Change how to train managers to get the job done.
11. Help individuals cope with frequent reassignments and role changes.
12. Strengthen the career development system.
13. Establish effective support systems.
14. Provide organisational support for individual coping.
15. Acknowledge and respond to the new diversity and new globalism.

---

* Extracted from Reading 1.1.

preparation and related activities, reappear for organizational consulting, executive counselling, evaluating change outcomes and processes, and recommending adjustments in change strategies. Exhibit 8.2 shows the most common additional roles and competencies that qualify partnering in each. Box 8.3 displays a fifteen-item agenda for trainers partnering with managers and policy-makers.

9

To Stay the Course: Learning Agendas for Policy-Makers and Change Managers

(In) a turbulent environment fresh appreciations have to be made frequently…to remain an open system in its environment [the organisation] has to maintain an open system within itself.

…The importance of self-regulating organisations has become much greater [with] increasing levels of interdependence, complexity and uncertainty…far more complex interactive webs of relationships… prompted the creation of the socio-ecological perspective.

…No organisation, however large, can go it alone in a turbulent environment. Dissimilar organisations become directively correlated… for the reduction of the turbulence and … [to] address 'meta-problems' at the 'domain' level.

—Eric Trist and Hugh Murray

Complexity, instability, and uncertainty are not removed or resolved by applying specialized knowledge to well-defined tasks. If anything, the effective use of specialized knowledge depends on a prior restructuring of situations.

...With this emphasis on problem-solving, we ignore problem *setting*, the process by which..., interactively, we *name* the things to which we will attend and *frame* the context in which we will attend to them. ...through the non-technical process of framing the problematic situation...we may organize and clarify both the ends to be achieved and the possible means of achieving them.

—Donald Schoen

So the habitual response policy-makers and change managers have at the ready—solving problems briskly and clearly as they come up, or better still, making sure somehow they don't—misleads more than it helps in turbulent environments. Not primarily because problems sprout too fast in it for retailing and will surely overwhelm the capacities and endurance of even the best and most devoted leader, staff, teams, and all. The very qualities that make problem-seeing and solving so very attractive—clarity, simplicity, gone-and-done-with, situation-now-under-control—fail where things are unclear and always changing, highly complex and interdependent, open-ended, and in no one's control. But if problems are not what policy-makers and managers are to look for, solve or avoid, how else to pay attention and do better instead, and how to get out of the one made and learn the other? Or, better, how to add the other and be master at both? This is what this final chapter is about.

THE NEW MODE TO MASTER

In the quotes at the head of this chapter, pioneer explorers set out the main features of this different world. That they had to wrestle their way through to formulate them like this adds credibility and weight.

The new-age organizations manage with 'fresh appreciations... [gathered] frequently', an 'open system' inside and out, and a 'socio-ecological perspective... to address meta-problems'. This is a big step from seeing that world as a giant mountain (volcano?) of problems to see and solve; big and definite, not like, say, a smooth slide up or down a ramp. A change of gear is the first good image to come to mind for the stepped-up awareness and levels of discourse and action required here. Or, better, a ratchet once moved up it *stays* up. These organizations take more things into account, gather more information to do it with, and use updated technologies—any and all from anywhere.

Not only do they see more out there to act on, they also see themselves differently. There is no more going it alone, but in 'inter-organisational networks'. These networks include even dissimilar organizations (unlike the familiar trade or professional associations of kin) and they are 'interactive' (no more just following the leader). They are for addressing 'meta-problems', each a whole 'domain' of interrelated issues. And this they cannot do by 'applying specialised technical knowledge to well-defined tasks' as before, but by more holistic, non-technical appreciation, and by making 'openness' the permanent state of the organization.

So these organizations become learning organizations and continue that way. '...to remain an open system in its environment it has to maintain an open system within itself.' And, we would add quite explicitly here, for an organization to be an open system internally too, its policy-makers and managers need to be open themselves. Learners, in short, learners life-long.

LEARNING ON THREE SCORES IN PARTICULAR

We see continuing learning required particularly on three scores. The personal is most basic and pervasive and may be the most difficult to accept and also to sustain. At issue here is how best to ease in and then confirm in daily practice the essential moves away from habitual, partial ways of looking and acting that, however unobtrusively, hold back openness to the new. The mushroom growth of executive counselling and coaching and the proliferation worldwide of personal and inter-personal training programs show that many people feel they need this personal learning.

The second level, by all signs much harder to make rigorous and keep up in sufficient detail, is good enough monitoring of one's own practice to keep on improving it. How well I understood the situation—X—in the first place and then behaved in line with that understanding is at issue here. Side effects, unintended consequences? What does the cluster of events centered on X tell about relationships in the organization and monitoring of my own for good enough diversity and intensity? Readiness of access is important to track and also how steps to improve things go in the light of that tracking. For policy-makers and managers, the focus here is on the organization and the larger system of which it is a direct part and on being the instrument for understanding and influencing the organization.

The third level of study, quite essential for good policy-making these times, is of the wider environment, especially (but not only or only directly—no knowing for sure in advance) as it impinges on *this* organization and opens opportunities for influence.

On all three scores identifying some situations as problematic and needing attention comes out of a holistic assessment, however well it is also informed technically. 'Both the ends to be achieved and the possible means of achieving them' become clearer in the process. It is this framing that makes or mars innovating at any point. It is a cut into the continuing process of seeing, assessing, and chosing, like a still cut from a movie. The process runs on.

With openness, innovation, and changing the aim, free imaging has much to contribute, both for getting at the frame that set the original appreciation of X and then also for suggesting the frame for the decision to intervene (or not) and how. Another implication of openness on all scores is that polarities can be in it together: what are either/ors, even opposites (that is, mutually exclusive options) in problem-solving images become and/ands in open-sytem thinking organizations. This particular shift may be the most difficult to achieve in industrial cultures in the West.

The Personal Score

Two pairs of eyes looking is better than one—in particular if the other's see things differently, out of another frame. A fresh angle is the essential help—not to prove one wrong but to add depth, raise questions, clarify essentials. So yes-men are of little use when taking a fresh look at matters, and still less for adding a new frame to one's permanent repertoire. Entertaining differences helps all see more truly.

Personal learning starts with a greater awareness of the frames one habitually brings and an open readiness to notice and try out others'—it makes for appreciating the situation better: more completely, more thoroughly. Seeing how they fit X is only one side of it. To make it part of my repertoire, they must fit me too—my disposition and style, my personal ways. Only then can it join the other frames I can call up from memory as I try to understand new situations that remind me of X.

We hold learning of this pervasive and permanent order in the greatest respect. Nothing excites us more than seeing even the glimmers of it; that mobilizes whatever support we can give to kindle them into flame and fire. It is an erratic process at best, and most starts suffocate in personal hesitations and cold reception. Even with personal openness and with colleagues eager and able to help, adding a major new frame and making it habitually available for use in new situations can be a drawn out and often anxious enterprise.

> Lynton has a 40 page-chapter on learning of this order: 'seeing systems—at last', he calls his case.[1] Knowledge about systems he already had aplenty for many years; had also worked in systems and even created and directed one. At issue now was really learning to use system thinking when he was long used to framing situations in personal and interpersonal terms. He describes how uneven progress with this can be as the still fresh and only partially tried and confirmed new competes for attention with the smoothly functioning old.
>
> Regular monitoring and reviewing problematic moments with this in actual practice helped greatly. When in contact with others, Lynton kept a running score of his intended purpose(s) and actual outcome(s); he also rated noteworthy effects on relationships and periodically reviewed the frames he used for each. Further details are in Reading 9.3, along with the instrument he used to keep the whole system constantly in view. With persistent correcting and sheer repetitive practice, systems thinking became as accessible a frame as the long-practised others.

Creating new situations, even hypothetical ones, helps the essential loosening up for creating space and readiness to test new frames. Brainstorming recognized this early: any thought whatever is valued there, far out or weird commend it. Fostering more 'creativity', also in adults, now has many forms (and many frauds). Effective programs highlight personal engagement in and reflection on the process and its wider meanings along with creating productions. In Future Search, participants construct the future they desire—the strategic issue is how to use the realities they project for framing.

Following well-tested preparatory steps, the mind map participants' construct of that future setting becomes the frame they use

---

[1] Rolf P. Lynton, *Social Science in Actual Practice: Themes on My Blue Guitar,* (New Delhi: Sage Publications, 1998), Chapter 6.

for, in Schoen's words again, 'the end to be achieved and the possible means for achieving them'.

An especially creative and yet so simple vehicle for questioning frames in habitual use and improving or replacing them are regular meetings of professionals with a skilled counsellor for the very purpose of looking again and together at problematic situations that recur despite interventions. That they recur strongly suggests a failure to understand and, with competent, experienced practitioners, that the presenter needed to look at the situation differently, that is, through a different frame.

The counsellor's particular function is to raise for possible examination the blindspots, assumptions, personal feelings, etc., that may have got in the way of a truer appreciation, and so sets the presenter and others off on deeper personal learning.

In some countries, e.g., Germany, physicians' groups like this are named for Michael Balint who pioneered them (in England) and are linked up in a network. They differ from the case conferences hospitals and clinics hold regularly, as they the focus on ordinary, undramatic situations—and so on the underlying personal learnings required to understand them better.

Monitoring and Learning More from Experience

Improved practice comes from a concerted effort to face questions that need answers, to search systematically for these answers, to test these answers rigorously, and to accept these tested answers then as the best available now and as a basis for further study and testing if required. This, in a nutshell, is the discipline of action research, i.e., research for improving practice directly. Policy-makers and managers can consider adding it for use side-by-side with the intuition they have developed from experience over the years, but more loosely and personally than the new complexities require.
Exhibit 9.1 states the beliefs that underlie action research and Exhibit 9.2 shows its components built into a complete feedback model.

In a program on organizational effectiveness in Indonesia, midlevel managers were set the task of constructing an effective organization from their experiences of working together in the program and then, individually, to rate their organizations back home on dimensions in the design that they considered relevant. Eight dimensions stood out, and rankings on a simple four-point scale produced the following results (mean values).

Exhibit 9.1
BELIEFS UNDERLYING ACTION RESEARCH

1. Action steps are more effective and enduring when they emerge from systematic search rather than from the authority or solely from a practitioner's intuition.
2. Research done by practitioners themselves on a question results in useful answers than research done by others.
3. Research consists of analyzing issues, searching for best answers, and testing and evaluating them. It uses skills which can be learned and developed by practitioners. Research is not the prerogative of experts.
4. Development of people's capabilities is basic to improvement in practice.

Exhibit 9.2
FEEDBACK MODEL OF ACTION RESEARCH

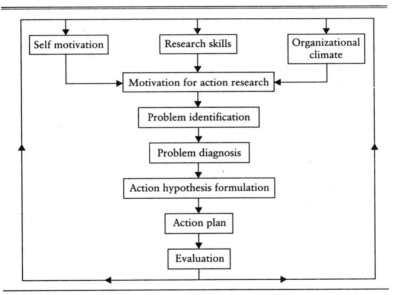

Mission orientation	3.8
Social benefit	3.4
Leadership	3.2
Client orientation	3.0
Innovation	2.8
Use of data and feedback	2.8
Expansion and growth	2.5
Competitive spirit	2.5

With the more general, abstract dimensions already so much better developed (in the participants' assessment) than innovation, achievement, and instrumentalities for them, trainers focused the remaining program sharply on the latter dimensions.

SOME ISSUES FOR ACTION RESEARCH IN ORGANIZATIONAL PRACTICE

Pinpointing an important issue in order to examine organizational experience with it and then also framing it right—these start off learnings which are worth policy-makers and managers focusing on: research in and for action. No sophistication later—whether in, method, sample size or instrumentation—can compensate for irrelevance or loose formulation of the issue at stake.

Here is a short list of issues which we see important for policy-makers and managers to study as they act on them and which are suitable for action research. Preferably they should actually do the research themselves, as stimulating and often important aspects crystallize in the process of doing it. If others do it, it is important that the reporting back goes beyond the bare end results. Problematic moments and insights gained along the way often tell much more.

The following list is just a sample, illustrative only: many more quite common and important issues could be included. They are ordered in sequence with this book and so allow us to walk over the same ground again, this time with action questions. Since issues for the organization in its environment is the particular focus of the next section, we start here with action research into some often taxing issues in making the organization into a learning system.

re: Making the Organization into a Learning System (Chapter 3)

1. In this conversion process, where (in the organization) are stresses most likely to occur, and how to recognize them in good time to avoid costly breaking points.
2. Where proceeding with incremental changes works well (enough) and where leapfrogging to a future position is better—and feasible.
3. Creating the new vision; choosing indicators within the organization as new points of reference to anchor it in; and making it and them widely known and supported.

4. Actual experiences with leaping dysjuctions that occur.
5. Creating and using prototypical situations for visualizing and practicing leaps forward.

In Indonesia we planned a program for greater organizational effectiveness. Mid-level managers of the provincial public health services were the participants. Instead of extracting standard criteria of excellence and effectiveness from foreign texts, the program set the participants themselves to research and work out characteristics of organizational effectiveness in Indonesia itself. This yielded the following list: collaborative and cooperative working, nurturing and effective leadership, realistic and detailed planning, effective human resources management (specifically acquiring good people, and their proper placement, utilization and training), high performance, and properly used control systems. These criteria were then used to design a program that proved highly effective.

re: *Policy Formulation in Practice (Chapter 4)*

6. The situational/background factors that stimulate the need and that influence the nature of the training policy.
7. Key persons who catalyze the process of policy formulation and the dynamics of the catalyzing process.
8. Factors that promote and retard implementation of the policy.
9. Monitoring and reviewing policy implementation, and making necessary changes in the policy in the light of the feedback received.

re: *Building a Training System (Chapter 5)*

10. How the training system composes, designs, and manages its linkages.
11. Designing, managing, evaluating, and refining internal components of the training system, e.g., internal structures, policies and processes; their interrelationships and flexibilities needed; practical options, their indicators and comparative costs (prominently including new and also imminent electronic options, 'distance learning', etc.).
12. Networking resources, boundary management, effective working mechanisms, e.g., retainer contracts.
13. Quality maintenance over time and providing for building further training system capacities.
14. Best practical indicators phase-to-phase for developing the training system for the predictable 'crises' and for their good enough 'resolutions'.

re: Making the Lead Institution Strong (Chapter 6)

15. Using in-house or outside resources: besides direct costs what considerations to take into account and how to weigh them.
16. Institutional leadership for successive phases of developing the institution; experiences with replacing a head; effective processes to retain talent and to reduce and manage internal disturbances.
17. Experiences with handling standard and innovative programs side by side.
18. Criteria for composing the leadership team and for advising and monitoring it.
19. Policies, structures, and processes for relating training with human resources development in the organization.
20. Influencing and monitoring the institution's linkages outside the organization and criteria for supporting that work.

re: Outcome Evaluation to Ensure High Benefits and Continuing Support (Chapter 7)

21. Benefits and costs of different approaches and methods to the organization and also inside the lead institution.
22. Best practices and other benchmarking and how they are best used.
23. Effective ways to ensure high attention to capacity-building in the organization (and by it in the training system) and to enforce planned performance with this.
24. Monitoring cost-benefits of innovative training strategies and programs, e.g., by electronic means.

re: Partnering Managers with Training Institution (Chapter 8)

25. Designing and managing training cost allocation to reflect operational plans and uses of training.
26. Valuing and supporting manager-training collaboration; learning from best practices.
27. Specifically for highly innovative training strategies and programs, record and learn about lower and higher management involvement and various scenarios for it.
28. Cost-benefit studies of different degrees and arrangements for managers' active involvement.
29. Specifically for developing full context-related task descriptions as basis for training, costs, and benefits of partnering to different degrees; effective methods.

30. Developing clear-headed support at the top for effective training and long-term capacity building.

SIMPLE METHODS FOR ACTION RESEARCH

Essential for action research are ready questioning and openness to alternative answers based on experience and information. Various devices can be used to stimulate, develop, and use this basic research spirit. Field research for a case exemplifies research of the clinical kind. There, in an ongoing working situation, an issue emerges that calls for understanding and decision. Whose responsibility is it to attend to it and act? Who are involved in its generation or implications? How do the main actors and others affected view the issues and options for decision? Researchers familiarize themselves with a situation and its background interview participants, and collect relevant documents. They draft a 'case' that sufficiently describes the situation and the happenings to make them 'real' to readers who can then understand the situation and think their way through to what they would do under similar circumstances. The original participants in the case modify and, usually, flesh out the draft to convey more accurately how it actually was. This is a meticulous, often protracted process. The manager/action researchers develop themselves through it and at the same time develop a potent vehicle for others to learn from the studied situation as well; the case is full and realistic enough for others too 'to see themselves in it'.

Another way to get into action research is to tap into the experiences different parties to an issue bring to it and go on to generate a simulation of it to experiment with, trying different approaches and seeing what all happens. Such self-generated simulations are often far more engaging and productive than materials from outside.

Instruments too have their use in action research and many are quite simple to use. Whole banks of them are now accessible electronically, with new ones added daily. Valid instruments can help managers, trainers, and others look at data about their own orientations, attitudes, values, and behavior and consider how they relate to their partners' dealing with the same issue or development dilemma.

In a programme to suit management to local culture, the managers of central and provincial health systems first rated their Indonesian culture individually, using the eight dimensions a major formal research had found significant. They next worked in small groups, discussed the dimensions and individual ratings, and worked out group ratings by consensus. Thereafter, published research data were made available. The two sets of findings were closely similar and validated each other. Later work on these dimensions, to strengthen the functional and reduce the dysfunctional, was very meaningful to the participants. Their evaluation confirmed that having generated the list and analyzed the functional and dysfunctional dimensions themselves strengthened their resolve to act on the issue.

The Changing Environment

For 'taking the environment in' these days, occasional or mostly anecdotal information about it is no longer enough. Pretty constant and systematic study of the organization's environment has become essential for keeping policies and development strategies and their management even reasonably well attuned to important changes outside. Certainly this is so for anticipating and preparing the organization for the ever greater range, complexities, and interdependencies there, and most of all for also influencing these developments on the organization's behalf. If influencing the environment still seems a curious idea and out of reach, it is worth remembering that any one organization's environment, after all, consists largely of other organizations, and that the changes and complexities in it come with what they do and do not do. How to keep track of the organization's relevant environment well enough—as a practical and economical ongoing condition—is the issue here.

re: Strategic Thrusts and Training for Transforming the Organization (Chapter 1)

1. Mapping the relevant environment, what to include and exclude, weighting of components, paring down to key elements.
2. Monitoring mapping for cost effectiveness, best practices.
3. Regular scanning of environment and readying the organization to reappraise it frequently and redraw the map and revise action strategies accordingly.
4. Effective mechanisms for information gathering and distribution in the organization and larger system.
5. Experiences with intervening in the environment in support of policies and management developments for developing into a learning organization.

6. Experiences with networking, particularly with networking among dissimilar organizations, differentiating parts and roles, and also keeping them integrated as a whole.

re: Assessing the Environmental and Cultural Contexts and the Opportunities to Change them (Chapter 2)

7. Indicators and diagnostic schema to test tolerances for change, both in the environment and internally in the organization.

8. Prototypes and pilot units for finding and confirming new paths: experiences with developing and also with positioning them (in the organization and vis-à-vis the environment); issues of differentiating and integrating them.

9. Mapping, managing, and monitoring linkages and the linkage system as a whole.

10. Inclusion/exclusion decisions about outside stakeholders; ways of handling later inclusions; costs and other consequences.

11. Experiences of middle-size organizations with interventions in their environments.

12. Experiences with expanding policy-makers' and managers' perspectives and ranges of appreciation; expanding incrementally and leapfrogging; using Future Searches.

Policy-makers and senior managers at least need to cast their learning nets even wider, beyond the currently relevant environment of their particular organization and the range of action research they can undertake themselves. Realistic appreciation of the wider political and societal cultures matters, how they influence each other and also the culture of their own organization, and how they can hope and plan to change it. What established cultural traits are well or badly attuned with current and imminent changes in technology, heightened interdependencies, roles of government, and the rest? Intergenerational issues abound, some highlighted by changes in education. How to pace organizational transformations in the light—and the unknowns and unpredictables—of so many forces is a constant issue along with making policy and managing ongoing operations in the midst of the uncertainties. When and how much to shield the organization from more environmental impact than it can cope with at any time and at the same time prepare it for desirable and even essential transformations is just one constant aspect of the task.

In Indonesia, as many examples have shown, intervention strategies made successful use of dominant cultural norms. Cross-cultural information too is useful, particularly across countries of the South, for there are many commonalities in the cultures and transformative patterns of developing countries. Processes of institutionalizing large-scale changes deserve study, especially the ways in which norms and values are reset and become pervasive and widely practiced. How far and how actively policy-makers and change managers interact with the cultural contexts often determines whether an initiative will spread far and permeate the wider culture, or will be still-born, or confined merely to the narrowly particular situation and at risk of getting overwhelmed by the larger forces beyond.

> The State Bank of India had more than 6,000 offices, employing more than 250,000 people. The office size varied from one employee to a work force of 20,000. Initially, the organisation tried to find universal solutions and practices. If a good practice was developed in one part of the organisation, there was a tendency to extend it to all other parts. Later the SBI provided autonomy to the different units, and extremely interesting practices came in vogue in different units to evolve their own practices. Consequently, a high degree of plurality and tolerance for divergence became a part of the SBI culture. What started as an experiment progressed to widespread experience, and policy makers have given local units more and more autonomy over the years.

In India, the State Bank—large, obiquitous, widely and officially supported—is easily recognized as a strategic organization. In turbulent conditions many much less known organizations turn out to be strategic too, including new-born organizations with quite untraditional features. Under these conditions, size and easy recognition matter less than the policies and ways of managing their development make powerful sense in the light of the new conditions. Modelling effective engagement with these novel conditions is what carries conviction even from small beginnings, not mere unorthodoxies which, like fashion, come and go.

Strategic organizations of all kinds demonstrate and model such plural ways of living and working. In fact, they must—if not they, who else? Organizations can influence political culture by emphasizing ethics and keeping organizational life and norms clean. If more and more strategic organizations adhere and practise high ethical standards, they will have a cascading impact on both societal and political cultures. A large proportion of the working life of people is spent in organizations and they carry the values of the organization to their homes. These values influence their families and, indirectly, societal culture. Thus whole organizations can become pilots for a new culture and spread values important and necessary for developing political culture and political ethics. They are in positions to influence public policy and political leadership as well. For this, policy-makers and change managers in organizations need to venture out, take up unconventional wider assignments and roles, and actively engage in the wider environments altogether.

It is a new world in many dimensions and that makes this a prime time for continued exploring and learning. Happily, the same disposition we identified earlier as the only essential for spicing practice with action research—of ready questioning and openness to various options that experience and new information suggest—also sustains and enhances effective policy-making and management in general. With repeated and increasingly habitual spiced-up practice, observation gets sharper, appreciation wider, interventions timelier and clearer, views longer, changing more routine, and futures steadier and full of promise.

Reading 9.1

Inter-organizational Domains and Referent Organizations

ERIC L. TRIST*

Complex societies in fast-changing environments give rise to sets or systems of problems (meta-problems) rather than discrete problems. These are beyond the capacity of single organizations to meet. Inter-organizational collaboration is required by groups of organizations at what is called the 'domain' level. The required capability at this level is mediated by 'referent organizations'....

... It is important to realize that domains are cognitive as well as organizational structures, else one can only too easily fall into the trap of thinking of them as objectively given, quasipermanent fixtures in the social fabric, rather than as ways we have chosen to construe various facets of it. Domains are based on what Vickers called 'acts of appreciation'. Appreciation is a complex perceptual and conceptual process which melds together judgements of reality and judgements of value. A new appreciation is made as a new meta-problem is recognized. As the appreciation becomes more widely

* From Eric Trist, 'Referent Organizations and the Development of Inter-Organizational Domains', *Human Relations*, Vol. 36, No. 3 (1983), pp. 269 and 273–76.

shared, a domain begins to be identified. It is most important that the identity of the domain is not mistaken through errors in the appreciative process, otherwise all subsequent social shaping becomes mismatched with what is required to deal with the meta-problem. As an identity is acquired, the domain begins to take a direction which makes a path into the future as to what may be attempted in the way of courses of action. All this entails some overall social shaping as regards boundaries and size: what organizations are to be included, heterogeneity, homogeneity, etc. Along with this, an internal structure evolves as the various stakeholders learn to accommodate their partially conflicting interests while securing their common ground. Locales begin to be established.

... Can we improve the work of appreciation? Can we learn to speed it up? When the locale is a region or a community, smaller scale and greater immediacy seem to enable more to be accomplished. Such locales may constitute our most accessible learning theatres for building domains.

Functions of Referent Organizations

There are two broad classes of domains which are complementary: those which display some kind of centering in terms of a referent organization (of which there are several variations) and those which remain uncentered and retain a purely network character. The latter comprise social movements concerned with the articulation of latent value alternatives...environmental probes into possible futures. But they are not in themselves purposeful...a referent organization must not usurp the functions of the constituent organizations; yet to be effective it must provide appropriate leadership.

... The first [function of a referent organization] is regulation as distinct from operation—operations are the business of the constituent organizations. Regulation entails setting the ground rules, determining the criteria for membership, maintaining the values from which goals and objectives are derived, undertaking conflict resolution, and sanctioning activities. But a referent organization also has a time perspective which tends to be longer term than that of the constituent organizations. It is consequence- rather than result-oriented ... so that it begins to assume considerable responsibility for the future of the domain. This entails the appreciation of emergent trends and issues and the working out with constituent organizations of desirable futures and modifying practice accordingly. Mobilization of resources may be an especially important item, as is developing a network of external relations. This is an interactive planning role which is an extension of the regulative function.

The life of referent organizations is by its very nature discontinuous, entailing the bringing together in various contexts of representatives of the constituent organizations. A staff is therefore necessary to provide infrastructure support, but the staff must be prevented from taking over the appreciative work of the leadership which is generalist rather than specialist.

Reading 9.2

National Strategies

ARTURO ISRAEL*

Usually, strategies for improving institutional performance focus on individual agencies or groups of them. This study, however, suggests that performance can be improved through countrywide policies and measures that affect most or all agencies. In fact, experience indicates that major improvements in performance often materialize in a country only after national policies and measures are established or modified.

When competition and specificity are taken as central explanations of institutional performance, the first and probably most important corollary is that low-specificity and noncompetitive activities cannot, by definition, achieve the same level or kind of performance as high-specificity and competitive ones. The effectiveness of low-specificity and noncompetitive activities has to be measured by different standards.

A second corollary of using the concepts of specificity and competition is that institutional improvement in low-specificity and noncompetitive activities will take longer than in high-specificity and competitive ones. If velocity of change is taken as a measure of performance, low-specificity and noncompetitive activities will be ranked as doing poorly. Evaluations of their performance will therefore have to use different measures.

A third corollary has to do with the possibility of substitution between specificity and competition as factors inducing better institutional performance....

A fourth corollary is that improved institutional performance is part and parcel of the process of modernization.... The challenge (for developing countries) is to modernize as fast as possible, but without unduly changing the character of their people-oriented activities.... Great progress could be made if key decision makers would change their attitude toward these issues and face insufficient institutional capacity as just one more of the resources lacking in a developing economy.

Emphasis on Low-specificity and Noncompetitive Activities

If increased awareness is the first order of business, the second is to give priority in institutional development strategies to the low-specificity (low-technology and people-oriented) activities. This priority is vital for countries

* From Arturo Israel, *Institutional Development: Incentives to Performance* (Baltimore: Johns Hopkins University Press, 1987), pp 111–17 and 150–61.

at lower levels of development, particularly if their high-technology activities operate as enclaves. The real intellectual challenge will be to design solutions for these activities without simply copying those that have worked in the high-specificity ones. Several biases will have to be overcome, such as the tendency to assume that progress will be made merely by introducing partial organizational improvements and a few management techniques or by concentrating on the quantifiable aspects of an operation and on planning and design instead of on implementation....

A question that arises now is whether this proposed emphasis on the institutional aspects of low-specificity and noncompetitive activities makes sense as a development strategy, since it neglects the modern sectors. To this, there are several answers. First, the low-specificity and noncompetitive activities in a developing economy will represent the largest proportion of the total activities, and the less developed the country, the larger that proportion; the strategy thus attempts to tackle the largest and weakest segments. Second, the modern and competitive activities will,... take care of themselves pretty well (relatively speaking, of course), and their effectiveness can be improved much more than those of the low-specificity and noncompetitive activities with relatively minor efforts. Third,...since many of the activities deal with the rural areas and the poorest segments of the population, emphasizing them is tantamount to reiterating the priority attached by the development community to the eradication of poverty; it coincides with the emphasis given to agriculture in the most recent development strategies; and it strengthens the argument that development programs oriented to agriculture and poverty eradication are among the most productive.

Perhaps the most difficult obstacle to this strategy is the long-standing belief in all societies, including developed ones, that hard technology deserves the highest priority. To conclude that low-specificity activities are the most important and in many ways the most difficult requires an intellectual jump which will be hard to achieve in practically all developing societies. At present, attitudes and incentives are oriented in the other direction.... Developing societies are dazzled with technology, but their real breakthrough will come at the other end of the spectrum.

Mechanisms to Compensate for Lack of Specificity

... the characteristics of low-specificity activities (e.g., human services) make it extremely difficult to arrive at clear operational guidelines for them, which is presumably why management science has neglected them... people-oriented activities need strong incentives, but their low-specificity makes the design and implementation of strong incentives almost impossible. Similarly, low-specificity activities need flexibility to operate effectively, which means that their objectives and incentives should not be specified in too much detail.

The techniques and approaches for simulating specificity can be divided into several categories: general strategies, recruitment, staff incentives, training, management, managerial techniques, and organizational structures. Undoubtedly, other classifications are possible, but the main interest here is the general thrust of the analysis.

Recruitment

One real dilemma is that many of the characteristics that make individuals especially effective in people-oriented activities are innate and cannot be taught... the difficulty comes in actually attempting to hire hundreds or thousands of poorly educated individuals to expand rural primary education or health services....

The problem may be less severe than it first appears. There is evidence that effectiveness in low-specificity activities is also heavily linked to motivation, particularly at low levels... that the abilities required are possessed by many people and [that these] are brought out by the greater professionalization and motivation which manifests itself in better work behavior.

Training

... Innate talent and successful practical experience should be valued more than educational background. This applies to the highest levels of management as well as to agents dealing with farmers and villagers. Experience in building primary health care systems strongly confirms this point... training has to be much more continuous in low-specificity activities because it is a matter of repeated adaptation to new situations. How continuous depends on the circumstances. The knowledge imparted is only partially cumulative and, especially in the case of staff with relatively little education, it is not realistic to expect low-level personnel to adapt their skills and solutions to the changing realities. Second, training for low-specificity activities should concentrate less on teaching specific techniques and more on offering a mixture of traditional-formal training in techniques, on-the-job training, and professional support to help the agents deal with operational problems. This structure of training is adapted to low-specificity activities and applies to all levels of staff....

Management

Management of low-specificity and especially people-oriented activities is distinguished, first, by a relatively greater need to deal with the political, economic, and cultural environments because it can affect people-oriented activities in many ways. High and middle-level managers constantly need to assess which external pressures are under their control and which are not and adapt their operations to changes in the external environment. In some instances, these external influences are such that the chief executive should be someone particularly capable of managing the political dimension, which should be his main concern, and someone else should be delegated to be in charge of operations....

The second characteristic of the management role in people-oriented activities is the more extreme need to adapt managerial techniques and approaches to the local culture... thorough knowledge of the locality and a sensitivity to local needs means that in most cases the managers should be local people.

... managers—especially at the middle level—need to cultivate a management style that is open to pressures, or 'incentives', from lower-level staff and from clients and beneficiaries. This will require important changes in the way most people-oriented activities are now managed, and changes in the managerial culture in many countries. Managers will need to improve communications with workers in the field and become much more oriented toward field operations; they will have to get used to leaving their offices in the capital or provincial city more often for direct contact with their subordinates in the small towns and villages.

... This point is at the heart of the differences between technology-oriented and people-oriented activities. Each decision made by an agent will have an element of uniqueness—whether advising a farmer on methods of production, persuading a villager to boil water, or solving a problem for a client of a ministry. The agent decides alone, on the spot. It is therefore essential that he gets professional support, in addition to continuous training and opportunities to compare his experience with other agents. Most agents have little education or experience and should not be left to make difficult decisions in isolation....

Managers in these cases should have as much feedback from their agents as possible, so as to monitor progress and change approach: they should take part in a continuous dialogue with each agent.... Managers in low-specificity activities should also put special emphasis on tracing and measuring the effects of the actions performed by their staff, either individually or in groups.

The best management styles... for people-oriented activities might have to be somewhat looser or more democratic than is desirable for technology-oriented ones—that is, it should not rely excessively on quantitative objectives and specific controls. A loose style does not preclude great precision and tightness in certain aspects of the operation however. In rural extension work, for example, management can ensure that visits to farmers are made on a strict schedule, but it cannot define too rigidly what the extensionist should do on each visit.

Reading 9.3

As Monitor/Researcher of his Own Praxis

ROLF P. LYNTON*

Data on scientific activities and programs, says an article in *Science* (1977), 'are frustratingly deficient. Record-keeping by science agencies has been designed primarily to account for money rather than to provide first for analyses of who went where and when'. And for what; and what happened when he/she/they did what they did that mattered to the purpose? My recording is a craftsman's tool in the first place; a researcher's only in the distant second. It helps me do the best work I can under the very exposed conditions of developing innovative institutions. I could not live with myself if, seeing the high risks that go with the high promise of building a truly community-oriented school (of public health), I did not do everything I could to sharpen my perception of current events around me, use the best conceptual formulations of what to anticipate, and monitor my own behavior in very orderly fashion. Most of all is this done with close colleagues, members of my 'core group', and a special consultant hired for the purpose from outside. But recording both stimulates my reflective self and feeds it. It also acknowledges that, as dean, I ultimately face my part in this innovative enterprise alone, that I indeed carry an individual responsibility.

By recording I mean not the daily log or journal that I also keep, but the systematic underpinning of data for it....

The antecedents of the present form (see Figure 1) take me back to 1961 in India, when I started work as a Ford Foundation consultant to a new institution, following a period of six years as founder-director of an international training center (Aloka). It was my wife, Ronnie, who suggested that it might be wise to keep track of this strategic change of role, to sustain an extra consciousness of it and so, presumably, also an extra capacity for sensitive behavior in the change-over from director to consultant and from director-in-charge to team member (between four and eight international consultants were attached at various times to the new institution, a staff college).

I started, simply enough, with keeping all documents—of those I sent I made sure to keep a copy—and a note of every contact I had with each work colleague, Indian and foreign. This produced a diary, and a more systematic one than most in that every contact had some notation.

Before long, this simple method threatened to become overwhelming and, for increasing numbers of contacts, also unnecessary: many contacts

*From Rolf P. Lynton, 'Boomerangs and Alligators: Professional Education in the Public Interest', Unpublished manuscript (1978), pp 75–84.

were brief and their contents routine and well-known. It was then that I developed a simple time/relationship matrix. It itemizes my colleagues in their main structural groups across the top of the page, leaving room for some 'other' and 'visitors' categories. Down the side on the left, it divides the day into half hours. With a simple red mark I can, as I go through my day, score every transaction on the matrix. I can also indicate by simple successive numbering any that I particularly want to make a diary note about when I have time.

As a result, my diary became selective—and manageable—while the basic recording—of *all* interactions—also continued. The time-matrix allowed me to distinguish, very simply, between long and short, large and small, meetings, and what colleagues (inside and outside the Institute) were involved in them. I can *see* patterns easily, including blanks (omissions).

This mode of scoring and diary keeping I kept up for the five years I worked with the Institute in India, half of it as team leader of the consultants. I valued the opportunity it offered to live my work life twice over. Usually I wrote my diary notes first thing in the morning and then felt well prepared to face the new day. There were certainly times when the whole relentless business felt like a strait-jacket; happily these were also the times when recording was most rewarding because so much was going on. I ended the five years with 4,500 pages of personal diary, all documents into and out of my office, and the complete interaction scores day by day.

Research into that whole body of data came later. Analysis anchored in more comprehensive conceptual schemes showed up a massive flaw in our work, an imbalance: we had concentrated attention on program development and the internal affairs of the Institute and neglected the Institute's external relationships. With that recognition, my interest in organization-environment linkages became vivid, systematic, and lasting.

For my more recent institution-building programs, the matrices comprehend more external relationships. The first step towards constructing the matrix (for the new school) was to identify the main classifications of colleagues, students, agencies, and other constituencies with which the school needed to relate. Most of these were obvious. For instance, the composition of an Advisory Committee determined one set of classifications in the general constituency of 'other colleges, schools, and departments'. It would clearly be important to monitor contacts with each of these eight academic units in USC, whereas grouping contacts with others together would suffice. It would also be important to track contacts with the heads of these units separately from contacts with their representatives on the Committee; so each of these units received three sub-classifications—dean or chair, committee representatives, and others. Similarly, three major State agencies were separately identified and room provided for specifying particular Divisions in each with which the school was to work most closely.

Such constituencies and subsets, liberally interspaced with spaces for 'other', that is emergent, constituents had columns across the matrix, the half hours of the day downwards. Five additional columns allowed for some rough and ready categorization of each contact as it took place. Figure 1 reproduces extracts of the completed matrix for one rather typical day.

The five categories I chose to categorize were: which party initiated the contact, the main contents and purpose of it, and my estimates as to the achievement of the immediate purpose and—very different, this—the estimated effects of this contact on the longer-term relationship with the constituent. The diary for this day (15 Jan 1976) has eight notes (for the contacts numbered in the margin on the left).

The matrix lay on my desk for marking up during the day, in the course of my contacts with people or just after. A vertical line in the column shows a meeting, face to face, its length and duration; T stands for telephone, M for a verbal message; four or five simple signs and letters fill the columns on the right. The full key is shown here. Each contact took about as much time to mark as saying hello. The result is a daily record which covers all kinds of personal contacts; and documents cover the rest. Making the marks in red made for easy scanning.

Key for Five Classificatory Columns

1. *'Initiated'*
   self = s
   other(s) = o
   joint = j
   unclear = blank
2. *'Content'*
   Program Activities = A
   Administration = Ad
   Colleagueship = Col
   Confrontation, conflict = C
   Diffuse linkage = D
   Future, scanning, long-term = F
   Normative development = N
   Organization structure = O
   Other Resources = OR
   Policy = Pol
   Relationship building = R
   Sanction, support = S
   Student Selection = SS
   Faculty Selection = FS
3. *'Purpose'*
   allocate = a
   advise = ad
   confront, for example,
      differences = c
   develop = d
   explore = e
   firm up, set = f
   inform = i
   implement = im
   maintain = m
   monitor/evaluate = mo
   obtain = o
   plan = p
   represent = r
   scan/visualize future = s
   teach = t
   think = th
4. *'Evaluate—immediate'*: +, -, blank = no comment
5. *'Evaluate—developmental'*: +, -, blank = no comment

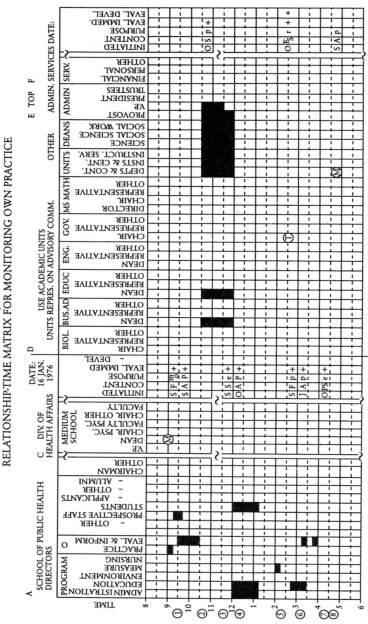

Figure 1

RELATIONSHIP-TIME MATRIX FOR MONITORING OWN PRACTICE

What the matrix and its regular use does most for me is to keep me aware of the full range of relationships with which I need to be concerned. Most of all they help me guard myself against neglecting external relationships. Because even if they are left only briefly unattended, relationships soon drop out of sight for good. The risks of this are especially high for 'underserved' constituencies who have every reason to expect that they will be neglected again, initial protestations to the contrary notwithstanding. But among the unintrusive, perhaps all too readily dormant, contextual relationships are also some of the most important and powerful for the new institutions mandate, e.g., key legislators, university budget planners—these people, agencies, etc., have to be known and noticed. Normative and diffuse linkages, which institution development studies show to be commonly neglected, are particularly important for innovative institutions to develop actively. So my own emphasis has shifted to managing linkages. Time and frequency of contacts continue to indicate where my attention flows, and the identification, classification, and regular review of the relationships of which my world of work consists have become central.

To sum up:

1. Quite basic is the *identification of the components of the institution's environment* which need to be included: this delineates the boundaries of my world of work to which I must pay attention. To offset any tendencies to draw the boundaries too narrowly, when in doubt about including a relationship in my regular surveillance. I have learned to include rather than exclude it. The extent of this world needs to be regularly reviewed because new components do emerge, for instance, through legislation of subtler processes: three to four monthly intervals seem right in the first year, twice a year after that. At least refinements in some categories will be required.

2. For proper *management and for letting this type of data influence action,* the matrix can be programmed for machine scanning, so it can reveal trends in the data for early discussions and use on a regular basis.

3. *Some characterizations of the contacts* is useful, even if it is rough. For instance, important dimensions of commitment and reciprocity in relationships are indicated by the pattern of initiatives in the contacts. I, therefore, score and periodically summarize, the balances of initiatives in each relationship. I also summarize the purposes for which a particular relationship is most often used.

4. Along with the scoring of all interactions, I keep up my *diary* for selected items daily. When, because of too many meetings and travel, the diary falls behind more than a day, I use the occasion for a systematic review of all relationships, ranging over recent events, and for assessing the quality of them for now and for the future (the diary for developing the new School includes five such systematic summaries in the three years).

Keeping the diary up to date takes me a little over an hour a day, a half-hour some days, as much as two hours on others. That time includes making notes for actions that come to mind while I write the diary and scan the record, to see where I am this morning and what I need to focus on for the day.

With the meticulous recording of my institution building experience I am also in the position to make a small contribution to filling the data gap that *Science* points to in the quote reproduced at the start of the piece. But that is a by-product. The primary objective of the recording effort is self-monitoring. It keeps me in top form, such as that is, helps me live my life twice in quick succession, an examined life, and so raises my critical awareness of the world around me and of myself in it....

INDEX

ABOUT THE AUTHORS

Rolf Lynton is now based in North Carolina. In his long career he has been Professor of Public Health and of Preventive Medicine at the University of South Carolina where, from 1974 to 1977, he was the founding Dean and Department Chairman. For five years he was team leader of the HRD project with the Ministry of Health, Government of Indonesia. He has been Johns Hopkins University/ USAID senior advisor working with the Ministry of Health and Family Welfare in India; Director of Aloka, an international training center for community development workers; and chairman of the International Association of Applied Social Scientists. Earlier he worked with the field research unit of the British Institute of Management, the European Youth Campaign based in France, and the Harvard Business School. He has authored many books and papers, has worked as a consultant with many international agencies, and is a professional member of the NTL Institute and of the Association for Creative Change.

Udai Pareek, author, researcher, and consultant, is currently Distinguished Visiting Professor at the Indian Institute of Health Management Research, Jaipur, India. During his career, he has been USAID Organization Development Advisor to the Ministry of Health in Indonesia, and Larsen and Toubro Professor of Organizational Behavior at the Indian Institute of Management, Ahmedabad. Udai Pareek has worked in the fields of education, agriculture, small industry, and public health. He has been a consultant to various Indian and international organizations, a Fellow of the NTL Institute, and has served on the editorial boards of the *Administrative Quarterly, Psychologia, Group and Organization Studies* and other journals. He is the editor of the *Journal of Health Management* besides having written or edited numerous books.

Both authors share current interests in systems change, institutional and organizational development, and human resource development.